MACAULAY

ON

WILLIAM PITT
EARL OF CHATHAM

THOMAS BABINGTON MACAULAY

WILLIAM PITT
EARL OF CHATHAM

EDITED BY

ARTHUR D. INNES, M.A.

CAMBRIDGE
AT THE UNIVERSITY PRESS
1907

CAMBRIDGE UNIVERSITY PRESS
Cambridge, New York, Melbourne, Madrid, Cape Town,
Singapore, São Paulo, Delhi, Mexico City

Cambridge University Press
The Edinburgh Building, Cambridge CB2 8RU, UK

Published in the United States of America by Cambridge University Press, New York

www.cambridge.org
Information on this title: www.cambridge.org/9781107621770

First edition 1897
First published 1897
Reprinted 1900, 1907
First paperback edition 2013

A catalogue record for this publication is available from the British Library

ISBN 978-1-107-62177-0 Paperback

CONTENTS.

INTRODUCTION.

I. MACAULAY; AND THE ESSAY

§ 1. *Biographical.*

THOMAS BABINGTON MACAULAY was born on October 25th, 1800. His father, Zachary Macaulay, was sprung of a Scotch Presbyterian stock; and was in his day well known as a philanthropist, an active worker for the abolition of the slave-trade, and a friend of many notable Whigs. Young Thomas was brought up in the eminently respectable and religious society for which Clapham in the days of Hannah More was famous. From his earliest youth he was an omnivorous reader, and being endowed with an amazing memory he accumulated vast quantities of knowledge with surprising ease. As a boy, his precocity was nothing short of portentous.

In due course he went to Cambridge, where his progress was highly successful; and commenced his literary career immediately after taking his degree. In 1825 appeared his Essay on Milton, in the *Edinburgh Review*, at that time perhaps the leading literary periodical. Politics however claimed him. He was an able and incisive speaker, and had won much applause in debate at Cambridge; and in 1830 he entered Parliament through the influence of the Hollands, on the Whig side, as member for Lord Lansdowne's pocket-borough of Calne. He took an active part in the Reform debates, and gained fresh reputation when he sat in the new Parliament for Leeds after

the great Reform Bill had been carried, in 1832. He was
placed on the Indian Board of Control, and in 1833 went out to
Calcutta as a Member of Council. Here he remained for five
years, till 1838, and in this time devoted his personal experience
to confirming all his previously formed ideas as to the history
and government of India. On his return to England he resumed his parliamentary career, and frequently held office, but
never attained fully to the very first rank as a parliamentarian.
Throughout these years he continued a constant and valuable
contributor to the *Edinburgh*, wherein one after another of his
Essays appeared. He was raised to the peerage in 1857, and
died in 1859.

§ 2. *Critical.*

Whatever judgment may be ultimately passed by posterity
on Macaulay as an historian, one great achievement may be
claimed for him, that he made history popular. His own
history and his biographical and historical essays have found
their way, and still find their way, where no predecessor of his
could get a hearing ; and wherever Macaulay has dealt with
any subject, his successors have been more or less compelled
to write with the deliberate intention of either removing or
confirming popular impressions for which he is responsible.

This means at least that Macaulay's literary excellence
is of a very high order. It means that he can excite interest
where others have failed to do so ; and that he makes a lasting
impression which, however erroneous, is singularly difficult to
eradicate.

This effect is due in the first place to his having formed a
style which is peculiarly lucid and coherent ; and while never
overloaded with ornament is still adorned with a wealth of apt
illustration which keeps the intellect pleasantly stimulated.

In the second place, Macaulay always writes with an air of
conviction and reasonableness combined which is in itself
convincing. The mere air of conviction does not convince;
it may merely arouse antagonism. It is possible to be so

reasonable that conviction is left quivering in the balance.
Conviction is conveyed by the conjunction. Now Macaulay
gives the impression that no one of his statements or opinions
has caused him a moment's hesitation, while there are always
sufficient facts and authorities in his favour to make them
plausible.

These qualities of style are combined with a mental characteristic which adds an immense persuasiveness. His point of
view is that which is also natural to the average reader : his
methods of thought are the same. He lives in the *via media*.
He approves of sobriety and order. He dislikes eccentricities.
He mistrusts ideals and enthusiasms which do not appeal to
him at sight; he does not feel that they demand careful
examination, that there may be some motive in them worth
penetrating after; he regards them in fact as a kind of craze.
Now this is precisely the attitude of the average Englishman
towards any political question in which he has no disturbing
purely personal interest. Consequently the view of any particular event or character which commends itself to Macaulay
is *primâ facie* the view likely to commend itself to the average
Englishman.

But style and mental attitude in combination would not
have sufficed to make Macaulay's position so strong, without
the immense industry and the prodigious memory which enabled
him to accumulate and to assort his facts. The facts as he
presents them may rest upon insufficient evidence, may be
coloured by prejudice, may be associated in a wholly misleading
manner; but at the worst they are gathered from sources in
which Macaulay believed, they have authority however untrust-
worthy, and as a rule, when stripped of rhetorical setting, the
bare facts have to be admitted. Macaulay's opinions and in-
ferences may be challenged to any extent; but to convict him
of mis-stating a date, a name, or a place is anything but an
easy task.

Such broadly are the reasons why Macaulay has secured
among the historians of England this unique position; that in
the main he has made his opinions the opinions of the average

man. We have now to examine those defects in his mental equipment which deprive him of the right to be placed actually in the first rank; which make it imperative for the serious student to revise with the utmost care the impressions produced on him whether by the History or by the Essays.

We have already dwelt upon the *average* character of his sympathies. This enables him not only to keep in touch with the average reader, but also to form a strikingly accurate judgment of average men and average movements; intelligent men actuated by commonplace motives; movements excited by commonplace desires. Both men and movements are often important enough. Somers and Walpole, the glorious Revolution and the 1832 Reform Bill, are excellent examples. These are subjects in dealing with which Macaulay was thoroughly in his element. But the very quality which enabled him to deal with these subjects with thorough understanding made him incompetent to treat adequately of greater men and greater causes. To him, the Cavaliers are little more than a crew of roystering swash-bucklers fighting for their own predominance : the Puritans, a collection of narrow-minded zealots. His sympathies are exclusively with the pure Parliamentarians who objected to being taxed against their will. To him, Cromwell is the man who used the prostration of the nation to place himself in the position of dictator—not the leader who raised his country, from the position of a third-rate power to which the incompetence of the Stuarts and the anarchy of civil war had reduced it, to the position of the arbiter of Europe. Chatham is a great orator, and a great war minister on the whole, but an impracticable politician. Yet Chatham found the country in a state of grovelling panic at the idea of a French war ; and in four years he had swept every rival fleet off the seas and annihilated, for good and all, all European rivalry in India and in America, besides striking the first blow at the oligarchy which forty years of Whig supremacy had built up.

That fancy then which plays freely among superficial and accidental ideas Macaulay had in abundance, and to it he owes in great part his power of picturesque description : but in the penetrating sympathetic imagination which gives a grip of fundamental moving ideas he was deficient. And this brings us to another aspect of his imaginative deficiency. It appears as though the range of his intellectual vision had become finally fixed when he was little more than a boy. No amount of experience altered him. As he had seen things when he was five-and-twenty, so he saw them when he was five-and-forty. The "Clive" might just as well have been written before he went to India as afterwards. No fresh ideas seem to touch him. The workmanship of his writing advances ; his wealth of illustration accumulates ; but there is hardly any discoverable advance in critical penetration. The essay on Milton is a brilliant Prize Essay ; that on Warren Hastings is a glorified Prize Essay. The rhetorical art is greater in the later essay than in the earlier one ; but the critical insight is of precisely the same order.

It is in these limitations that Macaulay's vital defect is to be found. Yet his worst fault is commonly held to be his want of impartiality. Still, paradoxical as it may sound, it is not altogether a fault for the historian to play the part of an advocate rather than a judge, provided that he is honest. The speeches of counsel are as necessary to the proper hearing of a case as the judge's summing up ; it is the business of the jury to discount the rhetoric. Macaulay is openly and palpably an advocate. He is a Whig, with certain political doctrines, so to speak, in his blood. Anyone with a policy which did not square with those doctrines is suspect : if there is a doubt he does not get the benefit of it. Also the historian was personally devoted to the Holland connexion, and all transactions associated with the name of Fox are coloured by the fact. His Evangelical up-bringing gave him a bias against all High Church-and-State doctrine, which colours all his views on ecclesiastical matters. And out of these several formative influences arose what can only be called personal animosities against particular individuals. But the bias is always open and palpable. That it is a fault is undeniable ; but from being so manifest it is less dangerous than the unconscious defect already named : and it leads to misrepresentation chiefly of individuals, while the other leads to misrepresentation of principles.

§ 3. *The Essays on William Pitt.*

These two essays display Macaulay's powers and limitations very characteristically. His sympathies are always appealed to most strongly by the men whose methods and aims were pre-eminently constitutional and regular. Pitt's methods and aims violated parliamentary practice, and sprang from motives which were more grandiose than conventional. Consequently, throughout both the essays, we find Macaulay constantly dwelling on the parliamentary aspect of politics, and more impressed by Pitt's failure as a parliamentarian than by his brief triumph as a dictator. The men and the times are drawn impressively, picturesquely, brilliantly, and on the whole truthfully; but the tremendous character of the stake which England and France were playing for is hardly alluded to in the earlier essay; while in the second we hear a good deal less of the great minister's projects than of the personal rivalries and the foibles of character which prevented him from embodying his projects in a policy.

Thus the real character of Pitt's great administration is inadequately treated. Between 1733 and 1763 one of the most momentous questions in the history of nations was decided. A great attempt was made to create in Europe a Bourbon league which should not only dominate the Continent, but should more particularly circumscribe the power and the expansion of Great Britain. Indirectly, at least, the war of 1739 was its outcome. That war was indecisive, but was followed by the thoroughly decisive war which began in 1756. From the time of the first Family Compact, it was certain that sooner or later Britain would have forced on her the alternative of submitting to the dictation of the combined Bourbons, or of fighting for her own dominion. Walpole attempted to defer the struggle as long as he could : yet it was forced on him, not by the deeper insight of his political opponents but by the mutual irritation of English

and Spanish. The nature of the stakes was not realised, and
the war was not brought to a decisive issue. But the essentials
of a lasting peace were lacking, and eight years later the struggle
was renewed. Pitt stood alone in grasping the essential fact
that the renewed war must be so carried out that on vital
questions its issue should be definitive. Macaulay fails to make
the reader realise—it is doubtful whether he realised himself—
that there was a problem demanding definitive settlement, in
which the sword alone could be arbiter. At the time Pitt was the
one man who did thoroughly realise that fact ; who further
perceived that a great and immediate development of overwhelming naval superiority was the sole means by which the
end could be achieved ; and so justified an enormous expenditure. Thus although Pitt had not himself designed the
conquest of India, it was due to his policy that France never
again found an opportunity of obtaining a footing there ; while
her expulsion from America was perhaps the most definite
object of his policy. The extraordinary folly of his successors
in office threw away the best of his gain in the West, but in
spite of the great rift, Canada remains to this day a monument
of Pitt's greatness. Yet Macaulay writes as if these achievements were at best the lucky outcome of a vigorously fought
combat, instead of being inherent parts in the great design of
a great statesman.

Failing as he did to recognise the largeness of Pitt's conception in this case, as well as to give due recognition to
the inevitability, sooner or later, of a duel *à outrance* between
the two expanding Powers, it is natural that Macaulay should
have failed also in other respects to attain a sympathetic
understanding of the subject of his biography. He betrays a
perpetual distrust ; his admiration has the air of being extorted ;
his censure has in it a note of satisfaction. The younger Fox
was one of Macaulay's heroes ; the fact makes him tender to
the memory of the elder Fox, and somewhat prejudiced against
the elder Fox's successful rival, all the more because Pitt's
moral superiority was unquestionable. For a corresponding
reason, the father of the younger Pitt was a person likely

a priori to excite the hostility of an ardent Foxite. Further, Macaulay's Whig traditions placed him thoroughly in sympathy with the Rockingham party, and he could not forgive Pitt for his treatment of the Rockinghams. As a result, wherever Chatham's motives are open to question, the biographer inclines to make the baser motive more prominent. Where fault may legitimately be found, he tends to exaggerate rather than to soften. Where praise may not be withheld, it is accompanied by some adverse suggestion. The tone throughout is that of a man who admires against his will, applauds because he must ; but is quick to find excuses for blame, and pleased by an oppor· tunity of depreciation.

II. HISTORICAL SURVEY.

[*See Appendix: Chronological table of events.*]

§ 1. *The reign of Walpole.*

IN the first of the two essays on William Pitt Macaulay devotes his attention to producing a brilliant picture of the. parliamentary chiefs from 1720 to 1760 ; from Walpole to Newcastle, their characters are presented with vivid portraiture ; but it is a remarkable fact that he gives no account at all of the national questions with which it was their business to deal.

Yet the period is one of supreme importance in the annals of empire : for it was during those years that the great struggle was fought out which decided whether the Anglo-Saxon or the Latin races should dominate North America, India, and the Sea : the third being the controlling factor in the other two.

When Walpole came into power in consequence of the discredit brought on his predecessors in office by the disaster known as the "South Sea Bubble," England was indubitably the first of the maritime powers, while both France and Spain had very considerable navies. In South America, where England had no footing, Spain exercised a commercial monopoly which was exceedingly irritating. In North America, British colonists held the long stretch of seaboard from Florida to Canada : but

Canada itself was French, Louisiana on the south was also French, and Florida was Spanish. Westward beyond the basins of the Ohio and Mississippi, all the interior was in dispute, French and British colonists being perpetually at feud. Nor was there in those days any probability of the contest being settled unless by the expulsion of one party or the other—the modern experiment of delimiting "spheres of influence" not having as yet been invented.

In India, trade was shared by the French and the British; but as yet neither had attempted to acquire territory or political influence. It was evident however that when one should lead the way, the other would have to follow suit on pain of extermination; and this would result in a struggle doomed to perpetual recurrence until one party or the other should be driven from the field altogether.

In the third place, naval superiority would have to decide the struggle which was already going on in a desultory fashion in America, and was not likely to be long deferred in India, though it had not yet entered into the calculations of statesmen. For the Power which developed on the sea sufficient superiority to enable it to pour reinforcements into the country where war was going on, and to prevent its antagonist from doing the same, was absolutely certain to drive the other out of the field; since it was only by sea that reinforcements could reach either America or India.

Now the direct rivalry in India was between France and England, but here it had not yet become a question of practical politics. In North America the rivalry between France and England was already acute: but Spain had little to say to it. In the West Indies, however, there was direct rivalry with Spain, and in the South Seas not a rivalry but a violent hostility to the Spanish monopolies. Added to this, the possession of Gibraltar was intensely galling to Spain.

Consequently there was direct friction with France on account of one set of interests, and with Spain on account of another. Neither could match us by sea single-handed. But if they should come to recognise Britain as the common enemy, their junction against us would be formidable—so much so that Walpole always declared we could not face it—while if they joined hands for other purposes it was not likely that they would be long in discovering that their mutual interests would be served by crippling British power.

There is indeed no sign at all that British statesmen, or, for the matter of that, foreign statesmen either, recognised that a fight for colonial empire was at hand. But during the "thirties" the signs of the times were pointing to a development of friendliness between France and Spain ; and Walpole at least knew that this had taken form in a secret treaty (1733) containing extremely anti-British clauses. But this knowledge was not public property : France was displaying no overt hostility to England. And in the meantime, any tendency to active interference in continental affairs was liable to be attributed to " Hanoverianism," i.e. to the king's desire to use England as a catspaw for Hanover. To these complicating factors it was always necessary at this time to add that a quarrel with France involved a serious risk of the revival of active Jacobitism : since the party of the exiled Stuarts necessarily looked to France for assistance.

Pitt entered parliament in 1735. By this time the secret treaty between France and Spain was an accomplished fact ; but while popular feeling against Spain was growing daily in consequence of the tales brought back by English sailors from the South Seas, there was no present belief that she would be joined by France in the event of a war. Walpole's knowledge of the secret treaty is probably to a great extent responsible for the intensity of his aversion to the Spanish war of 1739 ; but it must remain as the permanent blot upon his policy, that with his strenuous resistance to war he failed to join a strenuous preparation for it.

How it was that Fleury, the French minister, who had constructed the Franco-Spanish alliance, had failed equally to prepare for an event which he must have contemplated as early as 1733 remains something of a mystery. Probably he reckoned that Walpole would keep England out of war until his own plans were thoroughly matured; and that when once France could afford to throw off the mask and openly join in supporting Spanish demands, Great Britain would be afraid to face the united Bourbons.

§ 2. *From Walpole to Pitt.*

Happily the practical result of the declaration of war in 1739, although it was in no way the outcome of far-sighted statesmanship, was actually to improve the position of England as against Spain before France was ready to throw in her lot with the latter; and the "war of Jenkin's ears" was ended in 1748 without materially affecting the relative positions of these Powers—save that, incidentally, Jacobitism had received its death-blow at Culloden. Nevertheless, the war had revealed the fact that England was able to cope simultaneously with the navies of France and Spain; while the Franco-British struggle had opened in India with no tangible advantage to either side, though the honours so far rested with the French.

The Pelham administration, which succeeded the fall of Walpole after a brief interval, was distinguished by never possessing any positive policy at all. Its one rule was to do nothing that could be left undone, and to silence criticism by office. Foreign alliances and domestic departments were all left to take care of themselves; and when in 1754 Henry Pelham died and Newcastle became supreme, government became a mere chaos. Moreover in the meantime the hostilities of French and English in America and in India had attained an acuteness which must bring on a new war between England and France.

Spain was now governed by a king, Ferdinand, of pacific inclinations, and her neutrality might for the time be taken for granted. The superiority of the British to the French fleet was sufficiently marked; and it should therefore have appeared that a duel between France and England on the seas ought not to have offered any very alarming prospect to the latter. She would however be called upon in fairness to protect

Hanover, where France would probably seek to strike; nor was it reasonable to suppose that very efficient help in the field could come from Frederick of Prussia, who was himself threatened both by Russia on the east and Austria on the south. Taken altogether, however, it is evident that an intelligent and vigorous Government in England would at any rate have little to fear.

The Government, however, was neither vigorous nor intelligent, while there were no materials out of which an opposition could be constructed to take its place. Pitt had won popular favour, but he had not won a parliamentary backing. It was not till he had at last consented to a coalition with Newcastle, on the terms that he might do what he chose and Newcastle might spend what he chose, that a Government both vigorous and intelligent could be brought together. Happily France was little better off for leaders, and failed to use the time given her to work up her fleet, preferring to send armies to the Rhine; which did indeed bring disaster upon the Duke of Cumberland, who had been placed in command there, but enabled Pitt to put a definite naval policy in force without let or hindrance.

§ 3. *The Great War.*

The war between France and England began by the French capture of Minorca. The war on the Continent commenced later in the year with Frederick's invasion of Saxony, followed by the capture of Dresden.

Both Russia and Austria now made ready to fall upon Prussia; and a considerable French army advanced against Hanover, which was covered by Cumberland's army on the Weser. Frederick, on the other hand, made a dash upon Prague, before which he won a hotly contested battle; but shortly afterwards he met with a crushing reverse at Kolin.

Pitt and Newcastle had hardly formed their coalition, when Cumberland suffered a defeat at Hastenbeck; and in September (1757) was forced to dismiss half his army and retire beyond the Weser with the rest, by the Convention of Closterseven.

British and Prussians were now alike in a most precarious condition : but Frederick's power of recuperation was marvellous. After Kolin he reorganised his forces ; and first at Rossbach (Nov.), and a month later at Leuthen, inflicted severe defeats on his antagonists. Ferdinand of Brunswick being at the same time placed in command of the Hanover army, the French were at once held in check.

During 1758, both Ferdinand and Frederick did somewhat more than hold their own : the former winning a battle at Crefeld, and the latter driving back the Russian advance at Zorndorf. On the other hand, Frederick met with a defeat at Hochkirchen at the hands of Daun, but the Austrian failed to follow up his victory so as to turn it to any account.

In the meantime, the new spirit which Pitt was breathing into the British nation was beginning to take effect. Little as yet was actually achieved ; but our sailors were recalling the fact that their superior seamanship would enable them to deal not unsuccessfully with forces which might seem superior on paper : and the news of Clive's great victory at Plassey reminded the nation that it still possessed some fighting qualities. The tide was fairly on the turn.

By 1759, Britain had recovered the mastery though not yet an overwhelming supremacy on the sea. In the earlier part of the year, Goree in Africa and Guadaloupe in the West Indies were conquered. In August, Ferdinand won a decisive victory at Minden, greatly owing to the stubborn valour of the British regiments. In September, Boscawen broke up the Toulon fleet off Lagos. In September also, Wolfe scaled the heights of Abraham and captured Quebec at the price of his own life. In November Hawke decisively shattered the main French fleet from Brest at Quiberon. A couple of months later, the struggle in India, though it dragged on for another year, was virtually concluded by Coote's decisive victory over Lally at Wandewash. No French fleet could put to sea, and the years 1760 and 1761 were occupied in completing the conquests of

Canada and of the French in India, and in the absorption of the French possessions over seas.

Nevertheless, the years were serious ones for Frederick. In 1759, he suffered his worst reverse at Kunersdorf, a few days after Minden. In 1760, he was victorious at Liegnitz and Torgau, in August and November; but though these battles gave him breathing time, he had been steadily losing ground. 1761 was a year of exhaustion, which fortunately affected the Austrians as well as their stubborn opponent.

Happily for him also the opening of 1762 saw the withdrawal of Russia from the war; and he proved himself still more than a match for Austria alone. Consequently, when Bute made peace with France and Spain (the latter having been seduced into joining France, very much to her own loss, at the beginning of the year) Frederick was able to make satisfactory terms with Austria at the peace of Hubertsberg.

Thus ended the Seven Years' War. To Pitt and to Frederick were due primarily its triumphs; to Bute was due the shameless desertion of Prussia, and the resignation of not a little which had been won in a war which the country had entered upon in answer to a direct challenge.

§ 4. *Pitt's War Policy.*

Macaulay remarks that, though it can hardly be denied that Pitt was a great war minister, his achievements even in this field are liable to censure and not marked by any great profundity or dexterity. The historian has failed to note the fundamental characteristic of the Great Commoner's policy. We have learned to-day to understand the vital importance of complete naval supremacy; but it had been reserved for Pitt to assert in practice that great principle in its entirety. The whole fighting strength of the nation was for the first time in our French wars devoted exclusively to obtaining overwhelming maritime supremacy. British troops were but a small contingent in the army of Ferdinand; we fought on the Continent by means of subsidies. But the naval campaign was carried on with such vigour that the French fleet was virtually swept off the seas ; consequently reverses to the French arms in India and Canada found our rivals utterly without power of recuperation in both continents, thus securing Canada and the future Empire of India to the British. The capture of Quebec and the victory of Wandewash were decisive, because Boscawen and Hawke made the French fleet powerless. The glory of Pitt lay in this,—that he found the country in a panic, and inspired it with courage and resolution, whereby he approved himself a great man ; that he recognised naval supremacy as the grand aim to be achieved, and thereby approved himself a far-seeing statesman. He was the one man who saw how decisive victory could be achieved, and he achieved it triumphantly.

His success was due to the fact that in the supreme crisis the whole nation accepted his dictatorship and obeyed. But the country does not like dictatorships ; when the supreme crisis was past, and the arts of Parliamentary leadership were demanded to hold discordant elements together : when the struggle for place and power was renewed, and the idea of giving a vote adverse to the great minister was no longer terrifying and was indeed not unlikely to prove lucrative : Pitt could not adapt himself to the altered circumstances. He who had overawed opposition was unable to persuade and to conciliate, and he never regained control of the destinies of his country. Had the William Pitt of 1757 returned to power ten years later it may well be doubted whether the American colonies would ever have revolted, or England have found herself fighting for life with her back to the wall in 1780. But Pitt's statesmanship was the statesmanship of a dictator, not of a Parliamentary leader, when the latter was demanded by the times. So the king dominated Parliament, and Britain was shorn of her colonies.

This second part of Pitt's great career is narrated in the second of Macaulay's essays.

§ 5. *The King and the Parliamentary Groups.*

In the great epoch of William Pitt's power, imperial problems
and ideals had roused the enthusiasm of a great nation which
had for many years past been absorbed in very material aims.
Parliamentary intrigues had been quenched in the great contest;
minor personalities had been dwarfed by the towering figure of
the Great Commoner: he himself had found play for his
greatest qualities when he was free to exercise the control of
a dictator in achieving the ambitions of a patriot. Then came
reaction. The time that followed was a time of small men,
obstinate men, occasionally well-meaning men; but men one
and all lacking the heroic qualities and the large conceptions
which characterised Pitt. Parties were resolved into the
personal following of the king, of Chatham, of one group or
another of the Whig nobility.

First, there was the young king, bent on reasserting the
influence of the crown; backed by Bute, by the Tories, and by
the self-seeking group who came to be known as the king's
friends. His attempt to recover royal ascendency began by an
attack on the great representative of popular sentiment. Pitt's
war policy was challenged: the jealousy of the Whigs was
brought to bear against him: he was not allowed to declare war
against Spain, and he resigned along with Temple. Newcastle
was then attacked at his tenderest point. He found to his
dismay that Bute was giving away the comfortable appointments.
He found also that it was no longer intended to maintain the
subsidies to Frederick to which England was pledged by every
obligation of honour. Consequently Newcastle and his friends
followed Pitt.

But one section of the Whigs,—George Grenville and the
Bedfords—supported the king's party. Their conception of the
obligations of honour were controlled by their notions of legal
claims. Their objection to the continuance of the war was
based on a horror of expenditure. Bute meant to use them.
The discovery that they, not he, were masters of the situation

drove him effectively out of public life. They fell upon Wilkes; they passed the Stamp Act; but they bullied the king. They were indeed in general agreement with George on the leading questions of domestic and colonial politics, and of the war; but the king wished them to act as his servants, they wished him to act as theirs. The period from the fall of Bute to 1765 witnessed a series of unavailing struggles on George's part to deliver himself from the grip of the ministers whose policy outside was his own, but who bullied him privately in the closet.

Appeals to Pitt were vain; for Pitt first required the reinstatement along with him of members of the second Whig group; and then most unhappily laid down the quite impossible condition of association with Temple.

To escape from the Bedfords, the king admitted the Rockinghams to office; but since their policy, colonial and domestic, was opposed to his own, he used his influence to thwart them in every possible way.

At last Pitt took office with a hybrid ministry, but forthwith abdicated the functions of first minister. With no guiding mind the Government struggled along, consistently grasping at every opportunity to do the worst thing possible, while the king steadily gathered increasing influence; till in 1770 North became prime minister. North placed himself unreservedly in the king's hands; the king knew his own mind, and so got his own way; the administration in incompetent hands plunged the country into war, and then mismanaged that war completely.

A Whig domination was objectionable, both to the king and to Pitt. While the Whigs were banded together, George knew that he could not force his wishes on them; Pitt conceived that the nadir from which he had rescued the country was due to the power which had fallen into their hands. They had surrendered that power to him only under stress of a tremendous and vividly impressive national crisis. He was intensely opposed to their recovering it. Yet his arrogance and impracticability prevented him from forming a band of personal supporters who would submit to his dictatorship, nor would he have had the king's support in carrying out his own policy. Pitt, then, would not attempt to lead the Whigs; he could not lead the king's party. The king would not support the Rockingham Whigs, and could not endure the Grenvilles: so he adopted the policy of detaching miscellaneous members from the Whig sections and attaching them to the subservient body of the "king's friends," until he did succeed in getting a cabinet and a parliament which took their policy at his orders. The only escape from this would have lain in the coalition of Pitt with the Rockinghams; and the rejection of that alternative lies at Pitt's door. The only explanation to be found is in his exaggerated hatred of reconstructing the Whig connexion. But it must be remarked that this great blunder of Pitt's coincided in point of time with those strange vagaries of demeanour which can hardly be attributed to anything but some degree of mental derangement.

§ 6. *The Political Questions from* 1760—1770.

As the outcome of the great war, the two main branches of external politics had assumed a new aspect. These were the relations of Great Britain to the nations of Europe, and her relations to her own colonies.

On the Continent she was virtually in a position to stand out as a general arbiter. In alliance with Prussia no combination of powers could at this stage become dangerous to her. Bute succeeded in destroying the advantage won by deliberately deserting Frederick. Among the politicians of the day a general idea became prevalent that the affairs of Europe might be neglected—a doctrine which, so far as it can ever be true, depends strictly on Great Britain preserving such an overwhelming maritime supremacy as enables her to defy single-handed any possible combination of Powers. As a result, France in a very few years' time annexed Corsica; Poland was partitioned, with a complete disregard of British opinion; and England found herself in 1782 on the brink of overwhelming disaster, from which she was saved by the supreme skill of the men who managed her ships through every grade of the service: materially assisted by the downright blunders of opposing admirals. To sum up the situation, Bute flung away the power that Pitt had won, and Bute's successors ratified Bute's policy.

As regarded the colonies, however, the war had changed the situation in a different sense. It had annihilated the serious rivalry of France ; but in so doing it had relaxed the bond between the colonies and the mother country. That bond must always be of a double character : consisting partly in sentiment, partly in interest. Before the war, colonial interests lay in cultivating the goodwill of the mother country. The colonies could not afford to do without England. The American states were exposed to the rivalry of French colonists : supposing that they had taken umbrage at British interference with their commerce, and had achieved independence, their expansion would have been circumscribed by the whole power of France. Assisted by the mother country, it was possible to defy France: without her, it was not possible. But the war removed France as a factor in the situation. Commercial subjection had been the price paid for the defence of British fleets and armies. The fleets and armies were now no longer in demand, and the colonists, as a necessary consequence, were no longer prepared to pay the price for them—it had ceased to be in their interest to do so. Something of a parallel to the previous situation may be observed in South Africa to-day. If a South African republic were created, German rivalry to it—at present held in check by British fleets—would at once become active. The resources of a great European nation would be brought into play against the colonists—against the South African state bereft of the assistance of the British fleet.

In brief, the colonial situation before the war was, that the colonists depended for defence against a European Power upon the mother country, and paid for that defence by submitting to commercial restrictions in favour of Great Britain ; with the need of defence, the readiness to pay for it disappeared.

George Grenville seized the opportunity to demand increased

payment, with the result that the colonists kicked against the novel claim, and went on to reject the old recognised claim as well. In theory, the question raised was one of a technical constitutional right ; in *fact*, it was raised because the condition which had been the real sanction of that right—the need of defence—disappeared.

Besides these two great questions the old constitutional question of the powers of the crown was revived, as we have seen, but in a new form. The object of the Stuarts had been to override Parliaments, and to do without them. That was no longer possible. The object of king George was to get ministers to his own liking, with parliamentary majorities behind them. It cost him ten years of stubborn fighting to effect his object ; but when North came into power, the object was achieved. For a dozen years Parliament went with the king. The course of this struggle has already been described.

But further than these, two new questions were raised in the decade 1760—1770. Both were unfortunately associated with the name of a singularly unworthy champion of the right, John Wilkes. The first was the right of popular criticism, in connexion with Wilkes's paper, the *North Briton* : the second was the right of a majority of the Lower House to override free election, in connexion with the membership for Middlesex. The importance of both questions, as questions of practical politics, is often overrated, since in both cases the ultimate result was a foregone conclusion. But in both cases the existing Government took the wrong side, while the martyr of liberty was conspicuously not a hero, but a knave. From that fact, the Government derived all the colour obtainable for its action. A John Hampden might have criticised as vehemently as Wilkes, and even Grenville would not have ventured to touch him. Tyranny, doomed as it was to ultimate failure in a contest really decided in the previous century, found its opportunity solely in the character of its victim.

Yet one other question was to seriously engage the minds of statesmen—that of India. Between 1744 and 1761 French and English had fought for the mastery over each other, and in so doing the victor had won also the control of the great states of Southern India, and the lordship of the rich provinces of Bengal and Behar. The nature of that tremendous acquisition was as yet hardly understood. It was not realised that the responsibility for providing a population of many millions with a tolerable government necessarily fell upon those who had shaken the foundations of the wretched governments that existed. It was not realised that for the time being this gigantic task had fallen into the hands of the underpaid servants of a trading company, with overwhelming temptations to subordinate all other considerations to personal advantage. Clive knew the meaning of the problem ; to Pitt and to Burke it was a reality; to the other statesmen of the day it might almost be said that the conquests of Clive were incidents which derived their political importance from the number of rotten boroughs which the returning nabobs were enabled to purchase.

On every one of these questions Pitt held the views of sound statesmanship. On every one of them the Government acted on the view diametrically opposed to his. In the counsels of Europe the voice of England was silenced. The Indian problem was shelved for some years, and then dealt with only in hasty and ill-considered fashion by North's Regulating Acts. In these matters the Government sinned for the most part negatively—by leaving its duty undone. But in the affairs of the colonies and of Wilkes it transgressed positively ; it took active steps which were absolutely wrong and destructive.

The Wilkes affairs are treated with sufficient fulness by Macaulay. Here, it is sufficient to observe, that a scurrilous critic was transformed into a martyr by the employment of illegal and palpably vindictive methods in the attack made on him ; and secondly, that the House of Commons was discredited by arrogating to itself the power of nullifying an election on manifestly vindictive grounds. The greater question of the Colonies Macaulay has treated, apparently, as too familiar to demand full discussion, and it may well receive here some additional attention.

§ 7. *The Breach with America.*

The thirteen American colonies were established by Charter. In theory the colonists had been given leave to occupy certain territories on condition of their accepting a form of government arranged for them. That is to say, a privilege was granted in return for which the mother country claimed among other rights that of regulating commerce with an eye to her own advantage. Thus it was recognised as a legitimate demand that customs duties should be laid upon foreign goods so as to secure a preference for British goods in American markets; or that American goods must find their market in Great Britain, for the benefit of the British trader. The colonists regarded this as fair enough, while it gave England a sufficiently strong inducement to support them in their contests with French rivals. But Pitt had gone very much further than any previous ministers; he had aimed, and aimed successfully, at freeing the colonists from French rivalry altogether; he had paved the way for a union springing from a recognition of unity of interests, in which there would come to be no need for protection on the one side or for payment by commercial restrictions on the other.

But the result had been achieved at an immense outlay both in money and lives. Apart from all technicalities, it seemed reasonable that the whole burden should not be borne by England, especially as the main direct advantage was palpably with the colonists.

The natural course would appear to have been a settlement by mutual agreement. But there were difficulties. There was no existing body which represented the colonies as a whole. The individual colonies would probably take very different views of their own obligations. It was even conceivable, though not probable, that they would all repudiate any obligation, on the general ground that England had only fulfilled her share of the bargain implied in the existing commercial restrictions.

To arrive, then, at a friendly settlement would manifestly demand the exercise of tact and diplomacy. The effort might fail, and it would then become necessary to consider whether the situation should be accepted or an attempt be made to enforce the views of the British Treasury by an appeal to the technical powers of the sovereign established by the Constitution —the edict of Parliament and the Crown. Such an appeal would acquire a special effectiveness by remaining untried until the colonists had put themselves in the wrong by refusing a contribution.

But George Grenville elected to adopt a different method. He broadly asserted the right of the home Government to claim a contribution from the colonies, and to enforce that contribution by the simple method of imposing taxes, to be collected for the benefit of the British exchequer.

It does not at first sight appear obvious that this proposal involved a new principle. But a sharp distinction was immediately drawn between the right of taxation for commercial and for exchequer purposes. The principle for which John Hampden fell was, that the country should have the power of refusing to supply funds for a Government of which it disapproved. As long as the people's representatives held the purse-strings, they could resist tyranny. If the treasury could be filled without their assent, they became powerless. That was the fundamental justification of the struggle with the Stuarts. How could the political descendants of the Parliament men argue that the colonists were not in like manner entitled to claim control over their contributions to the national exchequer? The taxation hitherto admitted as justifiable had a different object. The national exchequer did not materially gain by it; the advantage was with the British merchants : Hampden's principles were not set aside by it as they were by the new taxation.

Grenville, in fact, was virtually in the position of the Crown after the judges had decided that it was within the Royal prerogative to levy ship-money. The existing law was on his side, but it set at defiance one of the root principles of free government. That principle had now been established for a century in theory. Hence Pitt in England was prepared to deny altogether the right of taxing the unrepresented. On the other hand, the Constitution recognised no power which could not be set aside by the united sanction of King, Lords and Commons. Hence Grenville's contention that he was within the law. The only formal way of getting rid of the constitutional difficulty lay in giving the colonists representation at Westminster; and that was manifestly impracticable. Under such circumstances, common sense demanded that the legal right should be abrogated as opposed to sound principle, and that appeal should be made to the colonists' loyalty and sense of justice.

But the mischief was done. The colonists felt the claim of the ministers to be incompatible with the principles of free government. They resisted: the Government would not retreat. The Rockingham ministry repealed the tax, but affirmed its legality: the Rockinghams went out, Charles Townshend became Chancellor of the Exchequer; more vexatious taxes were instituted. The spirit of disloyalty and defiance grew in America; the spirit of aggressive self-assertion grew in England till the breach became too great for patching up; the humiliation of retreat was too much for either party, and the war broke out.

The record of the time following the outbreak of the war is singularly uninspiring. The skirmish of Lexington opened the campaign in April, 1775. By the end of May the British troops in Boston were reinforced; within a month, the colonials were defeated at Bunker Hill; and then George Washington arrived to take the command. The British general, Howe, seemed to consider it quite needless to take the offensive, relying it may be supposed on the incapacity of the colonial volunteers for holding together. Early in the next year he evacuated Boston. Washington removed to New York; and on July 4 the Declaration of Independence was adopted. In the late summer Washington was forced to fall back from New York, which was occupied by the British; but, since the generals continued their scheme of inactivity, the American army succeeded in occupying improved positions during the winter. In '77, converging expeditions from the North and from New York were designed; but they were faultily carried out, and Bourgoyne was isolated and forced to surrender at Saratoga in October. In a few months France declared war in favour of the colonies; it was now too late for any but an extremely energetic Government to unite activity on the American continent with the naval activity demanded by the French intervention, especially as Spanish intervention also was soon to follow.

It was at this moment that the worn-out statesman made his dying effort to rouse the British nation to throw off its lethargy and rise to the crisis. But the effort was vain. Chatham had played his part for the last time, and the curtain fell upon a closing scene not unworthy of a great career.

Chatham's attitude towards the revolted colonies is not perhaps easy to grasp. He had declared that they could not be subdued; but when their arms were reinforced by those of France he would not hear of giving up the contest. The king's view was simple; the Americans were to be coerced into submission. The Rockingham view was also simple; reconciliation and coercion were alike impossible. Chatham appears to have trusted, as he had trusted once before with signal success, to the possibility of appealing to sentiments higher and deeper than the immediate passions of the combatants. He held on to a hope of reconciliation. His theory was that England was strong enough to conquer, great enough to own her injustice even while she showed her might. He had said that America could not be coerced, because she could never be compelled to submit to oppression; she could not be kept under. But justice might be rendered under circumstances which would prove that Britain was acting not from weakness but with magnanimity. Rightly led, the nation might defy the world in arms, repudiate the base objects with which she had entered on the American contest, and still refuse to suffer the severing of a sacred bond. The task was one which might have been accomplished by the William Pitt of 1757 ; but except to the man who once already had breathed his own mighty spirit into the whole body politic—who had turned what then seemed an impossible dream into a living reality— this dream of reunion appeared out of reach. His own life was ebbing fast, nor was there another man living on whom the mantle of inspiration could descend. The dream vanished when Chatham uttered his last speech. There was none left to achieve the impossible. England did indeed emerge from the struggle not ingloriously, thanks to her sailors ; but she emerged shorn of half a continent. Pitt in the day of his power had roused England to win America : when disease had broken him, and the shadow of death lay upon him he could not rouse her to preserve what she had won.

WILLIAM PITT, EARL OF CHATHAM.

*A History of the Right Honourable William Pitt, Earl of
Chatham, containing his Speeches in Parliament, a con-
siderable Portion of his Correspondence when Secretary
of State, upon French, Spanish, and American Affairs,
never before published; and an Account of the principal
Events and Persons of his Time, connected with his Life,
Sentiments and Administration.* By the Rev. FRANCIS
THACKERAY, A.M. 2 vols. 4to. London : 1827.

THOUGH several years have elapsed since the publication of
this work, it is still, we believe, a new publication to most
of our readers. Nor are we surprised at this. The book
is large, and the style heavy. The information which Mr
Thackeray has obtained from the State Paper Office is new ; 5
but much of it is very uninteresting. The rest of his
narrative is very little better than Gifford's or Tomline's
Life of the second Pitt, and tells us little or nothing that
may not be found quite as well told in the Parliamentary
History, the Annual Register, and other works equally 10
common.

Almost every mechanical employment, it is said, has a
tendency to injure some one or other of the bodily organs
of the artisan. Grinders of cutlery die of consumption ;
weavers are stunted in their growth ; smiths become 15

blear-eyed. In the same manner almost every intellectual employment has a tendency to produce some intellectual malady. Biographers, translators, editors, all, in short, who employ themselves in illustrating the lives or the writings of 5 others, are peculiarly exposed to the *Lues Boswelliana*, or disease of admiration. But we scarcely remember ever to have seen a patient so far gone in this distemper as Mr Thackeray. He is not satisfied with forcing us to confess that Pitt was a great orator, a vigorous minister, an honour-10 able and high-spirited gentleman. He will have it that all virtues and all accomplishments met in his hero. In spite of Gods, men, and columns, Pitt must be a poet, a poet capable of producing a heroic poem of the first order ; and we are assured that we ought to find many charms in such 15 lines as these :—

> "Midst all the tumults of the warring sphere,
> My light-charged bark may haply *glide;*
> Some gale may waft, some conscious thought shall cheer,
> And the small freight unanxious *glide*[1]."

20   Pitt was in the army for a few months in time of peace. Mr Thackeray accordingly insists on our confessing that, if the young cornet had remained in the service, he would have been one of the ablest commanders that ever lived. But this is not all. Pitt, it seems, was not merely a great poet 25 *in esse*, and a great general *in posse*, but a finished example of moral excellence, the just man made perfect. He was in the right when he attempted to establish an inquisition, and to give bounties for perjury, in order to get Walpole's head. He was in the right when he declared Walpole to have been 30 an excellent minister. He was in the right when, being in opposition, he maintained that no peace ought to be made

---

[1] The quotation is faithfully made from Mr Thackeray. Perhaps Pitt wrote *guide* in the fourth line.

with Spain, till she should formally renounce the right of search. He was in the right when, being in office, he silently acquiesced in a treaty by which Spain did not renounce the right of search. When he left the Duke of Newcastle, when he coalesced with the Duke of Newcastle, 5 when he thundered against subsidies, when he lavished subsidies with unexampled profusion, when he execrated the Hanoverian connection, when he declared that Hanover ought to be as dear to us as Hampshire, he was still invariably speaking the language of a virtuous and enlightened 10 statesman.

The truth is that there scarcely ever lived a person who had so little claim to this sort of praise as Pitt. He was undoubtedly a great man. But his was not a complete and well-proportioned greatness. The public life of Hampden 15 or of Somers resembles a regular drama, which can be criticized as a whole, and every scene of which is to be viewed in connection with the main action. The public life of Pitt, on the other hand, is a rude though striking piece, a piece abounding in incongruities, a piece without any 20 unity of plan, but redeemed by some noble passages, the effect of which is increased by the tameness or extravagance of what precedes and of what follows. His opinions were unfixed. His conduct at some of the most important conjunctures of his life was evidently determined by pride and 25 resentment. He had one fault, which of all human faults is most rarely found in company with true greatness. He was extremely affected. He was an almost solitary instance of a man of real genius, and of a brave, lofty, and commanding spirit, without simplicity of character. He was an 30 actor in the Closet, an actor at Council, an actor in Parliament; and even in private society he could not lay aside his theatrical tones and attitudes. We know that one of the

most distinguished of his partisans often complained that
he could never obtain admittance to Lord Chatham's room
till every thing was ready for the representation, till the
dresses and properties were all correctly disposed, till the
5 light was thrown with Rembrandt-like effect on the head of
the illustrious performer, till the flannels had been arranged
with the air of a Grecian drapery, and the crutch placed as
gracefully as that of Belisarius or Lear.

Yet, with all his faults and affectations, Pitt had, in a
10 very extraordinary degree, many of the elements of greatness. He had genius, strong passions, quick sensibility,
and vehement enthusiasm for the grand and the beautiful.
There was something about him which ennobled tergiversa-
tion itself. He often went wrong, very wrong. But, to
15 quote the language of Wordsworth,

> " He still retained,
> 'Mid such abasement, what he had received
> From nature, an intense and glowing mind."

In an age of low and dirty prostitution, in the age of
20 Dodington and Sandys, it was something to have a man
who might perhaps, under some strong excitement, have
been tempted to ruin his country, but who never would have
stooped to pilfer from her, a man whose errors arose, not
from a sordid desire of gain, but from a fierce thirst for
25 power, for glory, and for vengeance. History owes to him this
attestation, that, at a time when anything short of direct
embezzlement of the public money was considered as quite
fair in public men, he showed the most scrupulous disinterestedness; that, at a time when it seemed to be generally
30 taken for granted that Government could be upheld only by
the basest and most immoral arts, he appealed to the better
and nobler parts of human nature; that he made a brave
and splendid attempt to do, by means of public opinion,

what no other statesman of his day thought it possible to
do, except by means of corruption; that he looked for
support, not, like the Pelhams, to a strong aristocratical
connection, not, like Bute, to the personal favour of the
sovereign, but to the middle class of Englishmen; that he 5
inspired that class with a firm confidence in his integrity
and ability; that, backed by them, he forced an unwilling
court and an unwilling oligarchy to admit him to an ample
share of power; and that he used his power in such a
manner as clearly proved him to have sought it, not for the 10
sake of profit or patronage, but from a wish to establish for
himself a great and durable reputation by means of eminent
services rendered to the state.

The family of Pitt was wealthy and respectable. His
grandfather was Governor of Madras, and brought back 15
from India that celebrated diamond which the Regent
Orleans, by the advice of Saint Simon, purchased for
upwards of two millions of livres, and which is still considered as the most precious of the crown jewels of France.
Governor Pitt bought estates and rotten boroughs, and sat 20
in the House of Commons for Old Sarum. His son
Robert was at one time member for Old Sarum, and at
another for Oakhampton. Robert had two sons. Thomas,
the elder, inherited the estates and the parliamentary
interest of his father. The second was the celebrated 25
William Pitt.

He was born in November, 1708. About the early
part of his life little more is known than that he was
educated at Eton, and that at seventeen he was entered at
Trinity College, Oxford. During the second year of his 30
residence at the University, George the First died; and the
event was, after the fashion of that generation, celebrated
by the Oxonians in many middling copies of verses. On

this occasion Pitt published some Latin lines, which Mr
Thackeray has preserved. They prove that the young
student had but a very limited knowledge even of the
mechanical part of his art. All true Etonians will hear
5 with concern that their illustrious schoolfellow is guilty of
making the first syllable in *labenti* short[1]. The matter of
the poem is as worthless as that of any college exercise that
was ever written before or since. There is, of course, much
about Mars, Themis, Neptune, and Cocytus. The Muses
10 are earnestly entreated to weep over the urn of Cæsar; for
Cæsar, says the Poet, loved the Muses; Cæsar, who could
not read a line of Pope, and who loved nothing but punch
and fat women.

Pitt had been, from his school-days, cruelly tormented
15 by the gout, and was advised to travel for his health. He
accordingly left Oxford without taking a degree, and visited
France and Italy. He returned, however, without having
received much benefit from his excursion, and continued,
till the close of his life, to suffer most severely from his
20 constitutional malady.

His father was now dead, and had left very little to the
younger children. It was necessary that William should
choose a profession. He decided for the army, and a
cornet's commission was procured for him in the Blues.

25 But, small as his fortune was, his family had both the
power and the inclination to serve him. At the general
election of 1734, his elder brother Thomas was chosen
both for Old Sarum and for Oakhampton. When Parliament met in 1735, Thomas made his election to serve for
30 Oakhampton, and William was returned for Old Sarum.

Walpole had now been, during fourteen years, at the

---

[1] So Mr Thackeray has printed the poem. But it may be charitably
hoped that Pitt wrote *labanti*.

head of affairs. He had risen to power under the most
favourable circumstances. The whole of the Whig party,
of that party which professed peculiar attachment to the
principles of the Revolution, and which exclusively enjoyed
the confidence of the reigning house, had been united in 5
support of his administration.   Happily for him, he had
been out of office when the South Sea Act was passed ; and,
though he does not appear to have foreseen all the consequences of that measure, he had strenuously opposed it, as
he had opposed all the measures, good and bad, of Sunder- 10
land's administration.   When the South-Sea Company were
voting dividends of fifty per cent., when a hundred pounds
of their stock were selling for eleven hundred pounds, when
Threadneedle Street was daily crowded with the coaches of
dukes and prelates, when divines and philosophers turned 15
gamblers, when a thousand kindred bubbles were daily
blown into existence, the periwig-company, and the Spanish-
jackass - company, and the quicksilver-fixation-company,
Walpole's calm good sense preserved him from the general
infatuation.   He condemned the prevailing madness in 20
public, and turned a considerable sum by taking advantage
of it in private.   When the crash came, when ten thousand
families were reduced to beggary in a day, when the people,
in the frenzy of their rage and despair, clamoured, not only
against the lower agents in the juggle, but against the 25
Hanoverian favourites, against the English ministers, against
the King himself, when Parliament met, eager for confiscation and blood, when members of the House of Commons
proposed that the directors should be treated like parricides
in ancient Rome, tied up in sacks, and thrown into the 30
Thames, Walpole was the man on whom all parties turned
their eyes. Four years before he had been driven from
power by the intrigues of Sunderland and Stanhope ; and

the lead in the House of Commons had been intrusted to
Craggs and Aislabie. Stanhope was no more. Aislabie
was expelled from Parliament on account of his disgraceful
conduct regarding the South-Sea scheme. Craggs was
5 perhaps saved by a timely death from a similar mark of
infamy. A large minority in the House of Commons voted
for a severe censure on Sunderland, who, finding it impossible to withstand the force of the prevailing sentiment,
retired from office, and outlived his retirement but a very
10 short time. The schism which had divided the Whig party
was now completely healed. Walpole had no opposition to
encounter except that of the Tories; and the Tories were
naturally regarded by the King with the strongest suspicion
and dislike.

15 For a time business went on with a smoothness and a
despatch such as had not been known since the days of the
Tudors. During the session of 1724, for example, there
was hardly a single division except on private bills. It is
not impossible that, by taking the course which Pelham
20 afterwards took, by admitting into the Government all the
rising talents and ambition of the Whig party, and by
making room here and there for a Tory not unfriendly to
the House of Brunswick, Walpole might have averted the
tremendous conflict in which he passed the later years of his
25 administration, and in which he was at length vanquished.
The Opposition which overthrew him was an Opposition
created by his own policy, by his own insatiable love of
power.

In the very act of forming his Ministry he turned one
30 of the ablest and most attached of his supporters into a
deadly enemy. Pulteney had strong public and private
claims to a high situation in the new arrangement. His
fortune was immense. His private character was respectable.

He was already a distinguished speaker. He had acquired official experience in an important post. He had been, through all changes of fortune, a consistent Whig. When the Whig party was split into two sections, Pulteney had resigned a valuable place, and had followed the fortunes of 5 Walpole. Yet, when Walpole returned to power, Pulteney was not invited to take office. An angry discussion took place between the friends. The Ministry offered a peerage. It was impossible for Pulteney not to discern the motive of such an offer. He indignantly refused to accept it. 10 For some time he continued to brood over his wrongs, and to watch for an opportunity of revenge. As soon as a favourable conjuncture arrived he joined the minority, and became the greatest leader of Opposition that the House of Commons had ever seen. 15

Of all the members of the Cabinet Carteret was the most eloquent and accomplished. His talents for debate were of the first order; his knowledge of foreign affairs was superior to that of any living statesman; his attachment to the Protestant succession was undoubted. But there 20 was not room in one Government for him and Walpole. Carteret retired, and was, from that time forward, one of the most persevering and formidable enemies of his old colleague.

If there was any man with whom Walpole could have 25 consented to make a partition of power, that man was Lord Townshend. They were distant kinsmen by birth, near kinsmen by marriage. They had been friends from childhood. They had been schoolfellows at Eton. They were country neighbours in Norfolk. They had been in 30 office together under Godolphin. They had gone into opposition together when Harley rose to power. They had been persecuted by the same House of Commons. They had,

after the death of Anne, been recalled together to office.
They had again been driven out together by Sunderland,
and had again come back together when the influence of
Sunderland had declined.   Their opinions on public affairs
5 almost always coincided.   They were both men of frank,
generous, and compassionate natures.   Their intercourse
had been for many years affectionate and cordial.   But the
ties of blood, of marriage, and of friendship, the memory
of mutual services, the memory of common triumphs and
10 common disasters, were insufficient to restrain that ambition
which domineered over all the virtues and vices of Walpole.
He was resolved, to use his own metaphor, that the firm of
the house should be, not Townshend and Walpole, but
Walpole and Townshend.   At length the rivals proceeded
15 to personal abuse before a large company, seized each other
by the collar, and grasped their swords.   The women
squalled.   The men parted the combatants.   By friendly
intervention the scandal of a duel between cousins, brothers-
in-law, old friends, and old colleagues, was prevented.   But
20 the disputants could not long continue to act together.
Townshend retired, and, with rare moderation and public
spirit, refused to take any part in politics.   He could not,
he said, trust his temper.   He feared that the recollection
of his private wrongs might impel him to follow the example
25 of Pulteney, and to oppose measures which he thought
generally beneficial to the country.   He therefore never
visited London after his resignation, but passed the closing
years of his life in dignity and repose among his trees and
pictures at Rainham.

30   Next went Chesterfield.   He too was a Whig and a
friend of the Protestant succession.   He was an orator, a
courtier, a wit, and a man of letters.   He was at the head
of *ton* in days when in order to be at the head of *ton*, it was

not sufficient to be dull and supercilious. It was evident
that he submitted impatiently to the ascendancy of Walpole.
He murmured against the Excise Bill. His brothers voted
against it in the House of Commons. The Minister acted
with characteristic caution and characteristic energy ; caution 5
in the conduct of public affairs ; energy where his own
supremacy was concerned. He withdrew his Bill, and
turned out all his hostile or wavering colleagues. Chesterfield was stopped on the great staircase of St James's, and
summoned to deliver up the staff which he bore as Lord 10
Steward of the Household. A crowd of noble and powerful
functionaries, the Dukes of Montrose and Bolton, Lord
Burlington, Lord Stair, Lord Cobham, Lord Marchmont,
Lord Clinton, were at the same time dismissed from the
service of the Crown.   15

Not long after these events the Opposition was reinforced
by the Duke of Argyle, a man vainglorious indeed and
fickle, but brave, eloquent and popular. It was in a great
measure owing to his exertions that the Act of Settlement
had been peaceably carried into effect in England im- 20
mediately after the death of Anne, and that the Jacobite
rebellion which, during the following year, broke out in
Scotland, had been suppressed. He too carried over to
the minority the aid of his great name, his talents, and his
paramount influence in his native country.   25

In each of these cases taken separately, a skilful
defender of Walpole might perhaps make out a case for
him. But when we see that during a long course of years
all the footsteps are turned the same way, that all the most
eminent of those public men who agreed with the Minister 30
in their general views of policy left him, one after another,
with sore and irritated minds, we find it impossible not to
believe that the real explanation of the phænomenon is to

be found in the words of his son, "Sir Robert Walpole
loved power so much that he would not endure a rival."
Hume has described this famous minister with great felicity
in one short sentence,—"moderate in exercising power, not
5 equitable in engrossing it." Kind-hearted, jovial, and
placable as Walpole was, he was yet a man with whom no
person of high pretensions and high spirit could long
continue to act. He had, therefore, to stand against an
Opposition containing all the most accomplished statesmen
10 of the age, with no better support than that which he
received from persons like his brother Horace or Henry
Pelham, whose industrious mediocrity gave no cause for
jealousy, or from clever adventurers, whose situation and
character diminished the dread which their talents might
15 have inspired. To this last class belonged Fox, who was
too poor to live without office; Sir William Yonge, of
whom Walpole himself said, that nothing but such parts
could buoy up such a character, and that nothing but such
a character could drag down such parts; and Winnington,
20 whose private morals lay, justly or unjustly, under im-
putations of the worst kind.

The discontented Whigs were, not perhaps in number,
but certainly in ability, experience, and weight, by far
the most important part of the Opposition. The Tories
25 furnished little more than rows of ponderous foxhunters,
fat with Staffordshire or Devonshire ale, men who drank
to the King over the water, and believed that all the
fundholders were Jews, men whose religion consisted in
hating the Dissenters, and whose political researches had
30 led them to fear, like Squire Western, that their land
might be sent over to Hanover to be put in the sinking-
fund. The eloquence of these zealous squires, the remnant
of the once formidable October Club, seldom went beyond

a hearty Aye or No. Very few members of this party had distinguished themselves much in Parliament, or could, under any circumstances, have been called to fill any high office; and those few had generally, like Sir William Wyndham, learned in the company of their new associates 5 the doctrines of toleration and political liberty, and might indeed with strict propriety be called Whigs.

It was to the Whigs in Opposition, the Patriots, as they were called, that the most distinguished of the English youth who at this season entered into public life attached 10 themselves. These inexperienced politicians felt all the enthusiasm which the name of liberty naturally excites in young and ardent minds. They conceived that the theory of the Tory Opposition and the practice of Walpole's Government were alike inconsistent with the principles of 15 liberty. They accordingly repaired to the standard which Pulteney had set up. While opposing the Whig minister, they professed a firm adherence to the purest doctrines of Whiggism. He was the schismatic; they were the true Catholics, the peculiar people, the depositaries of the 20 orthodox faith of Hampden and Russell, the one sect which, amidst the corruptions generated by time and by the long possession of power, had preserved inviolate the principles of the Revolution. Of the young men who attached themselves to this portion of the Opposition the 25 most distinguished were Lyttelton and Pitt.

When Pitt entered Parliament, the whole political world was attentively watching the progress of an event which soon added great strength to the Opposition, and particularly to that section of the Opposition in which the young statesman 30 enrolled himself. The Prince of Wales was gradually becoming more and more estranged from his father and his father's ministers, and more and more friendly to the Patriots.

Nothing is more natural than that, in a monarchy where
a constitutional Opposition exists, the heir-apparent of the
throne should put himself at the head of that Opposition.
He is impelled to such a course by every feeling of
5 ambition and of vanity. He cannot be more than second
in the estimation of the party which is in. He is sure to
be the first member of the party which is out. The highest
favour which the existing administration can expect from
him is that he will not discard them. But, if he joins the
10 Opposition, all his associates expect that he will promote
them; and the feelings which men entertain towards one
from whom they hope to obtain great advantages which
they have not are far warmer than the feelings with which
they regard one who, at the very utmost, can only leave
15 them in possession of what they already have. An heir-
apparent, therefore, who wishes to enjoy, in the highest
perfection, all the pleasure that can be derived from
eloquent flattery and profound respect, will always join
those who are struggling to force themselves into power.
20 This is, we believe, the true explanation of a fact which
Lord Granville attributed to some natural peculiarity in the
illustrious House of Brunswick. "This family," said he at
Council, we suppose after his daily half-gallon of Burgundy,
"always has quarrelled, and always will quarrel, from
25 generation to generation." He should have known something of the matter; for he had been a favourite with three
successive generations of the royal house. We cannot
quite admit his explanation; but the fact is indisputable.
Since the accession of George the First, there have been
30 four Princes of Wales, and they have all been almost
constantly in Opposition.

Whatever might have been the motives which induced
Prince Frederic to join the party opposed to the govern-

ment, his support infused into many members of that party a courage and an energy of which they stood greatly in need. Hitherto it had been impossible for the discontented Whigs not to feel some misgivings when they found themselves dividing, night after night, with 5 uncompromising Jacobites who were known to be in constant communication with the exiled family, or with Tories who had impeached Somers, who had murmured against Harley and St John as too remiss in the cause of the Church and the landed interest, and who, if they were 10 not inclined to attack the reigning family, yet considered the introduction of that family as, at best, only the less of two great evils, as a necessary but painful and humiliating preservative against Popery. The Minister might plausibly say that Pulteney and Carteret, in the hope of gratifying 15 their own appetite for office and for revenge, did not scruple to serve the purposes of a faction hostile to the Protestant succession. The appearance of Frederic at the head of the patriots silenced this reproach. The leaders of the Opposition might now boast that their course was sanc- 20 tioned by a person as deeply interested as the King himself in maintaining the Act of Settlement, and that, instead of serving the purposes of the Tory party, they had brought that party over to the side of Whiggism. It must indeed be admitted that, though both the King and the Prince 25 behaved in a manner little to their honour, though the father acted harshly, the son disrespectfully, and both childishly, the royal family was rather strengthened than weakened by the disagreement of its two most distinguished members. A large class of politicians, who had considered 30 themselves as placed under sentence of perpetual exclusion from office, and who, in their despair, had been almost ready to join in a counter-revolution as the only mode of

removing the proscription under which they lay, now saw
with pleasure an easier and safer road to power opening
before them, and thought it far better to wait till, in the
natural course of things, the Crown should descend to the
5 heir of the House of Brunswick, than to risk their lands
and their necks in a rising for the House of Stuart. The
situation of the royal family resembled the situation of
those Scotch families in which father and son took opposite
sides during the rebellion, in order that, come what might,
10 the estate might not be forfeited.

In April 1736, Frederic was married to the Princess
of Saxe Gotha, with whom he afterwards lived on terms
very similar to those on which his father had lived with
Queen Caroline. The Prince adored his wife, and thought
15 her in mind and person the most attractive of her sex. But
he thought that conjugal fidelity was an unprincely virtue;
and, in order to be like Henry the Fourth and the Regent
Orleans, he affected a libertinism for which he had no taste,
and frequently quitted the only woman whom he loved for
20 ugly and disagreeable mistresses.

The address which the House of Commons presented
to the King on the occasion of the Prince's marriage was
moved, not by the Minister, but by Pulteney, the leader
of the Whigs in Opposition. It was on this motion that
25 Pitt, who had not broken silence during the session in
which he took his seat, addressed the House for the first
time. "A contemporary historian," says Mr Thackeray,
"describes Mr Pitt's first speech as superior even to the
models of ancient eloquence. According to Tindal, it was
30 more ornamented than the speeches of Demosthenes, and
less diffuse than those of Cicero." This unmeaning phrase
has been a hundred times quoted. That it should ever
have been quoted, except to be laughed at, is strange. The

vogue which it has obtained may serve to show in how
slovenly a way most people are content to think. Did
Tindal, who first used it, or Archdeacon Coxe and Mr
Thackeray, who have borrowed it, ever in their lives hear
any speaking which did not deserve the same compliment? 5
Did they ever hear speaking less ornamented than that of
Demosthenes, or more diffuse than that of Cicero? We
know no living orator, from Lord Brougham down to
Mr Hunt, who is not entitled to the same eulogy. It
would be no very flattering compliment to a man's figure 10
to say, that he was taller than the Polish Count, and shorter
than Giant O'Brien, fatter than the *Anatomie Vivante*, and
more slender than Daniel Lambert.

Pitt's speech, as it is reported in the Gentleman's
Magazine, certainly deserves Tindal's compliment, and 15
deserves no other. It is just as empty and wordy as a
maiden speech on such an occasion might be expected to
be. But the fluency and the personal advantages of the
young orator instantly caught the ear and eye of his audience. He was, from the day of his first appearance, 20
always heard with attention; and exercise soon developed
the great powers which he possessed.

In our time, the audience of a member of Parliament
is the nation. The three or four hundred persons who may
be present while a speech is delivered may be pleased or 25
disgusted by the voice and action of the orator; but, in
the reports which are read the next day by hundreds of
thousands, the difference between the noblest and the
meanest figure, between the richest and the shrillest tones,
between the most graceful and the most uncouth gesture, 30
altogether vanishes. A hundred years ago, scarcely any
report of what passed within the walls of the House of
Commons was suffered to get abroad. In those times,

therefore, the impression which a speaker might make on
the persons who actually heard him was everything. His
fame out of doors depended entirely on the report of those
who were within the doors. In the Parliaments of that
5 time, therefore, as in the ancient commonwealths, those
qualifications which enhance the immediate effect of a
speech, were far more important ingredients in the composition of an orator than at present. All those qualifications Pitt possessed in the highest degree. On the
10 stage, he would have been the finest Brutus or Coriolanus
ever seen. Those who saw him in his decay, when his
health was broken, when his mind was untuned, when he
had been removed from that stormy assembly of which he
thoroughly knew the temper, and over which he possessed
15 unbounded influence, to a small, a torpid, and an unfriendly audience, say that his speaking was then, for the
most part, a low, monotonous muttering, audible only to
those who sat close to him, that when violently excited, he
sometimes raised his voice for a few minutes, but that it
20 soon sank again into an unintelligible murmur. Such was
the Earl of Chatham; but such was not William Pitt. His
figure, when he first appeared in Parliament, was strikingly
graceful and commanding, his features high and noble, his
eve full of fire. His voice, even when it sank to a whisper,
25 was heard to the remotest benches; and when he strained
it to its full extent, the sound rose like the swell of the
organ of a great cathedral, shook the house with its peal,
and was heard through lobbies and down staircases, to the
Court of Requests and the precincts of Westminster Hall.
30 He cultivated all these eminent advantages with the most
assiduous care. His action is described by a very malignant
observer as equal to that of Garrick. His play of countenance was wonderful: he frequently disconcerted a hostile

orator by a single glance of indignation or scorn. Every
tone, from the impassioned cry to the thrilling aside was
perfectly at his command. It is by no means improbable
that the pains which he took to improve his great personal
advantages had, in some respects, a prejudicial operation, 5
and tended to nourish in him that passion for theatrical
effect which, as we have already remarked, was one of
the most conspicuous blemishes in his character.

But it was not solely or principally to outward accomplishments that Pitt owed the vast influence which, during 10
nearly thirty years, he exercised over the House of Commons.
He was undoubtedly a great orator; and, from the de-
scriptions given by his contemporaries, and the fragments
of his speeches which still remain, it is not difficult to
discover the nature and extent of his oratorical powers. 15

He was no speaker of set speeches. His few prepared
discourses were complete failures. The elaborate panegyric
which he pronounced on General Wolfe was considered as
the very worst of all his performances. "No man," says
a critic who had often heard him, "ever knew so little what 20
he was going to say." Indeed his facility amounted to a
vice. He was not the master, but the slave of his own
speech. So little self-command had he when once he felt
the impulse, that he did not like to take part in a debate
when his mind was full of an important secret of state. 25
"I must sit still," he once said to Lord Shelburne on such
an occasion; "for, when once I am up, everything that is
in my mind comes out."

Yet he was not a great debater. That he should not
have been so when first he entered the House of Commons 30
is not strange. Scarcely any person has ever become so
without long practice and many failures. It was by slow
degrees, as Burke said, that the late Mr Fox became the most

brilliant and powerful debater that ever lived. Charles Fox
himself attributed his own success to the resolution which he
formed when very young, of speaking, well or ill, at least
once every night. "During five whole sessions," he used to
5 say, "I spoke every night but one; and I regret only that
I did not speak on that night too." Indeed, with the
exception of Mr-Stanley, whose knowledge of the science
of parliamentary defence resembles an instinct, it would
be difficult to name any eminent debater who has not made
10 himself a master of his art at the expense of his audience.

But, as this art is one which even the ablest men have
seldom acquired without long practice, so it is one which
men of respectable abilities, with assiduous and intrepid
practice, seldom fail to acquire.   It is singular that, in such
15 an art, Pitt, a man of great parts, of great fluency, of great
boldness, a man whose whole life was passed in parliamentary conflict, a man who, during several years, was
the leading minister of the Crown in the House of Commons,
should never have attained to high excellence. He spoke
20 without premeditation; but his speech followed the course
of his own thoughts, and not the course of the previous
discussion. He could, indeed, treasure up in his memory
some detached expression of an opponent, and make it the
text for lively ridicule or solemn reprehension. Some of
25 the most celebrated bursts of his eloquence were called
forth by an unguarded word, a laugh, or a cheer. But this
was the only sort of reply in which he appears to have
excelled. He was perhaps the only great English orator
who did not think it any advantage to have the last word,
30 and who generally spoke by choice before his most formidable antagonists. His merit was almost entirely rhetorical. He did not succeed either in exposition or in
refutation; but his speeches abounded with lively illus-

trations, striking apophthegms, well told anecdotes, happy
allusions, passionate appeals. His invective and sarcasm
were terrific. Perhaps no English orator was ever so much
feared.

But that which gave most effect to his declamation was 5
the air of sincerity, of vehement feeling, of moral elevation,
which belonged to all that he said. His style was not
always in the purest taste. Several contemporary judges
pronounced it too florid. Walpole, in the midst of the
rapturous eulogy which he pronounces on one of Pitt's 10
greatest orations, owns that some of the metaphors were
too forced. Some of Pitt's quotations and classical stories
are too trite for a clever schoolboy. But these were niceties
for which the audience cared little. The enthusiasm of
the orator infected all who heard him; his ardour and his 15
noble bearing put fire into the most frigid conceit, and
gave dignity to the most puerile allusion.

His powers soon began to give annoyance to the Government; and Walpole determined to make an example of the
patriotic cornet. Pitt was accordingly dismissed from the 20
service. Mr Thackeray says that the Minister took this step
because he plainly saw that it would have been vain to
think of buying over so honourable and disinterested an
opponent. We do not dispute Pitt's integrity; but we do
not know what proof he had given of it when he was turned 25
out of the army; and we are sure that Walpole was not
likely to give credit for inflexible honesty to a young
adventurer who had never had an opportunity of refusing
anything. The truth is, that it was not Walpole's practice
to buy off enemies. Mr Burke truly says, in the Appeal 30
to the Old Whigs, that Walpole gained very few over
from the Opposition. Indeed that great minister knew his
business far too well. He knew that, for one mouth which

is stopped with a place, fifty other mouths will be instantly
opened.   He knew that it would have been very bad policy
in him to give the world to understand that more was to
be got by thwarting his measures than by supporting them.
5 These maxims are as old as the origin of parliamentary
corruption in England.   Pepys learned them, as he tells
us, from the counsellors of Charles the Second.

Pitt was no loser.   He was made Groom of the Bed-
chamber to the Prince of Wales, and continued to declaim
10 against the ministers with unabated violence and with increasing ability.   The question of maritime right, then
agitated between Spain and England, called forth all his
powers.   He clamoured for war with a vehemence which
it is not easy to reconcile with reason or humanity, but
15 which appears to Mr Thackeray worthy of the highest
admiration.   We will not stop to argue a point on which
we had long thought that all well informed people were
agreed.   We could easily show, we think, that, if any
respect be due to international law, if right, where societies
20 of men are concerned, be anything but another name for
might, if we do not adopt the doctrine of the Buccaneers,
which seems to be also the doctrine of Mr Thackeray, that
treaties mean nothing within thirty degrees of the line, the
war with Spain was altogether unjustifiable.   But the truth
25 is, that the promoters of that war have saved the historian
the trouble of trying them.   They have pleaded guilty.   " I
have seen," says Burke, "and with some care examined,
the original documents concerning certain important transactions of those times.   They perfectly satisfied me of the
30 extreme injustice of that war, and of the falsehood of the
colours which Walpole, to his ruin, and guided by a mistaken policy, suffered to be daubed over that measure.   Some
years after, it was my fortune to converse with many of

the principal actors against that minister, and with those
who principally excited that clamour.   None of them, no
not one, did in the least defend the measure, or attempt to
justify their conduct.   They condemned it as freely as they
would have done in commenting upon any proceeding in 5
history in which they were totally unconcerned."   Pitt, on
subsequent occasions, gave ample proof that he was one
of these penitents.   But his conduct, even where it appeared most criminal to himself, appears admirable to his
biographer.   10

The elections of 1741 were unfavourable to Walpole;
and after a long and obstinate struggle he found it necessary
to resign.   The Duke of Newcastle and Lord Hardwicke
opened a negotiation with the leading patriots, in the hope
of forming an administration on a Whig basis.   At this 15
conjuncture, Pitt and those persons who were most nearly
connected with him acted in a manner very little to their
honour.   They attempted to come to an understanding with
Walpole, and offered, if he would use his influence with
the King in their favour, to screen him from prosecution. 20
They even went so far as to engage for the concurrence
of the Prince of Wales.   But Walpole knew that the assistance of the Boys, as he called the young Patriots, would
avail him nothing if Pulteney and Carteret should prove
intractable, and would be superfluous if the great leaders 25
of the Opposition could be gained.   He, therefore, declined
the proposal.   It is remarkable that Mr Thackeray, who
has thought it worth while to preserve Pitt's bad college
verses, has not even alluded to this story, a story which
is supported by strong testimony, and which may be found 30
in so common a book as Coxe's *Life of Walpole*.

The new arrangements disappointed almost every member
of the Opposition, and none more than Pitt.   He was not

invited to become a placeman; and he therefore stuck
firmly to his old trade of patriot. Fortunate it was for
him that he did so. Had he taken office at this time, he
would in all probability have shared largely in the un-
5 popularity of Pulteney, Sandys, and Carteret. He was
now the fiercest and most implacable of those who called
for vengeance on Walpole. He spoke with great energy
and ability in favour of the most unjust and violent propositions which the enemies of the fallen minister could
10 invent. He urged the House of Commons to appoint a
secret tribunal for the purpose of investigating the conduct
of the late First Lord of the Treasury. This was done.
The great majority of the inquisitors were notoriously hostile
to the accused statesman. Yet they were compelled to own
15 that they could find no fault in him. They therefore called
for new powers, for a bill of indemnity to witnesses, or,
in plain words, for a bill to reward all who might give
evidence, true or false, against the Earl of Orford. This
bill Pitt supported, Pitt, who had himself offered to be a
20 screen between Lord Orford and public justice. These are
melancholy facts. Mr Thackeray omits them, or hurries
over them as fast as he can; and, as eulogy is his business,
he is in the right to do so. But, though there are many
parts of the life of Pitt which it is more agreeable to con-
25 template, we know none more instructive. What must have
been the general state of political morality, when a young
man, considered, and justly considered, as the most public-
spirited and spotless statesman of his time, could attempt
to force his way into office by means so disgraceful!

30   The Bill of Indemnity was rejected by the Lords.
Walpole withdrew himself quietly from the public eye; and
the ample space which he had left vacant was soon occupied
by Carteret. Against Carteret Pitt began to thunder with

as much zeal as he had ever manifested against Sir Robert. To Carteret he transferred most of the hard names which were familiar to his eloquence, sole minister, wicked minister, odious minister, execrable minister. The chief topic of Pitt's invective was the favour shown to the German do- 5 minions of the house of Brunswick. He attacked with great violence, and with an ability which raised him to the very first rank among the parliamentary speakers, the practice of paying Hanoverian troops with English money. The House of Commons had lately lost some of its most 10 distinguished ornaments. Walpole and Pulteney had accepted peerages; Sir William Wyndham was dead; and among the rising men none could be considered, as, on the whole, a match for Pitt.

During the recess of 1744, the old Duchess of Marl- 15 borough died. She carried to her grave the reputation of being decidedly the best hater of her time. Yet her love had been infinitely more destructive than her hatred. More than thirty years before, her temper had ruined the party to which she belonged and the husband whom she adored. 20 Time had made her neither wiser nor kinder. Whoever was at any moment great and prosperous was the object of her fiercest detestation. She had hated Walpole; she now hated Carteret. Pope, long before her death, predicted the fate of her vast property. 25

" To heirs unknown descends the unguarded store,
   Or wanders, heaven directed, to the poor."

Pitt was then one of the poor, and to him Heaven directed a portion of the wealth of the haughty Dowager. She left him a legacy of ten thousand pounds, in con- 30 sideration of " the noble defence he had made for the support of the laws of England and to prevent the ruin of his country."

The will was made in August. The Duchess died in
October. In November Pitt was a courtier. The Pelhams
had forced the King, much against his will, to part with
Lord Carteret, who had now become Earl Granville. They
5 proceeded, after this victory, to form the Government on
that basis, called by the cant name of "the broad bottom."
Lyttelton had a seat at the Treasury, and several other
friends of Pitt were provided for. But Pitt himself was,
for the present, forced to be content with promises. The
10 King resented most highly some expressions which the
ardent orator had used in the debate on the Hanoverian
troops. But Newcastle and Pelham expressed the strongest
confidence that time and their exertions would soften the
royal displeasure.

15   Pitt, on his part, omitted nothing that might facilitate
his admission to office. He resigned his place in the
household of Prince Frederic, and, when Parliament met,
exerted his eloquence in support of the Government. The
Pelhams were really sincere in their endeavours to remove
20 the strong prejudices which had taken root in the King's
mind. They knew that Pitt was not a man to be deceived
with ease or offended with impunity. They were afraid
that they should not be long able to put him off with
promises. Nor was it their interest so to put him off.
25 There was a strong tie between him and them. He was
the enemy of their enemy. The brothers hated and dreaded
the eloquent, aspiring, and imperious Granville. They had
traced his intrigues in many quarters. They knew his
influence over the royal mind. They knew that, as soon
30 as a favourable opportunity should arrive, he would be
recalled to the head of affairs. · They resolved to bring
things to a crisis; and the question on which they took
issue with their master was, whether Pitt should or should

not be admitted to office. They chose their time with more skill than generosity. It was when rebellion was actually raging in Britain, when the Pretender was master of the northern extremity of the island, that they tendered their resignations. The King found himself deserted, in one day, 5 by the whole strength of that party which had placed his family on the throne. Lord Granville tried to form a government; but it soon appeared that the parliamentary interest of the Pelhams was irresistible, and that the King's favourite statesman could count only on about thirty Lords 10 and eighty members of the House of Commons. The scheme was given up. Granville went away laughing. The ministers came back stronger than ever; and the King was now no longer able to refuse anything that they might be pleased to demand. He could only mutter that it was very hard 15 that Newcastle, who was not fit to be chamberlain to the most insignificant prince in Germany, should dictate to the King of England.

One concession the ministers graciously made. They agreed that Pitt should not be placed in a situation in 20 which it would be necessary for him to have frequent interviews with the King. Instead, therefore, of making their new ally Secretary-at-War as they had intended, they appointed him Vice-Treasurer of Ireland, and in a few months promoted him to the office of Paymaster of the 25 Forces.

This was, at that time, one of the most lucrative offices in the Government. The salary was but a small part of the emolument which the Paymaster derived from his place. He was allowed to keep a large sum, which, even in time of 30 peace, was seldom less than one hundred thousand pounds, constantly in his hands; and the interest on this sum he might appropriate to his own use. This practice was not

secret, nor was it considered as disreputable. It was the
practice of men of undoubted honour, both before and
after the time of Pitt. He, however, refused to accept one
farthing beyond the salary which the law had annexed to
5 his office. It had been usual for foreign princes who received the pay of England to give to the Paymaster of the
Forces a small per centage on the subsidies. These ignominious vails Pitt resolutely declined.

Disinterestedness of this kind was, in his days, very
10 rare. His conduct surprised and amused politicians. It
excited the warmest admiration throughout the body of the
people. In spite of the inconsistencies of which Pitt had
been guilty, in spite of the strange contrast between his
violence in Opposition and his tameness in office, he still
15 possessed a large share of the public confidence. The
motives which may lead a politician to change his connections or his general line of conduct are often obscure; but
disinterestedness in pecuniary matters every body can understand. Pitt was thenceforth considered as a man who
20 was proof to all sordid temptations. If he acted ill, it
might be from an error in judgment; it might be from
resentment; it might be from ambition. But poor as
he was, he had vindicated himself from all suspicion of
covetousness.

25   Eight quiet years followed, eight years during which the
minority, which had been feeble ever since Lord Granville
had been overthrown, continued to dwindle till it became
almost invisible. Peace was made with France and Spain
in 1748. Prince Frederic died in 1751; and with him
30 died the very semblance of opposition. All the most
distinguished survivors of the party which had supported
Walpole and of the party which had opposed him were
united under his successor. The fiery and vehement spirit

of Pitt had for a time been laid to rest. He silently
acquiesced in that very system of continental measures
which he had lately condemned.   He ceased to talk
disrespectfully about Hanover.   He did not object to the
treaty with Spain, though that treaty left us exactly where 5
we had been when he uttered his spirit-stirring harangues
against the pacific policy of Walpole.   Now and then
glimpses of his former self appeared; but they were few
and transient.   Pelham knew with whom he had to deal,
and felt that an ally, so little used to control, and so capable 10
of inflicting injury, might well be indulged in an occasional
fit of waywardness.

    Two men, little, if at all, inferior to Pitt in powers of
mind, held, like him, subordinate offices in the Government.
One of these, Murray, was successively Solicitor-General 15
and Attorney-General.   This distinguished person far surpassed Pitt in correctness of taste, in power of reasoning,
in depth and variety of knowledge.   His parliamentary
eloquence never blazed into sudden flashes of dazzling
brilliancy; but its clear, placid, and mellow splendour was 20
never for an instant overclouded.   Intellectually he was, we
believe, fully equal to Pitt; but he was deficient in the
moral qualities to which Pitt owed most of his success.
Murray wanted the energy, the courage, the all-grasping and
all-risking ambition, which make men great in stirring times. 25
His heart was a little cold, his temper cautious even to
timidity, his manners decorous even to formality.   He
never exposed his fortunes or his fame to any risk which
he could avoid.   At one time he might, in all probability,
have been Prime Minister.   But the object of his wishes 30
was the judicial bench.   The situation of Chief Justice
might not be so splendid as that of First Lord of the
Treasury; but it was dignified; it was quiet; it was

secure; and therefore it was the favourite situation of Murray.

Fox, the father of the great man whose mighty efforts in the cause of peace, of truth, and of liberty, have made that name immortal, was Secretary-at-War. He was a favourite with the King, with the Duke of Cumberland, and with some of the most powerful members of the great Whig connection. His parliamentary talents were of the highest order. As a speaker he was in almost all respects the very opposite to Pitt. His figure was ungraceful; his face, as Reynolds and Nollekens have preserved it to us, indicated a strong understanding; but the features were coarse, and the general aspect dark and lowering. His manner was awkward; his delivery was hesitating; he was often at a stand for want of a word; but as a debater, as a master of that keen, weighty, manly logic, which is suited to the discussion of political questions, he has perhaps never been surpassed except by his son. In reply he was as decidedly superior to Pitt as in declamation he was Pitt's inferior. Intellectually the balance was nearly even between the rivals. But here, again, the moral qualities of Pitt turned the scale. Fox had undoubtedly many virtues. In natural disposition as well as in talents, he bore a great resemblance to his more celebrated son. He had the same sweetness of temper, the same strong passions, the same openness, boldness, and impetuosity, the same cordiality towards friends, the same placability towards enemies. No man was more warmly or justly beloved by his family or by his associates. But unhappily he had been trained in a bad political school, in a school, the doctrines of which were, that political virtue is the mere coquetry of political prostitution, that every patriot has his price, that Government can be carried on only by means of corruption, and that the state is given as a prey to statesmen. These maxims were too much in vogue throughout the lower ranks of Walpole's party, and were too much encouraged by Walpole himself, who, from contempt of what is in our day vulgarly called *humbug*, often ran extravagantly and offensively into the opposite extreme. The loose political morality of Fox presented a remarkable contrast to the ostentatious purity of Pitt. The nation distrusted the former, and placed implicit confidence in the latter. But almost all the statesmen of the age had still to learn that the confidence of the nation was worth having. While things went on quietly, while there was no opposition, while every thing was given by the favour of a small ruling junto, Fox had a decided advantage over Pitt; but when dangerous times came, when Europe was convulsed with war, when Parliament was broken up into factions, when the public mind was violently excited, the favourite of the people rose to supreme power, while his rival sank into insignificance.

Early in the year 1754 Henry Pelham died unexpectedly. "Now I shall have no more peace," exclaimed the old King, when he heard the news. He was in the right. Pelham had succeeded in bringing together and keeping together all the talents of the kingdom. By his death, the highest post to which an English subject can aspire was left vacant; and at the same moment, the influence which had yoked together and reined in so many turbulent and ambitious spirits was withdrawn.

Within a week after Pelham's death, it was determined that the Duke of Newcastle should be placed at the head of the Treasury; but the arrangement was still far from complete. Who was to be the leading Minister of the Crown in the House of Commons? Was the office to be intrusted to a man of eminent talents? And would not

such a man in such a place demand and obtain a larger
share of power and patronage than Newcastle would be
disposed to concede? Was a mere drudge to be employed?
And what probability was there that a mere drudge would
5 be able to manage a large and stormy assembly, abounding
with able and experienced men?

Pope had said of that wretched miser Sir John Cutler,

"Cutler saw tenants break and houses fall
For very want: he could not build a wall."

10 Newcastle's love of power resembled Cutler's love of money.
It was an avarice which thwarted itself, a penny-wise and
pound-foolish cupidity.   An immediate outlay was so
painful to him that he would not venture to make the
most desirable improvement. If he could have found it
15 in his heart to cede at once a portion of his authority, he
might probably have ensured the continuance of what
remained. But he thought it better to construct a weak
and rotten government, which tottered at the smallest
breath, and fell in the first storm, than to pay the
20 necessary price for sound and durable materials.   He
wished to find some person who would be willing to
accept the lead of the House of Commons on terms
similar to those on which Secretary Craggs had acted
under Sunderland, five-and-thirty years before.   Craggs
25 could hardly be called a minister. He was a mere agent
for the Minister. He was not trusted with the higher
secrets of state, but obeyed implicitly the directions of
his superior, and was, to use Dodington's expression,
merely Lord Sunderland's man. But times were changed.
30 Since the days of Sunderland, the importance of the
House of Commons had been constantly on the increase.
During many years, the person who conducted the business
of the Government in that House had almost always been

Prime Minister. In these circumstances, it was not to be supposed that any person who possessed the talents necessary for the situation would stoop to accept it on such terms as Newcastle was disposed to offer.

Pitt was ill at Bath; and, had he been well and in London, neither the King nor Newcastle would have been disposed to make any overtures to him. The cool and wary Murray had set his heart on professional objects. Negotiations were opened with Fox. Newcastle behaved like himself, that is to say, childishly and basely. The proposition which he made was that Fox should be Secretary of State, with the lead of the House of Commons; that the disposal of the secret-service money, or in plain words, the business of buying members of Parliament should be left to the First Lord of the Treasury; but that Fox should be exactly informed of the way in which this fund was employed.

To these conditions Fox assented. But the next day every thing was in confusion. Newcastle had changed his mind. The conversation which took place between Fox and the Duke is one of the most curious in English history. "My brother," said Newcastle, "when he was at the Treasury, never told anybody what he did with the secret-service money. No more will I." The answer was obvious. Pelham had been, not only First Lord of the Treasury, but also manager of the House of Commons; and it was therefore unnecessary for him to confide to any other person his dealings with the members of that House. "But how," said Fox, "can I lead in the Commons without information on this head? How can I talk to gentle-men when I do not know which of them have received gratifications and which have not? And who," he continued, "is to have the disposal of places?"—"I myself,"

34 — WILLIAM PITT,

said the Duke.—"How then am I to manage the House
of Commons?"—"Oh, let the members of the House of
Commons come to me." Fox then mentioned the general
election which was approaching, and asked how the ministerial boroughs were to be filled up. "Do not trouble
yourself," said Newcastle; "that is all settled." This was
too much for human nature to bear. Fox refused to accept
the Secretaryship of State on such terms; and the Duke
confided the management of the House of Commons to a
dull, harmless man, whose name is almost forgotten in our
time, Sir Thomas Robinson.

When Pitt returned from Bath he affected great moderation, though his haughty soul was boiling with resentment.
He did not complain of the manner in which he had been
passed by, but said openly that, in his opinion, Fox was
the fittest man to lead the House of Commons. The rivals,
reconciled by their common interest and their common
enmities, concerted a plan of operations for the next session.
"Sir Thomas Robinson lead us!" said Pitt to Fox. "The
Duke might as well send his jack-boot to lead us."

The elections of 1754 were favourable to the administration. But the aspect of foreign affairs was threatening.
In India the English and the French had been employed,
ever since the peace of Aix-la-Chapelle, in cutting each
other's throats. They had lately taken to the same practice
in America. It might have been foreseen that stirring times
were at hand, times which would call for abilities very
different from those of Newcastle and Robinson.

In November the Parliament met; and before the end
of that month the new Secretary of State had been so
unmercifully baited by the Paymaster of the Forces and
the Secretary at War that he was thoroughly sick of his
situation. Fox attacked him with great force and acrimony.

Pitt affected a kind of contemptuous tenderness for Sir
Thomas, and directed his attacks principally against Newcastle. On one occasion he asked in tones of thunder
whether Parliament sat only to register the edicts of one
too powerful subject? The Duke was scared out of his 5
wits. He was afraid to dismiss the mutineers; he was
afraid to promote them; but it was absolutely necessary to
do something. Fox, as the less proud and intractable of
the refractory pair, was preferred. A seat in the Cabinet
was offered to him on condition that he would give efficient 10
support to the ministry in Parliament. In an evil hour
for his fame and his fortunes he accepted the offer, and
abandoned his connection with Pitt, who never forgave
this desertion.

Sir Thomas, assisted by Fox, contrived to get through 15
the business of the year without much trouble. Pitt was
waiting his time. The negotiations pending between France
and England took every day a more unfavourable aspect.
Towards the close of the session the King sent a message
to inform the House of Commons that he had found it 20
necessary to make preparations for war. The House returned an address of thanks, and passed a vote of credit.
During the recess, the old animosity of both nations was
inflamed by a series of disastrous events. An English force
was cut off in America; and several French merchantmen 25
were taken in the West Indian seas. It was plain that
an appeal to arms was at hand.

The first object of the King was to secure Hanover; and
Newcastle was disposed to gratify his master. Treaties were
concluded, after the fashion of those times, with several 30
petty German princes, who bound themselves to find soldiers
if England would find money; and, as it was suspected that
Frederic the Second had set his heart on the electoral

3—2

dominions of his uncle, Russia was hired to keep Prussia in awe.

When the stipulations of these treaties were made known, there arose throughout the kingdom a murmur from which 5 a judicious observer might easily prognosticate the approach of a tempest. Newcastle encountered strong opposition, even from those whom he had always considered as his tools. Legge, the Chancellor of the Exchequer, refused to sign the Treasury warrants which were necessary to give 10 effect to the treaties. Those persons who were supposed to possess the confidence of the young Prince of Wales and of his mother held very menacing language. In this perplexity Newcastle sent for Pitt, hugged him, patted him, smirked at him, wept over him, and lisped out the highest 15 compliments and the most splendid promises. The King who had hitherto been as sulky as possible, would be civil to him at the leeve ; he should be brought into the Cabinet ; he should be consulted about everything ; if he would only be so good as to support the Hessian subsidy in the House 20 of Commons. Pitt coldly declined the proffered seat in the Cabinet, expressed the highest love and reverence for the King, and said that, if his Majesty felt a strong personal interest in the Hessian treaty he would so far deviate from the line which he had traced out for himself as to give 25 that treaty his support. "Well, and the Russian subsidy," said Newcastle. "No," said Pitt, "not a system of subsidies." The Duke summoned Lord Hardwicke to his aid ; but Pitt was inflexible. Murray would do nothing. Robinson could do nothing. It was necessary to have 30 recourse to Fox. He became Secretary of State, with the full authority of a leader in the House of Commons ; and Sir Thomas was pensioned off on the Irish establishment.

In November, 1755, the Houses met. Public expectation was wound up to the height. After ten quiet years there was to be an Opposition, countenanced by the heir apparent of the throne, and headed by the most brilliant orator of the age. The debate on the address was long 5 remembered as one of the greatest parliamentary conflicts of that generation. It began at three in the afternoon, and lasted till five the next morning. It was on this night that Gerard Hamilton delivered that single speech from which his nickname was derived. His eloquence threw 10 into the shade every orator except Pitt, who declaimed against the subsidies for an hour and a half with extraordinary energy and effect. Those powers which had formerly spread terror through the majorities of Walpole and Carteret were now displayed in their highest perfection 15 before an audience long unaccustomed to such exhibitions. One fragment of this celebrated oration remains in a state of tolerable preservation. It is the comparison between the coalition of Fox and Newcastle, and the junction of the Rhone and the Saone. " At Lyons," said Pitt, " I 20 was taken to see the place where the two rivers meet, the one gentle, feeble, languid, and, though languid, yet of no depth, the other a boisterous and impetuous torrent : but different as they are, they meet at last." The amendment moved by the Opposition was rejected by a great majority ; 25 and Pitt and Legge were immediately dismissed from their offices.

During several months the contest in the House of Commons was extremely sharp. Warm debates took place on the estimates, debates still warmer on the subsidiary 30 treaties. The Government succeeded in every division ; but the fame of Pitt's eloquence, and the influence of his lofty and determined character, continued to increase through the Session; and the events which followed the prorogation made it utterly impossible for any other person to manage the Parliament or the country.

The war began in every part of the world with events
5 disastrous to England, and even more shameful than disastrous. But the most humiliating of these events was the loss of Minorca. The Duke of Richelieu, an old fop who had passed his life from sixteen to sixty in seducing women for whom he cared not one straw, landed on that island,
10 and succeeded in reducing it. Admiral Byng was sent from Gibraltar to throw succours into Port-Mahon; but he did not think fit to engage the French squadron, and sailed back without having effected his purpose. The people were inflamed to madness. A storm broke forth,
15 which appalled even those who remembered the days of Excise and of South-Sea. The shops were filled with libels and caricatures. The walls were covered with placards. The city of London called for vengeance, and the cry was echoed from every corner of the kingdom. Dorsetshire,
20 Huntingdonshire, Bedfordshire, Buckinghamshire, Somersetshire, Lancashire, Suffolk, Shropshire, Surrey, sent up strong addresses to the throne, and instructed their representatives to vote for a strict inquiry into the causes of the late disasters. In the great towns the feeling was as
25 strong as in the counties. In some of the instructions it was even recommended that the supplies should be stopped.

The nation was in a state of angry and sullen despondency, almost unparalleled in history. People have, in all ages, been in the habit of talking about the good old times
30 of their ancestors, and the degeneracy of their contemporaries. This is in general merely a cant. But in 1756 it was something more. At this time appeared Brown's *Estimate*, a book now remembered only by the allusions in

Cowper's *Table Talk* and in Burke's *Letters on a Regicide Peace*. It was universally read, admired, and believed. The author fully convinced his readers that they were a race of cowards and scoundrels; that nothing could save them; that they were on the point of being enslaved by their 5 enemies, and that they richly deserved their fate. Such were the speculations to which ready credence was given at the outset of the most glorious war in which England had ever been engaged.

Newcastle now began to tremble for his place, and for 10 the only thing which was dearer to him than his place, his neck. The people were not in a mood to be trifled with. Their cry was for blood. For this once they might be contented with the sacrifice of Byng. But what if fresh disasters should take place? What if an unfriendly sove- 15 reign should ascend the throne? What if a hostile House of Commons should be chosen?

At length, in October, the decisive crisis came. The new Secretary of State had been long sick of the perfidy and levity of the First Lord of the Treasury, and began 20 to fear that he might be made a scapegoat to save the old intriguer who, imbecile as he seemed, never wanted dexterity where danger was to be avoided. Fox threw up his office. Newcastle had recourse to Murray; but Murray had now within his reach the favourite object of his am- 25 bition. The situation of Chief-Justice of the King's Bench was vacant; and the Attorney-General was fully resolved to obtain it, or to go into opposition. Newcastle offered him any terms, the Duchy of Lancaster for life, a tellership of the Exchequer, any amount of pension, two thousand 30 a year, six thousand a year. When the Ministers found that Murray's mind was made up, they pressed for delay, the delay of a session, a month, a week, a day. Would

he only make his appearance once more in the House of Commons? Would he only speak in favour of the address? He was inexorable, and peremptorily said that they might give or withhold the Chief-Justiceship, but that he would
5 be Attorney-General no longer.

Newcastle now contrived to overcome the prejudices of the King, and overtures were made to Pitt, through Lord Hardwicke. Pitt knew his power, and showed that he knew it. He demanded as an indispensable condition
10 that Newcastle should be altogether excluded from the new arrangement.

The Duke was in a state of ludicrous distress. He ran about chattering and crying, asking advice and listening to none. In the mean time, the Session drew near. The
15 public excitement was unabated. Nobody could be found to face Pitt and Fox in the House of Commons. New-castle's heart failed him, and he tendered his resignation.

The King sent for Fox, and directed him to form the plan of an administration in concert with Pitt. But Pitt
20 had not forgotten old injuries, and positively refused to act with Fox.

The King now applied to the Duke of Devonshire, and this mediator succeeded in making an arrangement. He consented to take the Treasury. Pitt became Secretary
25 of State, with the lead of the House of Commons. The Great Seal was put into commission. Legge returned to the Exchequer; and Lord Temple, whose sister Pitt had lately married, was placed at the head of the Admiralty.

It was clear from the first that this administration would
30 last but a very short time. It lasted not quite five months; and, during those five months, Pitt and Lord Temple were treated with rudeness by the King, and found but feeble support in the House of Commons. It is a remarkable

fact, that the Opposition prevented the re-election of some of the new Ministers. Pitt, who sat for one of the boroughs which were in the Pelham interest, found some difficulty in obtaining a seat after his acceptance of the seals. So destitute was the new Government of that sort of influence without which no government could then be durable. One of the arguments most frequently urged against the Reform Bill was that, under a system of popular representation, men whose presence in the House of Commons was necessary to the conducting of public business might often find it impossible to find seats. Should this inconvenience ever be felt, there cannot be the slightest difficulty in devising and applying a remedy. But those who threatened us with this evil ought to have remembered that, under the old system, a great man called to power at a great crisis by the voice of the whole nation was in danger of being excluded, by an aristocratical cabal, from that House of which he was the most distinguished ornament.

The most important event of this short administration was the trial of Byng. On that subject public opinion is still divided. We think the punishment of the Admiral altogether unjust and absurd. Treachery, cowardice, ignorance amounting to what lawyers have called *crassa ignorantia*, are fit objects of severe penal inflictions. But Byng was not found guilty of treachery, of cowardice, or of gross ignorance of his profession. He died for doing what the most loyal subject, the most intrepid warrior, the most experienced seaman, might have done. He died for an error in judgment, an error such as the greatest commanders, Frederic, Napoleon, Wellington, have often committed, and have often acknowledged. Such errors are not proper objects of punishment, for this reason, that the punishing of such errors tends not to prevent them, but to produce them. The dread of an ignominious death may stimulate sluggishness to exertion, may keep a traitor to his standard, may prevent a coward from running away, but it has no tendency to bring out those qualities which 5 enable men to form prompt and judicious decisions in great emergencies. The best marksman may be expected to fail when the apple which is to be his mark is set on his child's head. We cannot conceive anything more likely to deprive an officer of his self-possession at the time when he most 10 needs it than the knowledge that, if the judgment of his superiors should not agree with his, he will be executed with every circumstance of shame. Queens, it has often been said, run far greater risk in childbed than private women, merely because their medical attendants are more 15 anxious. The surgeon who attended Marie Louise was altogether unnerved by his emotions. "Compose yourself," said Bonaparte; "imagine that you are assisting a poor girl in the Faubourg Saint Antoine." This was surely a far wiser course than that of the Eastern king in the *Arabian Nights'* 20 *Entertainments*, who proclaimed that the physicians who failed to cure his daughter should have their heads chopped off. Bonaparte knew mankind well; and, as he acted towards this surgeon, he acted towards his officers. No sovereign was ever so indulgent to mere errors of judg- 25 ment; and it is certain that no sovereign ever had in his service so many military men fit for the highest commands.

Pitt acted a brave and honest part on this occasion. He ventured to put both his power and his popularity to 30 hazard, and spoke manfully for Byng, both in Parliament and in the royal presence. But the King was inexorable. "The House of Commons, Sir," said Pitt, "seems inclined to mercy." "Sir," answered the King, "you have taught

me to look for the sense of my people in other places than
the House of Commons." The saying has more point
than most of those which are recorded of George the
Second, and, though sarcastically meant, contains a high
and just compliment to Pitt.   5

The King disliked Pitt, but absolutely hated Temple.
The new Secretary of State, his Majesty said, had never
read Vattel, and was tedious and pompous, but respectful.
The First Lord of the Admiralty was grossly impertinent.
Walpole tells one story, which, we fear, is much too good 10
to be true. He assures us that Temple entertained his
royal master with an elaborate parallel between Byng's
behaviour at Minorca, and his Majesty's behaviour at
Oudenarde, in which the advantage was all on the side of
the Admiral.   15

This state of things could not last. Early in April,
Pitt and all his friends were turned out, and Newcastle
was summoned to St James's. But the public discontent
was not extinguished. It had subsided when Pitt was
called to power. But it still glowed under the embers; 20
and it now burst at once into a flame. The stocks fell.
The Common Council met. The freedom of the city was
voted to Pitt. All the greatest corporate towns followed
the example. "For some weeks," says Walpole, "it rained
gold boxes."   25

This was the turning point of Pitt's life. It might have
been expected that a man of so haughty and vehement a
nature, treated so ungraciously by the Court, and supported
so enthusiastically by the people, would have eagerly taken
the first opportunity of showing his power and gratifying 30
his resentment; and an opportunity was not wanting. The
members for many counties and large towns had been
instructed to vote for an inquiry into the circumstances

which had produced the miscarriage of the preceding year.
A motion for inquiry had been carried in the House of
Commons, without opposition; and, a few days after Pitt's
dismissal, the investigation commenced, Newcastle and his
5 colleagues obtained a vote of acquittal; but the minority
were so strong that they could not venture to ask for a
vote of approbation, as they had at first intended; and it
was thought by some shrewd observers that, if Pitt had
exerted himself to the utmost of his power, the inquiry
10 might have ended in a censure, if not in an impeachment.

Pitt showed on this occasion a moderation and self-
government which was not habitual to him. He had
found by experience, that he could not stand alone. His
eloquence and his popularity had done much, very much
15 for him. Without rank, without fortune, without borough
interest, hated by the King, hated by the aristocracy, he
was a person of the first importance in the state. He
had been suffered to form a ministry, and to pronounce
sentence of exclusion on all his rivals, on the most powerful
20 nobleman of the Whig party, on the ablest debater in the
House of Commons. And he now found that he had
gone too far. The English Constitution was not, indeed,
without a popular element. But other elements generally
predominated. The confidence and admiration of the
25 nation might make a statesman formidable at the head of
an Opposition, might load him with framed and glazed
parchments and gold boxes, might possibly, under very
peculiar circumstances, such as those of the preceding
year, raise him for a time to power. But, constituted as
30 Parliament then was, the favourite of the people could not
depend on a majority in the people's own House. The
Duke of Newcastle, however contemptible in morals,
manners, and understanding, was a dangerous enemy.

His rank, his wealth, his unrivalled parliamentary interest, would alone have made him important. But this was not all. The Whig aristocracy regarded him as their leader. His long possession of power had given him a kind of prescriptive right to possess it still. The House of 5 Commons had been elected when he was at the head of affairs. The members for the ministerial boroughs had all been nominated by him. The public offices swarmed with his creatures.

Pitt desired power; and he desired it, we really believe, 10 from high and generous motives. He was, in the strict sense of the word, a patriot. He had none of that philanthropy which the great French writers of his time preached to all the nations of Europe. He loved England as an Athenian loved the City of the Violet Crown, as a 15 Roman loved the City of the Seven Hills. He saw his country insulted and defeated. He saw the national spirit sinking. Yet he knew what the resources of the empire, vigorously employed, could effect; and he felt that he was the man to employ them vigorously. "My Lord," he said 20 to the Duke of Devonshire, "I am sure that I can save this country, and that nobody else can."

Desiring, then, to be in power, and feeling that his abilities and the public confidence were not alone sufficient to keep him in power against the wishes of the Court and 25 of the aristocracy, he began to think of a coalition with Newcastle.

Newcastle was equally disposed to a reconciliation. He, too, had profited by his recent experience. He had found that the Court and the aristocracy, though powerful, 30 were not every thing in the state. A strong oligarchical connection, a great borough interest, ample patronage, and secret-service money, might, in quiet times, be all that a

Minister needed; but it was unsafe to trust wholly to such support in time of war, of discontent, and of agitation. The composition of the House of Commons was not wholly aristocratical; and, whatever be the composition of
5 large deliberative assemblies, their spirit is always in some degree popular. Where there are free debates, eloquence must have admirers, and reason must make converts. Where there is a free press, the governors must live in constant awe of the opinions of the governed.

10   Thus these two men, so unlike in character, so lately mortal enemies, were necessary to each other. Newcastle had fallen in November, for want of that public confidence which Pitt possessed, and of that parliamentary support which Pitt was better qualified than any man of his time
15 to give. Pitt had fallen in April, for want of that species of influence which Newcastle had passed his whole life in acquiring and hoarding. Neither of them had power enough to support himself. Each of them had power enough to overturn the other. Their union would be
20 irresistible. Neither the King nor any party in the state would be able to stand against them.

      Under these circumstances, Pitt was not disposed to proceed to extremities against his predecessors in office. Something, however, was due to consistency; and some-
25 thing was necessary for the preservation of his popularity. He did little; but that little he did in such manner as to produce great effect. He came down to the House in all the pomp of gout, his legs swathed in flannels, his arm dangling in a sling. He kept his seat through several
30 fatiguing days, in spite of pain and languor. He uttered a few sharp and vehement sentences; but during the greater part of the discussion, his language was unusually gentle.

When the inquiry had terminated without a vote either of approbation or of censure, the great obstacle to a coalition was removed. Many obstacles, however, remained. The King was still rejoicing in his deliverance from the proud and aspiring Minister who had been forced on him by the cry of the nation. His Majesty's indignation was excited to the highest point when it appeared that Newcastle, who had, during thirty years, been loaded with marks of royal favour, and who had bound himself, by a solemn promise, never to coalesce with Pitt, was meditating a new perfidy. Of all the statesmen of that age, Fox had the largest share of royal favour. A coalition between Fox and Newcastle was the arrangement which the King wished to bring about. But the Duke was too cunning to fall into such a snare. As a speaker in Parliament, Fox might perhaps be, on the whole, as useful to an administration as his great rival; but he was one of the most unpopular men in England. Then, again, Newcastle felt all that jealousy of Fox, which, according to the proverb, generally exists between two of a trade. Fox would certainly intermeddle with that department which the Duke was most desirous to reserve entire to himself, the jobbing department. Pitt, on the other hand, was quite willing to leave the drudgery of corruption to any who might be inclined to undertake it.

During eleven weeks England remained without a ministry, and in the mean time Parliament was sitting, and a war was raging. The prejudices of the King, the haughtiness of Pitt, the jealousy, levity, and treachery of Newcastle, delayed the settlement. Pitt knew the Duke too well to trust him without security. The Duke loved power too much to be inclined to give security. While they were haggling, the King was in vain attempting to produce a final ruputre between them, or to form a

Government without them. At one time he applied to
Lord Waldegrave, an honest and sensible man, but un-
practised in affairs. Lord Waldegrave had the courage to
accept the Treasury, but soon found that no administration
5 formed by him had the smallest chance of standing a single
week.

At length the King's pertinacity yielded to the necessity
of the case. After exclaiming with great bitterness, and
with some justice, against the Whigs, who ought, he said,
10 to be ashamed to talk about liberty while they submitted
to be the footmen of the Duke of Newcastle, his Majesty
submitted. The influence of Leicester House prevailed on
Pitt to abate a little, and but a little, of his high demands ;
and all at once, out of the chaos in which parties had for
15 some time been rising, falling, meeting, separating, arose
a government as strong at home as that of Pelham, as
successful abroad as that of Godolphin.

Newcastle took the Treasury. Pitt was Secretary of
State, with the lead in the House of Commons, and with
20 the supreme direction of the war and of foreign affairs.
Fox, the only man who could have given much annoyance
to the new Government, was silenced with the office of
Paymaster, which, during the continuance of that war, was
probably the most lucrative place in the whole Government.
25 He was poor, and the situation was tempting ; yet it
cannot but seem extraordinary that a man who had played
a first part in politics, and whose abilities had been found
not unequal to that part, who had sat in the Cabinet, who
had led the House of Commons, who had been twice
30 entrusted by the King with the office of forming a ministry,
who was regarded as the rival of Pitt, and who at one time
seemed likely to be a successful rival, should have consented,
for the sake of emolument, to take a subordinate place,

and to give silent votes for all the measures of a government to the deliberations of which he was not summoned.

The first acts of the new administration were characterized rather by vigour than by judgment. Expeditions were sent against different parts of the French coast with little success. 5 The small island of Aix was taken, Rochefort threatened, a few ships burned in the harbour of St Maloes, and a few guns and mortars brought home as trophies from the fortifications of Cherbourg. But soon conquests of a very different kind filled the kingdom with pride and rejoicing. 10 A succession of victories undoubtedly brilliant, and, as it was thought, not barren, raised to the highest point the fame of the minister to whom the conduct of the war had been entrusted. In July, 1758, Louisburg fell. The whole island of Cape Breton was reduced. The fleet to 15 which the Court of Versailles had confided the defence of French America was destroyed. The captured standards were borne in triumph from Kensington Palace to the city, and were suspended in St Paul's Church, amidst the roar of guns and kettle-drums, and the shouts of an immense 20 multitude. Addresses of congratulation came in from all the great towns of England. Parliament met only to decree thanks and monuments, and to bestow, without one murmur, supplies more than double of those which had been given during the war of the Grand Alliance. 25

The year 1759 opened with the conquest of Goree. Next fell Guadaloupe; then Ticonderoga; then Niagara. The Toulon squadron was completely defeated by Boscawen off Cape Lagos. But the greatest exploit of the year was the achievement of Wolfe on the heights of Abraham. 30 The news of his glorious death and of the fall of Quebec reached London in the very week in which the Houses met. All was joy and triumph. Envy and faction were

W. P.   4

forced to join in the general applause. Whigs and Tories
vied with each other in extolling the genius and energy of
Pitt. His colleagues were never talked of or thought of.
The House of Commons, the nation, the colonies, our allies,
5 our enemies, had their eyes fixed on him alone.

Scarcely had Parliament voted a monument to Wolfe
when another great event called for fresh rejoicings. The
Brest fleet, under the command of Conflans, had put out
to sea. It was overtaken by an English squadron under
10 Hawke. Conflans attempted to take shelter close under
the French coast. The shore was rocky: the night was
black: the wind was furious: the waves of the Bay of
Biscay ran high. But Pitt had infused into every branch
of the service a spirit which had long been unknown. No
15 British seaman was disposed to err on the same side with
Byng. The pilot told Hawke that the attack could not be
made without the greatest danger. "You have done your
duty in remonstrating," answered Hawke; "I will answer
for every thing. I command you to lay me alongside
20 the French admiral." Two French ships of the line struck.
Four were destroyed. The rest hid themselves in the
rivers of Britanny.

The year 1760 came; and still triumph followed
triumph. Montreal was taken; the whole province of
25 Canada was subjugated; the French fleets underwent a
succession of disasters in the seas of Europe and America.

In the meantime conquests equalling in rapidity, and
far surpassing in magnitude, those of Cortes and Pizarro,
had been achieved in the East. In the space of three years
30 the English had founded a mighty empire. The French
had been defeated in every part of India. Chandernagore
had surrendered to Clive, Pondicherry to Coote. Through
out Bengal, Bahar, Orissa, and the Carnatic, the authority

of the East India Company was more absolute than that of Acbar or Aurungzebe had ever been.

On the continent of Europe the odds were against England. We had but one important ally, the King of Prussia; and he was attacked, not only by France, but also by Russia and Austria. Yet even on the Continent the energy of Pitt triumphed over all difficulties. Vehemently as he had condemned the practice of subsidising foreign princes, he now carried that practice farther than Carteret himself would have ventured to do. The active and able Sovereign of Prussia received such pecuniary assistance as enabled him to maintain the conflict on equal terms against his powerful enemies. On no subject had Pitt ever spoken with so much eloquence and ardour as on the mischiefs of the Hanoverian connection. He now declared, not without much show of reason, that it would be unworthy of the English people to suffer their King to be deprived of his electoral dominions in an English quarrel. He assured his countrymen that they should be no losers, and that he would conquer America for them in Germany. By taking this line he conciliated the King, and lost no part of his influence with the nation. In Parliament, such was the ascendency which his eloquence, his success, his high situation, his pride, and his intrepidity had obtained for him, that he took liberties with the House of which there had been no example, and which have never since been imitated. No orator could there venture to reproach him with inconsistency. One unfortunate man made the attempt, and was so much disconcerted by the scornful demeanour of the Minister that he stammered, stopped, and sat down. Even the old Tory country gentlemen, to whom the very name of Hanover had been odious, gave their hearty Ayes to subsidy after subsidy. In a lively contemporary satire, much more lively indeed than delicate, this remarkable conversion is not unhappily described.

> " No more they make a fiddle-faddle
> About a Hessian horse or saddle.
> 5   No more of continental measures ;
> No more of wasting British treasures.
> Ten millions, and a vote of credit,
> 'Tis right. He can't be wrong who did it."

The success of Pitt's continental measures was such as 10 might have been expected from their vigour. When he came into power, Hanover was in imminent danger; and before he had been in office three months, the whole electorate was in the hands of France. But the face of affairs was speedily changed. The invaders were driven 15 out. An army, partly English, partly Hanoverian, partly composed of soldiers furnished by the petty princes of Germany, was placed under the command of Prince Ferdinand of Brunswick. The French were beaten in 1758 at Crevelt. In 1759 they received a still more 20 complete and humiliating defeat at Minden.

In the meantime, the nation exhibited all the signs of wealth and prosperity. The merchants of London had never been more thriving. The importance of several great commercial and manufacturing towns, of Glasgow 25 in particular, dates from this period. The fine inscription on the monument of Lord Chatham in Guildhall records the general opinion of the citizens of London, that under his administration commerce had been "united with and made to flourish by war."

30   It must be owned that these signs of prosperity were in some degree delusive. It must be owned that some of our conquests were rather splendid than useful. It must be owned that the expense of the war never entered

into Pitt's consideration.   Perhaps it would be more correct
to say that the cost of his victories increased the pleasure
with which he contemplated them.   Unlike other men in
his situation, he loved to exaggerate the sums which the
nation was laying out under his direction.   He was proud 5
of the sacrifices and efforts which his eloquence and his
success had induced his countrymen to make.   The price
at which he purchased faithful service and complete victory,
though far smaller than that which his son, the most
profuse and incapable of war ministers, paid for treachery, 10
defeat, and shame, was long and severely felt by the nation.

Even as a war minister, Pitt is scarcely entitled to all
the praise which his contemporaries lavished on him.
We, perhaps from ignorance, cannot discern in his arrangements any appearance of profound or dexterous combina- 15
tion.   Several of his expeditions, particularly those which
were sent to the coast of France, were at once costly and
absurd.   Our Indian conquests, though they add to the
splendour of the period during which he was at the head
of affairs, were not planned by him.   He had undoubtedly 20
great energy, great determination, great means at his
command.   His temper was enterprising; and, situated
as he was, he had only to follow his temper.   The wealth
of a rich nation, the valour of a brave nation, were ready
to support him in every attempt.   25

In one respect, however, he deserved all the praise
that he has ever received.   The success of our arms was
perhaps owing less to the skill of his dispositions than to
the national resources and the national spirit.   But that
the national spirit rose to the emergency, that the national 30
resources were contributed with unexampled cheerfulness,
this was undoubtedly his work.   The ardour of his soul
had set the whole kingdom on fire.   It inflamed every

soldier who dragged the cannon up the heights of Quebec, and every sailor who boarded the French ships among the rocks of Britanny. The Minister, before he had been long in office, had imparted to the commanders whom he employed his own impetuous, adventurous, and defying character. They, like him, were disposed to risk every thing, to play double or quits to the last, to think nothing done while any thing remained undone, to fail rather than not to attempt. For the errors of rashness there might be indulgence. For over-caution, for faults like those of Lord George Sackville, there was no mercy. In other times, and against other enemies, this mode of warfare might have failed. But the state of the French government and of the French nation gave every advantage to Pitt. The fops and intriguers of Versailles were appalled and bewildered by his vigour. A panic spread through all ranks of society. Our enemies soon considered it as a settled thing that they were always to be beaten. Thus victory begot victory; till, at last, wherever the forces of the two nations met, they met with disdainful confidence on one side, and with a craven fear on the other.

The situation which Pitt occupied at the close of the reign of George the Second was the most enviable ever occupied by any public man in English history. He had conciliated the King; he domineered over the House of Commons; he was adored by the people; he was admired by all Europe. He was the first Englishman of his time; and he had made England the first country in the world. The Great Commoner, the name by which he was often designated, might look down with scorn on coronets and garters. The nation was drunk with joy and pride. The Parliament was as quiet as it had been under Pelham. The old party distinctions were almost effaced;

nor was their place yet supplied by distinctions of a still more important kind. A new generation of country squires and rectors had arisen who knew not the Stuarts. The Dissenters were tolerated; the Catholics not cruelly perse-cuted. The Church was drowsy and indulgent. The 5 great civil and religious conflict which began at the Refor-mation seemed to have terminated in universal repose. Whigs and Tories, Churchmen and Puritans, spoke with equal reverence of the constitution, and with equal enthu-siasm of the talents, virtues, and services of the Minister. 10

A few years sufficed to change the whole aspect of affairs. A nation convulsed by faction, a throne assailed by the fiercest invective, a House of Commons hated and despised by the nation, England set against Scotland, Britain set against America, a rival legislature sitting 15 beyond the Atlantic, English blood shed by English bayonets, our armies capitulating, our conquests wrested from us, our enemies hastening to take vengeance for past humiliation, our flag scarcely able to maintain itself in our own seas, such was the spectacle which Pitt lived to see. 20 But the history of this great revolution requires far more space than we can at present bestow. We leave the Great Commoner in the zenith of his glory. It is not impossible that we may take some other opportunity of tracing his life to its melancholy, yet not inglorious close. 25

THE EARL OF CHATHAM.

MORE than ten years ago we commenced a sketch of the
political life of the great Lord Chatham.   We then stopped
at the death of George the Second, with the intention of
speedily resuming our task.   Circumstances, which it would
5 be tedious to explain, long prevented us from carrying this
intention into effect.   Nor can we regret the delay.   For
the materials which were within our reach in 1834 were
scanty and unsatisfactory, when compared with those which
we at present possess.   Even now, though we have had
10 access to some valuable sources of information which have
not yet been opened to the public, we cannot but feel that
the history of the first ten years of the reign of George
the Third is but imperfectly known to us.   Nevertheless,
we are inclined to think that we are in a condition to lay
15 before our readers a narrative neither uninstructive nor
uninteresting.   We therefore return with pleasure to our
long interrupted labour.

We left Pitt in the zenith of prosperity and glory, the

idol of England, the terror of France, the admiration of the whole civilised world.   The wind, from whatever quarter it blew, carried to England tidings of battles won, fortresses taken, provinces added to the empire.   At home, factions had sunk into a lethargy, such as had never been known 5 since the great religious schism of the sixteenth century had roused the public mind from repose.

In order that the events which we have to relate may be clearly understood, it may be desirable that we should advert to the causes which had for a time suspended the 10 animation of both the great English parties.

If, rejecting all that is merely accidental, we look at the essential characteristics of the Whig and the Tory, we may consider each of them as the representative of a great principle, essential to the welfare of. nations.   One is, in an 15 especial manner, the guardian of liberty, and the other, of order.   One is the moving power, and the other the steadying power of the state.   One is the sail, without which society would make no progress, the other the ballast, without which there would be small safety in a 20 tempest.   But, during the forty-six years which followed the accession of the House of Hanover, these distinctive peculiarities seemed to be effaced.   The Whig conceived that he could not better serve the cause of civil and religious freedom than by strenuously supporting the Pro- 25 testant dynasty.   The Tory conceived that he could not better prove his hatred of revolutions than by attacking a government to which a revolution had given birth.   Both came by degrees to attach more importance to the means than to the end.   Both were thrown into unnatural situa- 30 tions ; and both, like animals transported to an uncongenial climate, languished and degenerated.   The Tory, removed from the sunshine of the court, was as a camel in the snows

of Lapland. The Whig, basking in the rays of royal
favour, was as a reindeer in the sands of Arabia.

Dante tells us that he saw, in Malebolge, a strange
encounter between a human form and a serpent. The
5 enemies, after cruel wounds inflicted, stood for a time
glaring on each other. A great cloud surrounded them,
and then a wonderful metamorphosis began. Each creature
was transfigured into the likeness of its antagonist. The
serpent's tail divided itself into two legs; the man's legs
10 intertwined themselves into a tail. The body of the
serpent put forth arms; the arms of the man shrank into
his body. At length the serpent stood up a man, and
spake; the man sank down a serpent, and glided hissing
away. Something like this was the transformation which,
15 during the reign of George the First, befell the two English
parties. Each gradually took the shape and colour of its
foe, till at length the Tory rose up erect the zealot of
freedom, and the Whig crawled and licked the dust at the
feet of power.

20 It is true that, when these degenerate politicians discussed questions merely speculative, and, above all, when
they discussed questions relating to the conduct of their
own grandfathers, they still seemed to differ as their grandfathers had differed. The Whig, who, during three Parlia-
25 ments, had never given one vote against the court, and who
was ready to sell his soul for the Comptroller's staff or for
the Great Wardrobe, still professed to draw his political
doctrines from Locke and Milton, still worshipped the
memory of Pym and Hampden, and would still, on the
30 thirtieth of January, take his glass, first to the man in the
mask, and then to the man who would do it without a mask.
The Tory, on the other hand, while he reviled the mild and
temperate Walpole as a deadly enemy of liberty, could see

nothing to reprobate in the iron tyranny of Strafford and
Laud. But, whatever judgment the Whig or the Tory of
that age might pronounce on transactions long past, there
can be no doubt that, as respected the practical questions
then pending, the Tory was a reformer, and indeed an 5
intemperate and indiscreet reformer, while the Whig was
conservative even to bigotry. We have ourselves seen
similar effects produced in a neighbouring country by
similar causes. Who would have believed, fifteen years
ago, that M. Guizot and M. Villemain would have to 10
defend property and social order against the attacks of such
enemies as M. Genoude and M. de La Roche Jaquelin?

Thus the successors of the old Cavaliers had turned
demagogues; the successors of the old Roundheads had
turned courtiers. Yet was it long before their mutual 15
animosity began to abate; for it is the nature of parties to
retain their original enmities far more firmly than their
original principles. During many years, a generation of
Whigs, whom Sidney would have spurned as slaves, continue
to wage deadly war with a generation of Tories whom 20
Jeffreys would have hanged for republicans.

Through the whole reign of George the First, and
through nearly half of the reign of George the Second,
a Tory was regarded as an enemy of the reigning house,
and was excluded from all the favours of the crown. 25
Though most of the country gentlemen were Tories, none
but Whigs were created peers and baronets. Though
most of the clergy were Tories, none but Whigs were
appointed deans and bishops. In every county, opulent
and well descended Tory squires complained that their 30
names were left out of the commission of the peace, while
men of small estate and mean birth, who were for toleration
and excise, septennial parliaments and standing armies,

presided at quarter sessions, and became deputy lieutenants.

By degrees some approaches were made towards a
reconciliation. While Walpole was at the head of affairs,
5 enmity to his power induced a large and powerful body of
Whigs, headed by the heir apparent of the throne, to make
an alliance with the Tories, and a truce even with the
Jacobites. After Sir Robert's fall, the ban which lay on
the Tory party was taken off. The chief places in the
10 administration continued to be filled by Whigs, and,
indeed, could scarcely have been filled otherwise; for
the Tory nobility and gentry, though strong in numbers
and in property, had among them scarcely a single man
distinguished by talents, either for business or for debate.
15 A few of them, however, were admitted to subordinate
offices; and this indulgence produced a softening effect
on the temper of the whole body. The first levee of
George the Second after Walpole's resignation was a remarkable spectacle. Mingled with the constant supporters
20 of the House of Brunswick, with the Russells, the Cavendishes, and the Pelhams, appeared a crowd of faces utterly
unknown to the pages and gentlemen ushers, lords of rural
manors, whose ale and foxhounds were renowned in the
neighbourhood of the Mendip hills, or round the Wrekin,
25 but who had never crossed the threshold of the palace
since the days when Oxford, with the white staff in his
hand, stood behind Queen Anne.

During the eighteen years which followed this day, both
factions were gradually sinking deeper and deeper into
30 repose. The apathy of the public mind is partly to be
ascribed to the unjust violence with which the administration of Walpole had been assailed. In the body politic,
as in the natural body, morbid languor generally succeeds

morbid excitement. The people had been maddened by
sophistry, by calumny, by rhetoric, by stimulants applied
to the national pride. In the fulness of bread, they had
raved as if famine had been in the land. While enjoying
such a measure of civil and religious freedom as, till then, 5
no great society had ever known, they had cried out for a
Timoleon or a Brutus to stab their oppressor to the heart.
They were in this frame of mind when the change of
administration took place; and they soon found that there
was to be no change whatever in the system of government. 10
The natural consequences followed. To frantic zeal succeeded sullen indifference. The cant of patriotism had
not merely ceased to charm the public ear, but had become
as nauseous as the cant of Puritanism after the downfall
of the Rump. The hot fit was over: the cold fit had 15
begun: and it was long before seditious arts, or even real
grievances, could bring back the fiery paroxysm which had
run its course and reached its termination.

Two attempts were made to disturb this tranquillity.
The banished heir of the House of Stuart headed a rebel- 20
lion; the discontented heir of the House of Brunswick
headed an opposition. Both the rebellion and the opposition came to nothing. The battle of Culloden annihilated
the Jacobite party. The death of Prince Frederic dissolved
the faction which, under his guidance, had feebly striven to 25
annoy his father's government. His chief followers hastened
to make their peace with the ministry; and the political
torpor became complete.

Five years after the death of Prince Frederic, the public
mind was for a time violently excited. But this excitement 30
had nothing to do with the old disputes between Whigs and
Tories. England was at war with France. The war had
been feebly conducted. Minorca had been torn from us.

Our fleet had retired before the white flag of the House
of Bourbon. A bitter sense of humiliation, new to the
proudest and bravest of nations, superseded every other
feeling. The cry of all the counties and great towns of
5 the realm was for a government which would retrieve the
honour of the English arms. The two most powerful men
in the country were the Duke of Newcastle and Pitt.
Alternate victories and defeats had made them sensible
that neither of them could stand alone. The interest of
10 the state, and the interest of their own ambition, impelled
them to coalesce. By their coalition was formed the
ministry which was in power when George the Third
ascended the throne.

The more carefully the structure of this celebrated
15 ministry is examined, the more shall we see reason to
marvel at the skill or the luck which had combined in
one harmonious whole such various and, as it seemed,
incompatible elements of force. The influence which is
derived from stainless integrity, the influence which is
20 derived from the vilest arts of corruption, the strength
of aristocratical connection, the strength of democratical
enthusiasm, all these things were for the first time found
together. Newcastle brought to the coalition a vast mass
of power, which had descended to him from Walpole and
25 Pelham. The public offices, the church, the courts of law,
the army, the navy, the diplomatic service, swarmed with
his creatures. The boroughs, which long afterwards made
up the memorable schedules A and B, were represented
by his nominees. The great Whig families, which, during
30 several generations, had been trained in the discipline of
party warfare, and were accustomed to stand together in
a firm phalanx, acknowledged him as their captain. Pitt, on
the other hand, had what Newcastle wanted, an eloquence

which stirred the passions and charmed the imagination, a high reputation for purity, and the confidence and ardent love of millions.

The partition which the two ministers made of the powers of government was singularly happy. Each occu- pied a province for which he was well qualified; and neither had any inclination to intrude himself into the province of the other. Newcastle took the treasury, the civil and ecclesiastical patronage, and the disposal of that part of the secret service money which was then employed in bribing members of Parliament. Pitt was Secretary of State, with the direction of the war and of foreign affairs. Thus the filth of all the noisome and pestilential sewers of government was poured into one channel. Through the other passed only what was bright and stainless. Mean and selfish politicians, pining for commissionerships, gold sticks, and ribands, flocked to the great house at the corner of Lincoln's Inn Fields. There, at every levee, appeared eighteen or twenty pair of lawn sleeves; for there was not, it was said, a single Prelate who had not owed either his first elevation or some subsequent translation to Newcastle. There appeared those members of the House of Commons in whose silent votes the main strength of the government lay. One wanted a place in the excise for his butler. Another came about a prebend for his son. A third whispered that he had always stood by his Grace and the Protestant succession; that his last election had been very expensive; that potwallopers had now no conscience; that he had been forced to take up money on mortgage; and that he hardly knew where to turn for five hundred pounds. The Duke pressed all their hands, passed his arms round all their shoulders, patted all their backs, and sent away some with wages, and some with promises.

From this traffic Pitt stood haughtily aloof. Not only was he himself incorruptible, but he shrank from the loathsome drudgery of corrupting others. He had not, however, been twenty years in Parliament, and ten in office, without discovering how the government was carried on. He was perfectly aware that bribery was practised on a large scale by his colleagues. Hating the practice, yet despairing of putting it down, and doubting whether, in those times, any ministry could stand without it, he determined to be blind to it. He would see nothing, know nothing, believe nothing. People who came to talk to him about shares in lucrative contracts, or about the means of securing a Cornish corporation, were soon put out of countenance by his arrogant humility. They did him too much honour. Such matters were beyond his capacity. It was true that his poor advice about expeditions and treaties was listened to with indulgence by a gracious sovereign. If the question were, who should command in North America, or who should be ambassador at Berlin, his colleagues would probably condescend to take his opinion. But he had not the smallest influence with the Secretary of the Treasury, and could not venture to ask even for a tide-waiter's place.

It may be doubted whether he did not owe as much of his popularity to his ostentatious purity as to his eloquence, or to his talents for the administration of war. It was every where said with delight and admiration that the great Commoner, without any advantages of birth or fortune, had, in spite of the dislike of the Court and of the aristo-cracy, made himself the first man in England, and made England the first country in the world; that his name was mentioned with awe in every palace from Lisbon to Moscow; that his trophies were in all the four quarters of the globe;

yet that he was still plain William Pitt, without title or riband, without pension or sinecure place. Whenever he should retire, after saving the state, he must sell his coach horses and his silver candlesticks. Widely as the taint of corruption had spread, his hands were clean. They had 5 never received, they had never given, the price of infamy. Thus the coalition gathered to itself support from all the high and all the low parts of human nature, and was strong with the whole united strength of virtue and of Mammon.

Pitt and Newcastle were co-ordinate chief ministers. 10 The subordinate places had been filled on the principle of including in the government every party and shade of party, the avowed Jacobites alone excepted, nay, every public man who, from his abilities or from his situation, seemed likely to be either useful in office or formidable 15 in opposition.

The Whigs, according to what was then considered as their prescriptive right, held by far the largest share of power. The main support of the administration was what may be called the great Whig connection, a connection 20 which, during nearly half a century, had generally had the chief sway in the country, and which derived an immense authority from rank, wealth, borough interest, and firm union. To this connection, of which Newcastle was the head, belonged the houses of Cavendish, Lennox, Fitzroy, 25 Bentinck, Manners, Conway, Wentworth, and many others of high note.

There were two other powerful Whig connections, either of which might have been a nucleus for a strong opposition. But room had been found in the Government for both. 30 They were known as the Grenvilles and the Bedfords.

The head of the Grenvilles was Richard Earl Temple. His talents for administration and debate were of no high

order. But his great possessions, his turbulent and unscrupulous character, his restless activity, and his skill in
the most ignoble tactics of faction, made him one of the
most formidable enemies that a ministry could have. He
was keeper of the privy seal. His brother George was
treasurer of the navy. They were supposed to be on terms
of close friendship with Pitt, who had married their sister,
and was the most uxorious of husbands.

The Bedfords, or, as they were called by their enemies,
the Bloomsbury gang, professed to be led by John Duke
of Bedford, but in truth led him wherever they chose, and
very often led him where he never would have gone of his
own accord. He had many good qualities of head and
heart, and would have been certainly a respectable, and
possibly a distinguished man, if he had been less under
the influence of his friends, or more fortunate in choosing
them. Some of them were indeed, to do them justice,
men of parts. But here, we are afraid, eulogy must end.
Sandwich and Rigby were able debaters, pleasant boon
companions, dexterous intriguers, masters of all the arts
of jobbing and electioneering, and, both in public and
private life, shamelessly immoral. Weymouth had a natural eloquence, which sometimes astonished those who
knew how little he owed to study. But he was indolent
and dissolute, and had early impaired a fine estate with
the dice-box, and a fine constitution with the bottle. The
wealth and power of the Duke, and the talents and audacity
of some of his retainers, might have seriously annoyed the
strongest ministry. But his assistance had been secured.
He was Lord Lieutenant of Ireland; Rigby was his secretary; and the whole party dutifully supported the measures
of the Government.

Two men had, a short time before, been thought likely

to contest with Pitt the lead of the House of Commons, William Murray and Henry Fox. But Murray had been removed to the Lords, and was Chief Justice of the King's Bench. Fox was indeed still in the Commons : but means had been found to secure, if not his strenuous support, at 5 least his silent acquiescence. He was a poor man ; he was a doting father. The office of Paymaster-General during an expensive war was, in that age, perhaps the most lucrative situation in the gift of the government. This office was bestowed on Fox. The prospect of making a noble fortune 10 in a few years, and of providing amply for his darling boy Charles, was irresistibly tempting. To hold a subordinate place, however profitable, after having led the House of Commons, and having been entrusted with the business of forming a ministry, was indeed a great descent. But a 15 punctilious sense of personal dignity was no part of the character of Henry Fox.

We have not time to enumerate all the other men of weight who were, by some tie or other, attached to the government. We may mention Hardwicke, reputed the 20 first lawyer of the age ; Legge, reputed the first financier of the age ; the acute and ready Oswald ; the bold and humorous Nugent ; Charles Townshend, the most brilliant and versatile of mankind ; Elliot, Barrington, North, Pratt. Indeed, as far as we recollect, there were in the whole 25 House of Commons only two men of distinguished abilities who were not connected with the government ; and those two men stood so low in public estimation, that the only service which they could have rendered to any government would have been to oppose it. We speak of Lord George 30 Sackville and Bubb Dodington.

Though most of the official men, and all the members of the cabinet, were reputed Whigs the Tories were by no

5—2

means excluded from employment. Pitt had gratified many
of them with commands in the militia, which increased both
their income and their importance in their own counties;
and they were therefore in better humour than at any time
5 since the death of Anne. Some of the party still continued
to grumble over their punch at the Cocoa Tree; but in the
House of Commons not a single one of the malecontents
durst lift his eyes above the buckle of Pitt's shoe.

Thus there was absolutely no opposition. Nay, there
10 was no sign from which it could be guessed in what quarter
opposition was likely to arise. Several years passed during
which Parliament seemed to have abdicated its chief functions. The Journals of the House of Commons, during
four sessions, contain no trace of a division on a party
15 question. The supplies, though beyond precedent great,
were voted without discussion. The most animated debates
of that period were on road bills and inclosure bills.

The old King was content; and it mattered little
whether he were content or not. It would have been
20 impossible for him to emancipate himself from a ministry
so powerful, even if he had been inclined to do so. But
he had no such inclination. He had once, indeed, been
strongly prejudiced against Pitt, and had repeatedly been
ill used by Newcastle; but the vigour and success with
25 which the war had been waged in Germany, and the
smoothness with which all public business was carried on,
had produced a favourable change in the royal mind.

Such was the posture of affairs when, on the twenty-fifth
of October, 1760, George the Second suddenly died, and
30 George the Third, then twenty-two years old, became King.
The situation of George the Third differed widely from that
of his grandfather and that of his great-grandfather. Many
years had elapsed since a sovereign of England had been

an object of affection to any part of his people. The first
two Kings of the House of Hanover had neither those
hereditary rights which have often supplied the defect of
merit, nor those personal qualities which have often supplied
the defect of title. A prince may be popular with little 5
virtue or capacity, if he reigns by birthright derived from
a long line of illustrious predecessors. An usurper may be
popular, if his genius has saved or aggrandised the nation
which he governs. Perhaps no rulers have in our time had
a stronger hold on the affection of subjects than the 10
Emperor Francis, and his son-in-law the Emperor Napoleon.
But imagine a ruler with no better title than Napoleon, and
no better understanding than Francis. Richard Cromwell
was such a ruler; and, as soon as an arm was lifted up
against him, he fell without a struggle, amidst universal 15
derision. George the First and George the Second were
in a situation which bore some resemblance to that of
Richard Cromwell. They were saved from the fate of
Richard Cromwell by the strenuous and able exertions of
the Whig party, and by the general conviction that the 20
nation had no choice but between the House of Brunswick
and popery. But by no class were the Guelphs regarded
with that devoted affection, of which Charles the First,
Charles the Second, and James the Second, in spite of
the greatest faults, and in the midst of the greatest misfor- 25
tunes, received innumerable proofs. Those Whigs who stood
by the new dynasty so manfully with purse and sword did so
on principles independent of, and indeed almost incompatible
with, the sentiment of devoted loyalty. The moderate Tories
regarded the foreign dynasty as a great evil, which must be 30
endured for fear of a greater evil. In the eyes of the high
Tories, the Elector was the most hateful of robbers and
tyrants. The crown of another was on his head; the blood

of the brave and loyal was on his hands. Thus, during many years, the Kings of England were objects of strong personal aversion to many of their subjects, and of strong personal attachment to none. They found, indeed, firm 5 and cordial support against the pretender to their throne: but this support was given, not at all for their sake, but for the sake of a religious and political system which would have been endangered by their fall. This support, too, they were compelled to purchase by perpetually sacrificing their 10 private inclinations to the party which had set them on the throne, and which maintained them there.

At the close of the reign of George the Second, the feeling of aversion with which the House of Brunswick had long been regarded by half the nation had died away; but 15 no feeling of affection to that house had yet sprung up. There was little, indeed, in the old King's character to inspire esteem or tenderness. He was not our countryman. He never set foot on our soil till he was more than thirty years old. His speech bewrayed his foreign origin and 20 breeding. His love for his native land, though the most amiable part of his character, was not likely to endear him to his British subjects. He was never so happy as when he could exchange St James's for Hernhausen. Year after year, our fleets were employed to convoy him to the 25 Continent, and the interests of his kingdom were as nothing to him when compared with the interests of his Electorate. As to the rest, he had neither the qualities which make dulness respectable, nor the qualities which make libertinism attractive. He had been a bad son and a worse father, an 30 unfaithful husband and an ungraceful lover. Not one magnanimous or humane action is recorded of him; but many instances of meanness, and of a harshness which, but for the strong constitutional restraints under

which he was placed, might have made the misery of
his people.

He died; and at once a new world opened. The young
King was a born Englishman. All his tastes and habits,
good or bad, were English. No portion of his subjects had 5
anything to reproach him with. Even the remaining
adherents of the House of Stuart could scarcely impute
to him the guilt of usurpation. He was not responsible
for the Revolution, for the Act of Settlement, for the
suppression of the risings of 1715 and of 1745. He was 10
innocent of the blood of Derwentwater and Kilmarnock, of
Balmerino and Cameron. Born fifty years after the old
line had been expelled, fourth in descent and third in
succession of the Hanoverian dynasty, he might plead
some show of hereditary right. His age, his appearance, 15
and all that was known of his character, conciliated public
favour. He was in the bloom of youth; his person and
address were pleasing. Scandal imputed to him no vice;
and flattery might, without any glaring absurdity, ascribe to
him many princely virtues. 20

It is not strange, therefore, that the sentiment of loyalty,
a sentiment which had lately seemed to be as much out of
date as the belief in witches or the practice of pilgrimage,
should, from the day of his accession, have begun to revive.
The Tories in particular, who had always been inclined to 25
King-worship, and who had long felt with pain the want of
an idol before whom they could bow themselves down, were
as joyful as the priests of Apis, when, after a long interval,
they had found a new calf to adore. It was soon clear that
George the Third was regarded by a portion of the nation 30
with a very different feeling from that which his two predecessors had inspired. They had been merely First
Magistrates, Doges, Stadtholders; he was emphatically a

King, the anointed of heaven, the breath of his people's
nostrils. The years of the widowhood and mourning of
the Tory party were over. Dido had kept faith long
enough to the cold ashes of a former lord; she had at
5 last found a comforter, and recognised the vestiges of the
old flame. The golden days of Harley would return. The
Somersets, the Lees, and the Wyndhams would again
surround the throne. The latitudinarian Prelates, who
had not been ashamed to correspond with Doddridge and
10 to shake hands with Whiston, would be succeeded by
divines of the temper of South and Atterbury. The de-
votion which had been so signally shown to the House of
Stuart, which had been proof against defeats, confiscations,
and proscriptions, which perfidy, oppression, ingratitude,
15 could not weary out, was now transferred entire to the
House of Brunswick. If George the Third would but
accept the homage of the Cavaliers and High Churchmen,
he should be to them all that Charles the First and Charles
the Second had been.

20   The Prince, whose accession was thus hailed by a great
party long estranged from his house, had received from
nature a strong will, a firmness of temper to which a
harsher name might perhaps be given, and an understanding not, indeed, acute or enlarged, but such as qualified
25 him to be a good man of business. But his character had
not yet fully developed itself. He had been brought up in
strict seclusion. The detractors of the Princess Dowager
of Wales affirmed that she had kept her children from
commerce with society, in order that she might hold an
30 undivided empire over their minds. She gave a very
different explanation of her conduct. She would gladly,
she said, see her sons and daughters mix in the world, if
they could do so without risk to their morals. But the

profligacy of the people of quality alarmed her. The young men were all rakes; the young women made love, instead of waiting till it was made to them. She could not bear to expose those whom she loved best to the contaminating influence of such society. The moral ad- 5 vantages of the system of education which formed the Duke of York, the Duke of Cumberland, and the Queen of Denmark, may perhaps be questioned. George the Third was indeed no libertine; but he brought to the throne a mind only half opened, and was for some time entirely 10 under the influence of his mother and of his Groom of the Stole, John Stuart, Earl of Bute.

The Earl of Bute was scarcely known, even by name, to the country which he was soon to govern. He had indeed, a short time after he came of age, been chosen to fill a 15 vacancy which in the middle of a parliament, had taken place among the Scotch representative peers. He had disobliged the Whig ministers by giving some silent votes with the Tories, had consequently lost his seat at the next dissolution, and had never been re-elected. Near twenty 20 years had elapsed since he had borne any part in politics. He had passed some of those years at his seat in one of the Hebrides, and from that retirement he had emerged as one of the household of Prince Frederic. Lord Bute, excluded from public life, had found out many ways of amusing his 25 leisure. He was a tolerable actor in private theatricals, and was particularly successful in the part of Lothario. A handsome leg, to which both painters and satirists took care to give prominence, was among his chief qualifications for the stage. He devised quaint dresses for masquerades. 30 He dabbled in geometry, mechanics, and botany. He paid some attention to antiquities and works of art, and was considered in his own circle as a judge of painting, architecture, and poetry. It is said that his spelling was incorrect. But though, in our time, incorrect spelling is justly considered as a proof of sordid ignorance, it would be unjust to apply the same rule to people who lived a century ago. The novel of Sir Charles Grandison was published about the time at which Lord Bute made his appearance at Leicester House. Our readers may perhaps remember the account which Charlotte Grandison gives of her two lovers. One of them, a fashionable baronet who talks French and Italian fluently, cannot write a line in his own language without some sin against orthography; the other, who is represented as a most respectable specimen of the young aristocracy, and something of a virtuoso, is described as spelling pretty well for a lord. On the whole, the Earl of Bute might fairly be called a man of cultivated mind. He was also a man of undoubted honour. But his understanding was narrow, and his manners cold and haughty. His qualifications for the part of a statesman were best described by Frederic, who often indulged in the unprincely luxury of sneering at his dependents. "Bute," said his Royal Highness, "you are the very man to be envoy at some small proud German court where there is nothing to do."

Scandal represented the Groom of the Stole as the favoured lover of the Princess Dowager. He was undoubtedly her confidential friend. The influence which the two united exercised over the mind of the King was for a time unbounded. The Princess, a woman and a foreigner, was not likely to be a judicious adviser about affairs of state. The Earl could scarcely be said to have served even a noviciate in politics. His notions of government had been acquired in the society which had been in the habit of assembling round Frederic at Kew and Leicester House. That society consisted principally of

Tories, who had been reconciled to the House of Hanover by the civility with which the Prince had treated them, and by the hope of obtaining high preferment when he should come to the throne.   Their political creed was a peculiar modification of Toryism.   It was the creed neither of the 5 Tories of the seventeenth nor of the Tories of the nineteenth century.   It was the creed, not of Filmer and Sacheverell, not of Perceval and Eldon, but of the sect of which Bolingbroke may be considered as the chief doctor.   This sect deserves commendation for having pointed out and 10 justly reprobated some great abuses which sprang up during the long domination of the Whigs.   But it is far easier to point out and reprobate abuses than to propose beneficial reforms : and the reforms which Bolingbroke proposed would either have been utterly inefficient, or would have 15 produced much more mischief than they would have removed.

The Revolution had saved the nation from one class of evils, but had at the same time—such is the imperfection of all things human—engendered or aggravated another class 20 of evils which required new remedies.   Liberty and property were secure from the attacks of prerogative.   Conscience was respected.   No government ventured to infringe any of the rights solemnly recognised by the instrument which had called William and Mary to the throne.   But it cannot be 25 denied that, under the new system, the public interests and the public morals were seriously endangered by corruption and faction.   During the long struggle against the Stuarts, the chief object of the most enlightened statesmen had been to strengthen the House of Commons.   The struggle was 30 over ; the victory was won ; the House of Commons was supreme in the state ; and all the vices which had till then been latent in the representative system were rapidly

developed by prosperity and power. Scarcely had the executive government become really responsible to the House of Commons, when it began to appear that the House of Commons was not really responsible to the nation.
5 Many of the constituent bodies were under the absolute control of individuals; many were notoriously at the command of the highest bidder. The debates were not published. It was very seldom known out of doors how a gentleman had voted. Thus, while the ministry was accountable to
10 the Parliament, the majority of the Parliament was accountable to nobody. In such circumstances, nothing could be more natural than that the members should insist on being paid for their votes, should form themselves into combinations for the purpose of raising the price of their votes,
15 and should at critical conjunctures extort large wages by threatening a strike. Thus the Whig ministers of George the First and George the Second were compelled to reduce corruption to a system, and to practise it on a gigantic scale.

20   If we are right as to the cause of these abuses, we can scarcely be wrong as to the remedy. The remedy was surely not to deprive the House of Commons of its weight in the state. Such a course would undoubtedly have put an end to parliamentary corruption and to parliamentary
25 factions: for, when votes cease to be of importance, they will cease to be bought; and, when knaves can get nothing by combining, they will cease to combine. But to destroy corruption and faction by introducing despotism would have been to cure bad by worse. The proper remedy evidently
30 was, to make the House of Commons responsible to the nation; and this was to be effected in two ways; first, by giving publicity to parliamentary proceedings, and thus placing every member on his trial before the tribunal of

public opinion; and secondly, by so reforming the constitution of the House that no man should be able to sit in
it who had not been returned by a respectable and independent body of constituents.

Bolingbroke and Bolingbroke's disciples recommended a 5
very different mode of treating the diseases of the state.
Their doctrine was that a vigorous use of the prerogative by
a patriot King would at once break all factious combinations,
and supersede the pretended necessity of bribing members
of Parliament. The King had only to resolve that he 10
would be master, that he would not be held in thraldom by
any set of men, that he would take for ministers any persons
in whom he had confidence, without distinction of party,
and that he would restrain his servants from influencing
by immoral means either the constituent bodies or the 15
representative body. This childish scheme proved that
those who proposed it knew nothing of the nature of the
evil with which they pretended to deal. The real cause of
the prevalence of corruption and faction was that a House
of Commons, not accountable to the people, was more 20
powerful than the King. Bolingbroke's remedy could be
applied only by a King more powerful than the House of
Commons. How was the patriot Prince to govern in
defiance of the body without whose consent he could not
equip a sloop, keep a battalion under arms, send an embassy, 25
or defray even the charges of his own household? Was he
to dissolve the Parliament? And what was he likely to
gain by appealing to Sudbury and Old Sarum against the
venality of their representatives? Was he to send out privy
seals? Was he to levy ship-money? If so, this boasted 30
reform must commence in all probability by civil war, and,
if consummated, must be consummated by the establishment
of absolute monarchy. Or was the patriot King to carry the

House of Commons with him in his upright designs? By what means? Interdicting himself from the use of corrupt influence, what motive was he to address to the Dodingtons and Winningtons? Was cupidity, strengthened by habit, to 5 be laid asleep by a few fine sentences about virtue and union?

Absurd as this theory was, it had many admirers, particularly among men of letters. It was now to be reduced to practice; and the result was, as any man of sagacity must 10 have foreseen, the most piteous and ridiculous of failures.

On the **very** day of the young King's accession, appeared some signs which indicated the approach of a great change. The speech which he made to his council was not submitted to the cabinet. It was drawn up by Bute, and contained 15 some expressions which might be construed into reflections on the conduct of affairs during the late reign. Pitt remonstrated, and begged that these expressions might be softened down in the printed copy; but it was not till after some hours of altercation that Bute yielded; and, even after Bute 20 had yielded, the King affected to hold out till the following afternoon. On the same day on which this singular contest took place, Bute was not only sworn of the privy council, but introduced into the cabinet.

Soon after this, Lord Holdernesse, one of the Secretaries 25 of State, in pursuance of a plan concerted with the court, resigned the seals. Bute was instantly appointed to the vacant place. A general election speedily followed, and the new Secretary entered parliament in the only way in which he then could enter it, as one of the sixteen representative 30 peers of Scotland*.

* In the reign of Anne, the House of Lords had resolved that under the 23rd article of Union no Scotch peer could be created a peer of Great Britain. This resolution was not annulled till the year 1782.

Had the ministers been firmly united it can scarcely be doubted that they would have been able to withstand the court. The parliamentary influence of the Whig aristocracy, combined with the genius, the virtue, and the fame of Pitt, would have been irresistible. But there had been in the 5 cabinet of George the Second latent jealousies and enmities, which now began to show themselves. Pitt had been estranged from his old ally Legge, the Chancellor of the Exchequer. Some of the ministers were envious of Pitt's popularity. Others were, not altogether without cause, 10 disgusted by his imperious and haughty demeanour. Others, again, were honestly opposed to some parts of his policy. They admitted that he had found the country in the depths of humiliation, and had raised it to the height of glory: they admitted that he had conducted the war with energy, 15 ability, and splendid success; but they began to hint that the drain on the resources of the state was unexampled, and that the public debt was increasing with a speed at which Montague or Godolphin would have stood aghast. Some of the acquisitions made by our fleets and armies were, it 20 was acknowledged, profitable as well as honourable; but, now that George the Second was dead, a courtier might venture to ask why England was to become a party in a dispute between two German powers. What was it to her whether the House of Hapsburg or the House of Branden- 25 burg ruled in Silesia? Why were the best English regiments fighting on the Main? Why were the Prussian battalions paid with English gold? The great minister seemed to think it beneath him to calculate the price of victory. As long as the Tower guns were fired, as the streets were 30 illuminated, as French banners were carried in triumph through London, it was to him matter of indifference to what extent the public burdens were augmented. Nay, he

seemed to glory in the magnitude of those sacrifices which the people, fascinated by his eloquence and success, had too readily made, and would long and bitterly regret. There was no check on waste or embezzlement. Our commissaries
5 returned from the camp of Prince Ferdinand to buy boroughs, to rear palaces, to rival the magnificence of the old aristocracy of the realm. Already had we borrowed, in four years of war, more than the most skilful and economical government would pay in forty years of peace. But the prospect of
10 peace was as remote as ever. It could not be doubted that France, smarting and prostrate, would consent to fair terms of accommodation; but this was not what Pitt wanted. War had made him powerful and popular; with war, all that was brightest in his life was associated: for war his talents
15 were peculiarly fitted. He had at length begun to love war for its own sake, and was more disposed to quarrel with neutrals than to make peace with enemies.

Such were the views of the Duke of Bedford and of the Earl of Hardwicke; but no member of the government
20 held these opinions so strongly as George Grenville, the treasurer of the navy. George Grenville was brother-in-law of Pitt, and had always been reckoned one of Pitt's personal and political friends. But it is difficult to conceive two men of talents and integrity more utterly unlike each other.
25 Pitt, as his sister often said, knew nothing accurately except Spenser's Fairy Queen. He had never applied himself steadily to any branch of knowledge. He was a wretched financier. He never became familiar even with the rules of that House of which he was the brightest
30 ornament. He had never studied public law as a system; and was, indeed, so ignorant of the whole subject, that George the Second, on one occasion, complained bitterly that a man who had never read Vattel should presume to

undertake the direction of foreign affairs. But these defects
were more than redeemed by high and rare gifts, by a
strange power of inspiring great masses of men with confidence and affection, by an eloquence which not only
delighted the ear, but stirred the blood, and brought tears 5
into the eyes, by originality in devising plans, by vigour in
executing them. Grenville, on the other hand, was by
nature and habit a man of details. He had been bred
a lawyer; and he had brought the industry and acuteness
of the Temple into official and parliamentary life. He 10
was supposed to be intimately acquainted with the whole
fiscal system of the country. He had paid especial attention to the law of Parliament, and was so learned in all
things relating to the privileges and orders of the House
of Commons that those who loved him least pronounced 15
him the only person competent to succeed Onslow in the
Chair. His speeches were generally instructive, and sometimes, from the gravity and earnestness with which he
spoke, even impressive, but never brilliant, and generally
tedious. Indeed, even when he was at the head of affairs, 20
he sometimes found it difficult to obtain the ear of the
House. In disposition as well as in intellect, he differed
widely from his brother-in-law. Pitt was utterly regardless
of money. He would scarcely stretch out his hand to take
it; and, when it came, he threw it away with childish 25
profusion. Grenville, though strictly upright, was grasping
and parsimonious. Pitt was a man of excitable nerves,
sanguine in hope, easily elated by success and popularity,
keenly sensible of injury, but prompt to forgive; Grenville's
character was stern, melancholy, and pertinacious. Nothing 30
was more remarkable in him than his inclination always
to look on the dark side of things. He was the raven
of the House of Commons, always croaking defeat in the

midst of triumphs, and bankruptcy with an overflowing
exchequer. Burke, with general applause, compared him,
in a time of quiet and plenty, to the evil spirit whom Ovid
described looking down on the stately temples and wealthy
5 haven of Athens, and scarce able to refrain from weeping
because she could find nothing at which to weep. Such
a man was not likely to be popular. But to unpopularity
Grenville opposed a dogged determination, which sometimes
forced even those who hated him to respect him.

10   It was natural that Pitt and Grenville, being such as
they were, should take very different views of the situation
of affairs. Pitt could see nothing but the trophies; Grenville
could see nothing but the bill. Pitt boasted that England
was victorious at once in America, in India, and in Germany,
15 the umpire of the Continent, the mistress of the sea.
Grenville cast up the subsidies, sighed over the army
extraordinaries, and groaned in spirit to think that the
nation had borrowed eight millions in one year.

With a ministry thus divided it was not difficult for Bute
20 to deal. Legge was the first who fell. He had given
offence to the young King in the late reign, by refusing to
support a creature of Bute at a Hampshire election. He
was now not only turned out, but in the closet, when he
delivered up his seal of office, was treated with gross
25 incivility.

Pitt, who did not love Legge, saw this event with
indifference. But the danger was now fast approaching
himself. Charles the Third of Spain had early conceived
a deadly hatred of England. Twenty years before, when
30 he was King of the Two Sicilies, he had been eager to join
the coalition against Maria Theresa. But an English fleet
had suddenly appeared in the Bay of Naples. An English
captain had landed, had proceeded to the palace, had laid a

watch on the table, and had told his majesty that, within an hour, a treaty of neutrality must be signed, or a bombardment would commence. The treaty was signed; the squadron sailed out of the bay twenty-four hours after it had sailed in; and from that day the ruling passion 5 of the humbled Prince was aversion to the English name. He was at length in a situation in which he might hope to gratify that passion. He had recently become King of Spain and the Indies. He saw, with envy and apprehension, the triumphs of our navy, and the rapid extension of our 10 colonial Empire. He was a Bourbon, and sympathized with the distress of the house from which he sprang. He was a Spaniard; and no Spaniard could bear to see Gibraltar and Minorca in the possession of a foreign power. Impelled by such feelings, Charles concluded a 15 secret treaty with France. By this treaty, known as the Family Compact, the two powers bound themselves, not in express words, but by the clearest implication, to make war on England in common. Spain postponed the declaration of hostilities only till her fleet, laden with the treasures 20 of America, should have arrived.

The existence of the treaty could not be kept a secret from Pitt. He acted as a man of his capacity and energy might be expected to act. He at once proposed to declare war against Spain, and to intercept the American fleet. He 25 had determined, it is said, to attack without delay both Havanna and the Philippines.

His wise and resolute counsel was rejected. Bute was foremost in opposing it, and was supported by almost the whole cabinet. Some of the ministers doubted, or affected 30 to doubt, the correctness of Pitt's intelligence; some shrank from the responsibility of advising a course so bold and decided as that which he proposed; some were weary of his ascendency, and were glad to be rid of him on any pretext. One only of his colleagues agreed with him, his brother-in-law, Earl Temple.

Pitt and Temple resigned their offices. To Pitt the young King behaved at parting in the most gracious manner. Pitt, who, proud and fiery every where else, was always meek and humble in the closet, was moved even to tears. The King and the favourite urged him to accept some substantial mark of royal gratitude. Would he like to be appointed governor of Canada? A salary of five thousand pounds a year should be annexed to the office. Residence would not be required. It was true that the governor of Canada, as the law then stood, could not be a member of the House of Commons. But a bill should be brought in, authorising Pitt to hold his government together with a seat in Parliament, and in the preamble should be set forth his claims to the gratitude of his country. Pitt answered, with all delicacy, that his anxieties were rather for his wife and family than for himself, and that nothing would be so acceptable to him as a mark of royal goodness which might be beneficial to those who were dearest to him. The hint was taken. The same Gazette which announced the retirement of the Secretary of State announced also that, in consideration of his great public services, his wife had been created a peeress in her own right, and that a pension of three thousand pounds a year, for three lives, had been bestowed on himself. It was doubtless thought that the rewards and honours conferred on the great minister would have a conciliatory effect on the public mind. Perhaps, too, it was thought that his popularity, which had partly arisen from the contempt which he had always shown for money, would be damaged by a pension; and, indeed, a crowd of libels instantly appeared, in which he was accused of having sold his country. Many of his true friends thought that he would have best consulted the dignity of his character by refusing to accept any pecuniary reward from the court. Nevertheless, the general opinion of his talents, virtues, and 5 services, remained unaltered. Addresses were presented to him from several large towns. London showed its admiration and affection in a still more marked manner. Soon after his resignation came the Lord Mayor's day. The King and the royal family dined at Guildhall. Pitt was 10 one of the guests. The young Sovereign, seated by his bride in his state coach, received a remarkable lesson. He was scarcely noticed. All eyes were fixed on the fallen minister; all acclamations directed to him. The streets, the balconies, the chimney tops, burst into a roar 15 of delight as his chariot passed by. The ladies waved their handkerchiefs from the windows. The common people clung to the wheels, shook hands with the footmen, and even kissed the horses. Cries of "No Bute!" "No Newcastle salmon!" were mingled with the shouts of "Pitt 20 for ever!" When Pitt entered Guildhall, he was welcomed by loud huzzas and clapping of hands, in which the very magistrates of the city joined. Lord Bute, in the mean time, was hooted and pelted through Cheapside, and would, it was thought, have been in some danger, if he had not 25 taken the precaution of surrounding his carriage with a strong body guard of boxers. Many persons blamed the conduct of Pitt on this occasion as disrespectful to the King. Indeed, Pitt himself afterwards owned that he had done wrong. He was led into this error, as he was 30 afterwards led into more serious errors, by the influence of his turbulent and mischievous brother-in-law, Temple.

The events which immediately followed Pitt's retirement

raised his fame higher than ever. War with Spain proved
to be, as he had predicted, inevitable. News came from
the West Indies that Martinique had been taken by an
expedition which he had sent forth. Havanna fell; and
5 it was known that he had planned an attack on Havanna.
Manilla capitulated; and it was believed that he had
meditated a blow against Manilla. The American fleet,
which he had proposed to intercept, had unloaded an
immense cargo of bullion in the haven of Cadiz, before
10 Bute could be convinced that the Court of Madrid really
entertained hostile intentions.

The session of Parliament which followed Pitt's retirement passed over without any violent storm. Lord Bute
took on himself the most prominent part in the House of
15 Lords. He had become Secretary of State, and indeed
prime minister, without having once opened his lips in
public except as an actor. There was, therefore, no small
curiosity to know how he would acquit himself. Members
of the House of Commons crowded the bar of the Lords,
20 and covered the steps of the throne. It was generally
expected that the orator would break down; but his most
malicious hearers were forced to own that he had made
a better figure than they expected. They, indeed, ridiculed
his action as theatrical, and his style as tumid. They
25 were especially amused by the long pauses which, not
from hesitation, but from affectation, he made at all the
emphatic words, and Charles Townshend cried out, "Minute
guns!" The general opinion however was, that, if Bute
had been early practised in debate, he might have become
30 an impressive speaker.

In the Commons, George Grenville had been entrusted
with the lead. The task was not, as yet, a very difficult
one: for Pitt did not think fit to raise the standard of

opposition. His speeches at this time were distinguished, not only by that eloquence in which he excelled all his rivals, but also by a temperance and a modesty which had too often been wanting to his character. When war was declared against Spain, he justly laid claim to the merit of having foreseen what had at length become manifest to all, but he carefully abstained from arrogant and acrimonious expressions; and this abstinence was the more honourable to him, because his temper, never very placid, was now severely tried, both by gout and by calumny. The courtiers had adopted a mode of warfare, which was soon turned with far more formidable effect against themselves. Half the inhabitants of the Grub Street garrets paid their milk scores, and got their shirts out of pawn, by abusing Pitt. His German war, his subsidies, his pension, his wife's peerage, were shin of beef and gin, blankets and baskets of small coal, to the starving poetasters of the Fleet. Even in the House of Commons, he was, on one occasion during this session, assailed with an insolence and malice which called forth the indignation of men of all parties; but he endured the outrage with majestic patience. In his younger days he had been but too prompt to retaliate on those who attacked him; but now, conscious of his great services, and of the space which he filled in the eyes of all mankind, he would not stoop to personal squabbles. "This is no season," he said, in the debate on the Spanish war, "for altercation and recrimination. A day has arrived when every Englishman should stand forth for his country. Arm the whole; be one people; forget everything but the public. I set you the example. Harassed by slanderers, sinking under pain and disease, for the public I forget both my wrongs and my infirmities!" On a general

review of his life, we are inclined to think that his genius
and virtue never shone with so pure an effulgence as during
the session of 1762.

The session drew towards the close; and Bute, em-
5 boldened by the acquiescence of the Houses, resolved
to strike another great blow, and to become first minister
in name as well as in reality. That coalition, which a
few months before had seemed all powerful, had been
dissolved. The retreat of Pitt had deprived the govern-
10 ment of popularity. Newcastle had exulted in the fall
of the illustrious colleague whom he envied and dreaded,
and had not foreseen that his own doom was at hand. He
still tried to flatter himself that he was at the head of
the government; but insults heaped on insults at length
15 undeceived him. Places which had always been considered
as in his gift, were bestowed without any reference to him.
His expostulations only called forth significant hints that
it was time for him to retire. One day he pressed on Bute
the claims of a Whig Prelate to the archbishopric of York.
20 "If your grace thinks so highly of him," answered Bute,
"I wonder that you did not promote him when you had
the power." Still the old man clung with a desperate
grasp to the wreck. Seldom, indeed, have Christian
meekness and Christian humility equalled the meekness
25 and humility of his patient and abject ambition. At length
he was forced to understand that all was over. He quitted
that Court where he had held high office during forty-five
years, and hid his shame and regret among the cedars of
Claremont. Bute became first lord of the treasury.

30   The favourite had undoubtedly committed a great error.
It is impossible to imagine a tool better suited to his
purposes than that which he thus threw away, or rather
put into the hands of his enemies. If Newcastle had

been suffered to play at being first minister, Bute might securely and quietly have enjoyed the substance of power. The gradual introduction of Tories into all the departments of the government might have been effected without any violent clamour, if the chief of the great Whig connection had been ostensibly at the head of affairs. This was strongly represented to Bute by Lord Mansfield, a man who may justly be called the father of modern Toryism, of Toryism modified to suit an order of things under which the House of Commons is the most powerful body in the state. The theories which had dazzled Bute could not impose on the fine intellect of Mansfield. The temerity with which Bute provoked the hostility of powerful and deeply rooted interests, was displeasing to Mansfield's cold and timid nature. Expostulation, however, was vain. Bute was impatient of advice, drunk with success, eager to be, in show as well as in reality, the head of the government. He had engaged in an undertaking in which a screen was absolutely necessary to his success, and even to his safety. He found an excellent screen ready in the very place where it was most needed; and he rudely pushed it away.

And now the new system of government came into full operation. For the first time since the accession of the House of Hanover, the Tory party was in the ascendant. The prime minister himself was a Tory. Lord Egremont, who had succeeded Pitt as Secretary of State, was a Tory, and the son of a Tory. Sir Francis Dashwood, a man of slender parts, of small experience, and of notoriously immoral character, was made Chancellor of the Exchequer, for no reason that could be imagined, except that he was a Tory, and had been a Jacobite. The royal household was filled with men whose favourite toast, a

few years before, had been the King over the water. The
relative position of the two great national seats of learning
was suddenly changed. The University of Oxford had
long been the chief seat of disaffection. In troubled
5 times, the High Street had been lined with bayonets;
the colleges had been searched by the King's messengers.
Grave doctors were in the habit of talking very Ciceronian
treason in the theatre; and the undergraduates drank
bumpers to Jacobite toasts, and chanted Jacobite airs.
10 Of four successive Chancellors of the University, one
had notoriously been in the Pretender's service; the other
three were fully believed to be in secret correspondence
with the exiled family. Cambridge had therefore been
especially favoured by the Hanoverian Princes, and had
15 shown herself grateful for their patronage. George the
First had enriched her library; George the Second had
contributed munificently to her Senate House. Bishoprics
and deaneries were showered on her children. Her Chancellor was Newcastle, the chief of the Whig aristocracy;
20 her High Steward was Hardwicke, the Whig head of the
law. Both her burgesses had held office under the Whig
ministry. Times had now changed. The University of
Cambridge was received at St. James's with comparative
coldness. The answers to the addresses of Oxford were
25 all graciousness and warmth.

The watchwords of the new government were prerogative and purity. The sovereign was no longer to be
a puppet in the hands of any subject, or of any combination of subjects. George the Third would not be forced
30 to take ministers whom he disliked, as his grandfather
had been forced to take Pitt. George the Third would
not be forced to part with any whom he delighted to
honour, as his grandfather had been forced to part with

Carteret. At the same time, the system of bribery which had grown up during the late reigns was to cease. It was ostentatiously proclaimed that, since the accession of the young King, neither constituents nor representatives had been bought with the secret service money. To free 5 Britain from corruption and oligarchical cabals, to detach her from continental connections, to bring the bloody and expensive war with France and Spain to a close, such were the specious objects which Bute professed to procure. 10

Some of these objects he attained. England withdrew, at the cost of a deep stain on her faith, from her German connections. The war with France and Spain was terminated by a peace, honourable indeed and advantageous to our country, yet less honourable and less advantageous 15 than might have been expected from a long and almost unbroken series of victories, by land and sea, in every part of the world. But the only effect of Bute's domestic administration was to make faction wilder, and corruption fouler than ever. 20

The mutual animosity of the Whig and Tory parties had begun to languish after the fall of Walpole, and had seemed to be almost extinct at the close of the reign of George the Second. It now revived in all its force. Many Whigs, it is true, were still in office. The Duke 25 of Bedford had signed the treaty with France. The Duke of Devonshire, though much out of humour, still continued to be Lord Chamberlain. Grenville, who led the House of Commons, and Fox, who still enjoyed in silence the immense gains of the Pay Office, had always been regarded 30 as strong Whigs. But the bulk of the party throughout the country regarded the new minister with abhorrence. There was, indeed, no want of popular themes for

invective against his character. He was a favourite; and
favourites have always been odious in this country. No
mere favourite had been at the head of the government
since the dagger of Felton had reached the heart of the
5 Duke of Buckingham. After that event the most arbitrary
and the most frivolous of the Stuarts had felt the necessity
of confiding the chief direction of affairs to men who
had given some proof of parliamentary or official talent.
Strafford, Falkland, Clarendon, Clifford, Shaftesbury, Lau-
10 derdale, Danby, Temple, Halifax, Rochester, Sunderland,
whatever their faults might be, were all men of acknowledged ability. They did not owe their eminence merely
to the favour of the sovereign. On the contrary, they
owed the favour of the sovereign to their eminence.
15 Most of them, indeed, had first attracted the notice of
the court by the capacity and vigour which they had
shown in opposition. The Revolution seemed to have
for ever secured the state against the domination of a
Carr or a Villiers. Now, however, the personal regard
20 of the King had at once raised a man who had seen
nothing of public business, who had never opened his
lips in Parliament, over the heads of a crowd of eminent
orators, financiers, diplomatists. From a private gentleman,
this fortunate minion had at once been turned into a
25 Secretary of State. He had made his maiden speech
when at the head of the administration. The vulgar
resorted to a simple explanation of the phenomenon,
and the coarsest ribaldry against the Princess Mother
was scrawled on every wall and sung in every alley.
30   This was not all. The spirit of party, roused by
impolitic provocation from its long sleep, roused in turn
a still fiercer and more malignant Fury, the spirit of
national animosity. The grudge of Whig against Tory

was mingled with the grudge of Englishman against Scot.
The two sections of the great British people had not yet
been indissolubly blended together. The events of 1715
and of 1745 had left painful and enduring traces. The
tradesmen of Cornhill had been in dread of seeing their 5
tills and warehouses plundered by barelegged mountaineers
from the Grampians. They still recollected that Black
Friday, when the news came that the rebels were at Derby,
when all the shops in the city were closed, and when the
Bank of England began to pay in sixpences. The Scots, 10
on the other hand, remembered with natural resentment,
the severity with which the insurgents had been chastised,
the military outrages, the humiliating laws, the heads fixed
on Temple Bar, the fires and quartering blocks on Ken-
nington Common. The favourite did not suffer the English 15
to forget from what part of the island he came. The cry
of all the south was that the public offices, the army, the
navy, were filled with high-cheeked Drummonds and
Erskines, Macdonalds and Macgillivrays, who could not
talk a Christian tongue, and some of whom had but lately 20
begun to wear Christian breeches. All the old jokes on
hills without trees, girls without stockings, men eating the
food of horses, pails emptied from the fourteenth story,
were pointed against these lucky adventurers. To the
honour of the Scots it must be said, that their prudence 25
and their pride restrained them from retaliation. Like
the princess in the Arabian tale, they stopped their ears
tight, and, unmoved by the shrillest notes of abuse, walked
on, without once looking round, straight towards the Golden
Fountain. 30

Bute, who had always been considered as a man of
taste and reading, affected, from the moment of his elevation, the character of a Mæcenas. If he expected to

conciliate the public by encouraging literature and art, he
was grievously mistaken. Indeed, none of the objects of
his munificence, with the single exception of Johnson, can
be said to have been well selected ; and the public, not
5 unnaturally, ascribed the selection of Johnson rather to
the Doctor's political prejudices than to his literary merits :
for a wretched scribbler named Shebbeare, who had nothing
in common with Johnson except violent Jacobitism, and
who had stood in the pillory for a libel on the Revolution,
10 was honoured with a mark of royal approbation, similar
to that which was bestowed on the author of the *English
Dictionary*, and of the *Vanity of Human Wishes*. It was
remarked that Adam, a Scotchman, was the court architect,
and that Ramsay, a Scotchman, was the court painter, and
15 was preferred to Reynolds. Mallet, a Scotchman, of no
high literary fame, and of infamous character, partook
largely of the liberality of the government. John Home,
a Scotchman, was rewarded for the tragedy of Douglas,
both with a pension and with a sinecure place. But, when
20 the author of the *Bard* and of the *Elegy in a Country
Churchyard*, ventured to ask for a Professorship, the emoluments of which he much needed, and for the duties of
which he was, in many respects, better qualified than any
man living, he was refused ; and the post was bestowed on
25 the pedagogue under whose care the favourite's son-in-law,
Sir James Lowther, had made such signal proficiency in
the graces and in the humane virtues.

Thus, the first lord of the treasury was detested by
many as a Tory, by many as a favourite, and by many as
30 a Scot. All the hatred which flowed from these various
sources soon mingled, and was directed in one torrent of
obloquy against the treaty of peace. The Duke of Bedford,
who had negotiated that treaty, was hooted through the

streets. Bute was attacked in his chair, and was with
difficulty rescued by a troop of the guards. He could
hardly walk the streets in safety without disguising himself.
A gentleman who died not many years ago used to say
that he once recognised the favourite Earl in the piazza of 5
Covent Garden, muffled in a large coat, and with a hat
and wig drawn over his brows. His lordship's established
type with the mob was a jack boot, a wretched pun on
his Christian name and title. A jack boot, generally
accompanied by a petticoat, was sometimes fastened on a 10
gallows, and sometimes committed to the flames. Libels
on the court, exceeding in audacity and rancour any that
had been published for many years, now appeared daily
both in prose and verse. Wilkes, with lively insolence,
compared the mother of George the Third to the mother 15
of Edward the Third, and the Scotch minister to the gentle
Mortimer. Churchill, with all the energy of hatred, de-
plored the fate of his country, invaded by a new race of
savages, more cruel and ravenous than the Picts or the
Danes, the poor, proud children of Leprosy and Hunger. 20
It is a slight circumstance, but deserves to be recorded,
that in this year pamphleteers first ventured to print at
length the names of the great men whom they lampooned.
George the Second had always been the K——. His
ministers had been Sir R—— W——, Mr P——, and the 25
Duke of N——. But the libellers of George the Third,
of the Princess Mother, and of Lord Bute did not give
quarter to a single vowel.

It was supposed that Lord Temple secretly encouraged
the most scurrilous assailants of the government. In truth, 30
those who knew his habits tracked him as men track a
mole. It was his nature to grub underground. Whenever
a heap of dirt was flung up, it might well be suspected

that he was at work in some foul crooked labyrinth below.
Pitt turned away from the filthy work of opposition, with
the same scorn with which he had turned away from the
filthy work of government. He had the magnanimity to
5 proclaim everywhere the disgust which he felt at the insults
offered by his own adherents to the Scottish nation, and
missed no opportunity of extolling the courage and fidelity
which the Highland regiments had displayed through the
whole war. But, though he disdained to use any but lawful
10 and honourable weapons, it was well known that his fair
blows were likely to be far more formidable than the privy
thrusts of his brother-in-law's stiletto.

Bute's heart began to fail him. The Houses were about
to meet. The treaty would instantly be the subject of
15 discussion. It was probable that Pitt, the great Whig
connection, and the multitude, would all be on the same
side. The favourite had professed to hold in abhorrence
those means by which preceding ministers had kept the
House of Commons in good humour. He now began to
20 think that he had been too scrupulous. His Utopian
visions were at an end. It was necessary, not only to
bribe, but to bribe more shamelessly and flagitiously than
his predecessors, in order to make up for lost time. A
majority must be secured, no matter by what means. Could
25 Grenville do this? Would he do it? His firmness and
ability had not yet been tried in any perilous crisis. He
had been generally regarded as a humble follower of his
brother Temple, and of his brother-in-law Pitt, and was
supposed, though with little reason, to be still favourably
30 inclined towards them. Other aid must be called in. And
where was other aid to be found?

There was one man, whose sharp and manly logic had
often in debate been found a match for the lofty and

impassioned rhetoric of Pitt, whose talents for jobbing were not inferior to his talents for debate, whose dauntless spirit shrank from no difficulty or danger, and who was as little troubled with scruples as with fears. Henry Fox, or nobody, could weather the storm which was about to 5 burst. Yet was he a person to whom the court, even in that extremity, was unwilling to have recourse. He had always been regarded as a Whig of the Whigs. He had been the friend and disciple of Walpole. He had long been connected by close ties with William Duke 10 of Cumberland. By the Tories he was more hated than any man living. So strong was their aversion to him that when, in the late reign, he had attempted to form a party against the Duke of Newcastle, they had thrown all their weight into Newcastle's scale. By the Scots, Fox was 15 abhorred as the confidential friend of the conqueror of Culloden. He was, on personal grounds, most obnoxious to the Princess Mother. For he had, immediately after her husband's death, advised the late King to take the education of her son, the heir apparent, entirely out of 20 her hands. He had recently given, if possible, still deeper offence; for he had indulged, not without some ground, the ambitious hope that his beautiful sister-in-law, the Lady Sarah Lennox, might be queen of England. It had been observed that the King at one time rode every morning 25 by the grounds of Holland House, and that, on such occasions, Lady Sarah, dressed like a shepherdess at a masquerade, was making hay close to the road, which was then separated by no wall from the lawn. On account of the part which Fox had taken in this singular love affair, 30 he was the only member of the Privy Council who was not summoned to the meeting at which his Majesty announced his intended marriage with the Princess of

Mecklenburg. Of all the statesmen of the age, therefore, it seemed that Fox was the last with whom Bute, the Tory, the Scot, the favourite of the Princess Mother, could, under any circumstances, act. Yet to Fox Bute was now com-
5 pelled to apply.

Fox had many noble and amiable qualities, which in private life shone forth in full lustre, and made him dear to his children, to his dependents, and to his friends; but as a public man he had no title to esteem. In him the
10 vices which were common to the whole school of Walpole appeared, not perhaps in their worst, but certainly in their most prominent form; for his parliamentary and official talents made all his faults conspicuous. His courage, his vehement temper, his contempt for appearances, led him
15 to display much that others, quite as unscrupulous as himself, covered with a decent veil. He was the most unpopular of the statesmen of his time, not because he sinned more than many of them, but because he canted less.

He felt his unpopularity; but he felt it after the fashion
20 of strong minds. He became, not cautious, but reckless, and faced the rage of the whole nation with a scowl of inflexible defiance. He was born with a sweet and generous temper; but he had been goaded and baited into a savageness which was not natural to him, and which amazed
25 and shocked those who knew him best. Such was the man to whom Bute, in extreme need, applied for succour.

That succour Fox was not unwilling to afford. Though by no means of an envious temper, he had undoubtedly contemplated the success and popularity of Pitt with bitter
30 mortification. He thought himself Pitt's match as a debater, and Pitt's superior as a man of business. They had long been regarded as well-paired rivals. They had started fair in the career of ambition. They had long run side by side.

At length Fox had taken the lead, and Pitt had fallen behind. Then had come a sudden turn of fortune, like that in Virgil's foot-race. Fox had stumbled in the mire, and had not only been defeated, but befouled. Pitt had reached the goal, and received the prize. The emoluments 5 of the Pay Office might induce the defeated statesman to submit in silence to the ascendancy of his competitor, but could not satisfy a mind conscious of great powers, and sore from great vexations. As soon, therefore, as a party arose adverse to the war and to the supremacy of the great 10 war minister, the hopes of Fox began to revive. His feuds with the Princess Mother, with the Scots, with the Tories, he was ready to forget, if by the help of his old enemies, he could now regain the importance which he had lost, and confront Pitt on equal terms.   15

The alliance was, therefore, soon concluded. Fox was assured that, if he would pilot the government out of its embarrassing situation, he should be rewarded with a peerage, of which he had long been desirous. He undertook on his side to obtain, by fair or foul means, a vote 20 in favour of the peace. In consequence of this arrangement he became leader of the House of Commons; and Grenville, stifling his vexation as well as he could, sullenly acquiesced in the change.

Fox had expected that his influence would secure to 25 the court the cordial support of some eminent Whigs who were his personal friends, particularly of the Duke of Cumberland and of the Duke of Devonshire. He was disappointed, and soon found that, in addition to all his other difficulties, he must reckon on the opposition of the ablest 30 prince of the blood, and of the great house of Cavendish.

But he had pledged himself to win the battle; and he

was not a man to go back. It was no time for squeamish-
ness. Bute was made to comprehend that the ministry
could be saved only by practising the tactics of Walpole
to an extent at which Walpole himself would have stared.
5 The Pay Office was turned into a mart for votes. Hundreds
of members were closeted there with Fox, and, as there is
too much reason to believe, departed carrying with them the
wages of infamy. It was affirmed by persons who had the
best opportunities of obtaining information, that twenty-five
10 thousand pounds were thus paid away in a single morning.
The lowest bribe given, it was said, was a bank-note for two
hundred pounds.

Intimidation was joined with corruption. All ranks,
from the highest to the lowest, were to be taught that
15 the King would be obeyed. The Lords Lieutenants of
several counties were dismissed. The Duke of Devonshire
was especially singled out as the victim by whose fate the
magnates of England were to take warning. His wealth,
rank, and influence, his stainless private character, and the
20 constant attachment of his family to the House of Hanover
did not secure him from gross personal indignity. It was
known that he disapproved of the course which the government had taken; and it was accordingly determined to
humble the Prince of the Whigs, as he had been nicknamed
25 by the Princess Mother. He went to the Palace to pay his
duty. "Tell him," said the King to a page, "that I will
not see him." The page hesitated. "Go to him," said the
King, "and tell him those very words." The message was
delivered. The Duke tore off his gold key, and went
30 away boiling with anger. His relations who were in office
instantly resigned. A few days later, the King called for
the list of Privy Councillors, and with his own hand struck
out the Duke's name.

In this step there was at least courage, though little wisdom or good nature. But, as nothing was too high for the revenge of the court, so also was nothing too low. A persecution, such as had never been known before, and has never been known since, raged in every public depart- 5 ment. Great numbers of humble and laborious clerks were deprived of their bread, not because they had neglected their duties, not because they had taken an active part against the ministry, but merely because they had owed their situations to the recommendation of some nobleman 10 or gentleman who was against the peace. The proscription extended to tidewaiters, to gaugers, to door-keepers. One poor man to whom a pension had been given for his gallantry in a fight with smugglers, was deprived of it because he had been befriended by the Duke of Grafton. 15 An aged widow, who, on account of her husband's services in the navy, had, many years before, been made housekeeper to a public office, was dismissed from her situation, because it was imagined that she was distantly connected by marriage with the Cavendish family. The public clamour, as may 20 well be supposed, grew daily louder and louder. But the louder it grew, the more resolutely did Fox go on with the work which he had begun. His old friends could not conceive what had possessed him. "I could forgive," said the Duke of Cumberland, "Fox's political vagaries; 25 but I am quite confounded by his inhumanity. Surely he used to be the best-natured of men."

At last Fox went so far as to take a legal opinion on the question, whether the patents granted by George the Second were binding on George the Third. It is said that, if his 30 colleagues had not flinched, he would at once have turned out the Tellers of the Exchequer and Justices in Eyre.

Meanwhile the Parliament met. The ministers, more

hated by the people than ever, were secure of a majority, and they had also reason to hope that they would have the advantage in the debates as well as in the divisions; for Pitt was confined to his chamber by a severe attack of gout.
5 His friends moved to defer the consideration of the treaty till he should be able to attend: but the motion was rejected.   The great day arrived.   The discussion had lasted some time, when a loud huzza was heard in Palace Yard.   The noise came nearer and nearer, up the stairs,
10 through the lobby.   The door opened, and from the midst of a shouting multitude came forth Pitt, borne in the arms of his attendants.   His face was thin and ghastly, his limbs swathed in flannel, his crutch in his hand.   The bearers set him down within the bar.   His friends instantly surrounded
15 him, and with their help he crawled to his seat near the table.   In this condition he spoke three hours and a half against the peace.   During that time he was repeatedly forced to sit down and to use cordials.   It may well be supposed that his voice was faint, that his action was
20 languid, and that his speech, though occasionally brilliant and impressive, was feeble when compared with his best oratorical performances.   But those who remembered what he had done, and who saw what he suffered, listened to him with emotions stronger than any that mere eloquence can
25 produce.   He was unable to stay for the division, and was carried away from the House amidst shouts as loud as those which had announced his arrival.

A large majority approved the peace.   The exultation of the court was boundless.   "Now," exclaimed the Princess
30 Mother, "my son is really King."   The young sovereign spoke of himself as freed from the bondage in which his grandfather had been held.   On one point, it was announced, his mind was unalterably made up.   Under no circumstances

whatever should those Whig grandees, who had enslaved his predecessors and endeavoured to enslave himself, be restored to power.

This vaunting was premature. The real strength of the favourite was by no means proportioned to the number of 5 votes which he had, on one particular division, been able to command. He was soon again in difficulties. The most important part of his budget was a tax on cider. This measure was opposed, not only by those who were generally hostile to his administration, but also by many 10 of his supporters. The name of excise had always been hateful to the Tories. One of the chief crimes of Walpole, in their eyes, had been his partiality for this mode of raising money. The Tory Johnson had in his Dictionary given so scurrilous a definition of the word Excise, that the Com- 15 missioners of Excise had seriously thought of prosecuting him. The counties which the new impost particularly affected had always been Tory counties. It was the boast of John Philips, the poet of the English vintage, that the Cider-land had ever been faithful to the throne, and that all 20 the pruning-hooks of her thousand orchards had been beaten into swords for the service of the ill fated Stuarts. The effect of Bute's fiscal scheme was to produce an union between the gentry and yeomanry of the Cider-land and the Whigs of the capital. Herefordshire and Worcestershire 25 were in a flame. The city of London, though not so directly interested, was, if possible, still more excited. The debates on this question irreparably damaged the government. Dashwood's financial statement had been confused and absurd beyond belief, and had been received by the 30 House with roars of laughter. He had sense enough to be conscious of his unfitness for the high situation which he held, and exclaimed in a comical fit of despair, "What

shall I do? The boys will point at me in the street, and
cry, 'There goes the worst Chancellor of the Exchequer
that ever was.'" George Grenville came to the rescue, and
spoke strongly on his favourite theme, the profusion with
5 which the late war had been carried on. That profusion,
he said, had made taxes necessary. He called on the
gentlemen opposite to him to say where they would have a
tax laid, and dwelt on this topic with his usual prolixity.
"Let them tell me where," he repeated in a monotonous
10 and somewhat fretful tone. "I say, sir, let them tell me
where. I repeat it, sir; I am entitled to say to them, Tell
me where." Unluckily for him, Pitt had come down to the
House that night, and had been bitterly provoked by the
reflections thrown on the war. He revenged himself by
15 murmuring, in a whine resembling Grenville's, a line of a
well known song, "Gentle Shepherd, tell me where." "If,"
cried Grenville, "gentlemen are to be treated in this
way——" Pitt, as was his fashion, when he meant to
mark extreme contempt, rose deliberately, made his bow,
20 and walked out of the House, leaving his brother-in-law in
convulsions of rage, and every body else in convulsions of
laughter. It was long before Grenville lost the nickname
of the Gentle Shepherd.

But the ministry had vexations still more serious to
25 endure. The hatred which the Tories and Scots bore to
Fox was implacable. In a moment of extreme peril, they
had consented to put themselves under his guidance. But
the aversion with which they regarded him broke forth as
soon as the crisis seemed to be over. Some of them
30 attacked him about the accounts of the Pay Office. Some
of them rudely interrupted him when speaking, by laughter
and ironical cheers. He was naturally desirous to escape
from so disagreeable a situation, and demanded the

peerage which had been promised as the reward of his
services.

It was clear that there must be some change in the
composition of the ministry.   But scarcely any, even of
those who, from their situation, might be supposed to be 5
in all the secrets of the government, anticipated what really
took place.   To the amazement of the Parliament and the
nation, it was suddenly announced that Bute had resigned.

Twenty different explanations of this strange step were
suggested.   Some attributed it to profound design, and 10
some to sudden panic.   Some said that the lampoons of
the Opposition had driven the Earl from the field ; some
that he had taken office only in order to bring the war to
a close, and had always meant to retire when that object
had been accomplished.   He publicly assigned ill health 15
as his reason for quitting business, and privately complained
that he was not cordially seconded by his colleagues, and
that Lord Mansfield, in particular, whom he had himself
brought into the cabinet, gave him no support in the House
of Peers.   Mansfield was, indeed, far too sagacious not to 20
perceive that Bute's situation was one of great peril, and
far too timorous to thrust himself into peril for the sake of
another.   The probability, however, is that Bute's conduct
on this occasion, like the conduct of most men on most
occasions, was determined by mixed motives.   We suspect 25
that he was sick of office ; for this is a feeling much more
common among ministers than persons who see public life
from a distance are disposed to believe; and nothing could
be more natural than that this feeling should take possession
of the mind of Bute.   In general, a statesman climbs by 30
slow degrees.   Many laborious years elapse before he
reaches the topmost pinnacle of preferment.   In the earlier
part of his career, therefore, he is constantly lured on by

seeing something above him.   During his ascent he
gradually becomes inured to the annoyances which belong
to a life of ambition.   By the time that he has attained
the highest point, he has become patient of labour and
5 callous to abuse.   He is kept constant to his vocation, in
spite of all its discomforts, at first by hope, and at last by
habit.   It was not so with Bute.   His whole public life
lasted little more than two years.   On the day on which
he became a politician he became a cabinet minister.   In
10 a few months he was, both in name and in show, chief of
the administration.   Greater than he had been he could
not be.   If what he already possessed was vanity and
vexation of spirit, no delusion remained to entice him
onward.   He had been cloyed with the pleasures of
15 ambition before he had been seasoned to its pains.   His
habits had not been such as were likely to fortify his mind
against obloquy and public hatred.   He had reached his
forty-eighth year in dignified ease, without knowing, by
personal experience, what it was to be ridiculed and
20 slandered.   All at once, without any previous initiation,
he had found himself exposed to such a storm of invective
and satire as had never burst on the head of any statesman.
The emoluments of office were now nothing to him ; for he
had just succeeded to a princely property by the death of
25 his father-in-law.   All the honours which could be bestowed
on him he had already secured.   He had obtained the
Garter for himself, and a British peerage for his son.   He
seems also to have imagined that by quitting the treasury
he should escape from danger and abuse without really
30 resigning power, and should still be able to exercise in
private supreme influence over the royal mind.

Whatever may have been his motives, he retired.   Fox
at the same time took refuge in the House of Lords ; and

George Grenville became First Lord of the Treasury and Chancellor of the Exchequer.

We believe that those who made this arrangement fully intended that Grenville should be a mere puppet in the hands of Bute; for Grenville was as yet very imperfectly known even to those who had observed him long. He passed for a mere official drudge; and he had all the industry, the minute accuracy, the formality, the tediousness, which belong to the character. But he had other qualities which had not yet shown themselves, devouring ambition, dauntless courage, self-confidence amounting to presumption, and a temper which could not endure opposition. He was not disposed to be any body's tool; and he had no attachment, political or personal, to Bute. The two men had, indeed, nothing in common, except a strong propensity towards harsh and unpopular courses. Their principles were fundamentally different. Bute was a Tory. Grenville would have been very angry with any person who should have denied his claim to be a Whig. He was more prone to tyrannical measures than Bute; but he loved tyranny only when disguised under the forms of constitutional liberty. He mixed up, after a fashion then not very unusual, the theories of the republicans of the seventeenth century with the technical maxims of English law, and thus succeeded in combining anarchical speculation with arbitrary practice. The voice of the people was the voice of God; but the only legitimate organ through which the voice of the people could be uttered was the Parliament. All power was from the people; but to the Parliament the whole power of the people had been delegated. No Oxonian divine had ever, even in the years which immediately followed the Restoration, demanded for the King so abject, so unreasoning a homage, as Grenville, on what he considered as the purest Whig principles, demanded for the Parliament. As he wished to see the Parliament despotic over the nation, so he wished to see it also despotic over the court. In his view the prime minister, possessed of the confidence of the House of Commons, ought to be Mayor of the Palace. The King was a mere Childeric or Chilperic, who might well think himself lucky in being permitted to enjoy such handsome apartments at Saint James's, and so fine a park at Windsor. Thus the opinions of Bute and those of Grenville were diametrically opposed. Nor was there any private friendship between the two statesmen. Grenville's nature was not forgiving; and he well remembered how, a few months before, he had been compelled to yield the lead of the House of Commons to Fox.

We are inclined to think, on the whole, that the worst administration which has governed England since the Revolution was that of George Grenville. His public acts may be classed under two heads, outrages on the liberty of the people, and outrages on the dignity of the crown.

He began by making war on the press. John Wilkes, member of Parliament for Aylesbury, was singled out for persecution. Wilkes had, till very lately, been known chiefly as one of the most profane, licentious, and agreeable rakes about town. He was a man of taste, reading, and engaging manners. His sprightly conversation was the delight of green rooms and taverns, and pleased even grave hearers when he was sufficiently under restraint to abstain from detailing the particulars of his amours, and from breaking jests on the New Testament. His expensive debaucheries forced him to have recourse to the Jews. He was soon a ruined man, and determined to try his chance as a political adventurer. In Parliament he did not succeed. His speaking, though pert, was feeble, and by no means interested his hearers so much as to make them forget his face, which was so hideous that the caricaturists were forced, in their own despite, to flatter him. As a writer, he made 5 a better figure. He set up a weekly paper, called the *North Briton*. This journal, written with some pleasantry, and great audacity and impudence, had a considerable number of readers. Forty-four numbers had been published when Bute resigned; and, though almost every number had 10 contained matter grossly libellous, no prosecution had been instituted. The forty-fifth number was innocent when compared with the majority of those which had preceded it, and indeed contained nothing so strong as may in our time be found daily in the leading articles of the *Times* and 15 *Morning Chronicle*. But Grenville was now at the head of affairs. A new spirit had been infused into the administration. Authority was to be upheld. The government was no longer to be braved with impunity. Wilkes was arrested under a general warrant, conveyed to the Tower, 20 and confined there with circumstances of unusual severity. His papers were seized, and carried to the Secretary of State. These harsh and illegal measures produced a violent outbreak of popular rage, which was soon changed to delight and exultation. The arrest was pronounced un- 25 lawful by the Court of Common Pleas, in which Chief Justice Pratt presided, and the prisoner was discharged. This victory over the government was celebrated with enthusiasm both in London and in the cider counties.

While the ministers were daily becoming more odious 30 to the nation, they were doing their best to make themselves also odious to the court. They gave the King plainly to understand that they were determined not to be Lord Bute's

creatures, and exacted a promise that no secret adviser
should have access to the royal ear. They soon found
reason to suspect that this promise had not been observed.
They remonstrated in terms less respectful than their master
5 had been accustomed to hear, and gave him a fortnight to
make his choice between his favourite and his cabinet.

George the Third was greatly disturbed. He had but a
few weeks before exulted in his deliverance from the yoke
of the great Whig connection. He had even declared that
10 his honour would not permit him ever again to admit the
members of that connection into his service. He now
found that he had only exchanged one set of masters for
another set still harsher and more imperious. In his distress
he thought on Pitt. From Pitt it was possible that better
15 terms might be obtained than either from Grenville, or from
the party of which Newcastle was the head.

Grenville, on his return from an excursion into the
country, repaired to Buckingham House. He was astonished to find at the entrance a chair, the shape of which
20 was well known to him, and indeed to all London. It was
distinguished by a large boot, made for the purpose of
accommodating the Great Commoner's gouty leg. Grenville
guessed the whole. His brother-in-law was closeted with
the King. Bute, provoked by what he considered as the
25 unfriendly and ungrateful conduct of his successors, had
himself proposed that Pitt should be summoned to the
palace.

Pitt had two audiences on two successive days. What
passed at the first interview led him to expect that the
30 negotiation would be brought to a satisfactory close ; but on
the morrow he found the King less complying. The best
account, indeed the only trustworthy account of the con-
ference, is that which was taken from Pitt's own mouth by

Lord Hardwicke. It appears that Pitt strongly represented
the importance of conciliating those chiefs of the Whig
party who had been so unhappy as to incur the royal displeasure. They had, he said, been the most constant
friends of the House of Hanover. Their power was great; 5
they had been long versed in public business. If they were
to be under sentence of exclusion, a solid administration
could not be formed. His Majesty could not bear to think
of putting himself into the hands of those whom he had
recently chased from his court with the strongest marks of 10
anger. "I am sorry, Mr Pitt," he said, "but I see this will
not do. My honour is concerned. I must support my
honour." How his Majesty succeeded in supporting his
honour we shall soon see.

Pitt retired, and the King was reduced to request the 15
ministers, whom he had been on the point of discarding, to
remain in office. During the two years which followed,
Grenville, now closely leagued with the Bedfords, was the
master of the court; and a hard master he proved. He
knew that he was kept in place only because there was no 20
choice except between himself and the Whigs. That under
any circumstances the Whigs would be forgiven, he thought
impossible. The late attempt to get rid of him had roused
his resentment; the failure of that attempt had liberated
him from all fear. He had never been very courtly. He 25
now began to hold a language, to which, since the days of
Cornet Joyce and President Bradshaw, no English King
had been compelled to listen.

In one matter, indeed, Grenville, at the expense of
justice and liberty, gratified the passions of the court while 30
gratifying his own. The persecution of Wilkes was eagerly
pressed. He had written a parody on Pope's *Essay on
Man*, entitled the *Essay on Woman*, and had appended to

it notes, in ridicule of Warburton's famous Commentary.
This composition was exceedingly profligate, but not more
so, we think, than some of Pope's own works, the imitation
of the second satire of the first book of Horace, for
5 example ; and, to do Wilkes justice, he had not, like Pope,
given his ribaldry to the world. He had merely printed at
a private press a very small number of copies, which he
meant to present to some of his boon companions, whose
morals were in no more danger of being corrupted by a
10 loose book than a negro of being tanned by a warm sun.
A tool of the government, by giving a bribe to the printer,
procured a copy of this trash, and placed it in the hands of
the ministers. The ministers resolved to visit Wilkes's
offence against decorum with the utmost rigour of the law.
15 What share piety and respect for morals had in dictating
this resolution, our readers may judge from the fact that no
person was more eager for bringing the libertine poet to
punishment than Lord March, afterwards Duke of Queens-
berry. On the first day of the session of Parliament, the
20 book, thus disgracefully obtained, was laid on the table of
the Lords by the Earl of Sandwich, whom the Duke of
Bedford's interest had made Secretary of State. The unfortunate author had not the slightest suspicion that his
licentious poem had ever been seen, except by his printer
25 and by a few of his dissipated companions, till it was produced in full Parliament. Though he was a man of easy
temper, averse from danger, and not very susceptible of
shame, the surprise, the disgrace, the prospect of utter ruin,
put him beside himself. He picked a quarrel with one
30 of Lord Bute's dependents, fought a duel, was seriously
wounded, and when half recovered, fled to France. His
enemies had now their own way both in the Parliament and
in the King's Bench. He was censured, expelled from the

House of Commons, outlawed. His works were ordered to be burned by the common hangman. Yet was the multitude still true to him. In the minds even of many moral and religious men, his crime seemed light when compared with the crime of his accusers. The conduct of Sandwich, 5 in particular, excited universal disgust. His own vices were notorious; and, only a fortnight before he laid the Essay on Woman before the House of Lords, he had been drinking and singing loose catches with Wilkes at one of the most dissolute clubs in London. Shortly after the meeting of 10 Parliament, the Beggar's Opera was acted at Covent Garden theatre. When Macheath uttered the words—" That Jemmy Twitcher should peach me I own surprised me,"— pit, boxes, and galleries, burst into a roar which seemed likely to bring the roof down. From that day Sandwich 15 was universally known by the nickname of Jemmy Twitcher. The ceremony of burning the North Briton was interrupted by a riot. The constables were beaten; the paper was rescued; and, instead of it, a jackboot and a petticoat were committed to the flames. Wilkes had instituted an action 20 for the seizure of his papers against the Undersecretary of State. The jury gave a thousand pounds damages. But neither these nor any other indications of public feeling had power to move Grenville. He had the Parliament with him: and, according to his political creed, the sense of the 25 nation was to be collected from the Parliament alone.

Soon, however, he found reason to fear that even the Parliament might fail him. On the question of the legality of general warrants, the Opposition, having on its side all sound principles, all constitutional authorities, and the 30 voice of the whole nation, mustered in great force, and was joined by many who did not ordinarily vote against the Government. On one occasion the ministry, in a very

full House, had a majority of only fourteen votes. The
storm, however, blew over. The spirit of the Opposition,
from whatever cause, began to flag at the moment when
success seemed almost certain. The session ended without
5 any change. Pitt, whose eloquence had shone with its
usual lustre in all the principal debates, and whose
popularity was greater than ever, was still a private man.
Grenville, detested alike by the court and by the people,
was still minister.

10   As soon as the Houses had risen, Grenville took a step
which proved, even more signally than any of his past acts,
how despotic, how acrimonious, and how fearless his nature
was. Among the gentlemen not ordinarily opposed to the
Government, who, on the great constitutional question of
15 general warrants, had voted with the minority, was Henry
Conway, brother of the Earl of Hertford, a brave soldier,
a tolerable speaker, and a well-meaning, though not a wise
or vigorous politician. He was now deprived of his
regiment, the merited reward of faithful and gallant service
20 in two wars. It was confidently asserted that in this
violent measure the King heartily concurred.

    But whatever pleasure the persecution of Wilkes, or
the dismissal of Conway, may have given to the royal
mind, it is certain that his Majesty's aversion to his
25 ministers increased day by day. Grenville was as frugal
of the public money as of his own, and morosely refused
to accede to the King's request, that a few thousand pounds
might be expended in buying some open fields to the west
of the gardens of Buckingham House. In consequence of
30 this refusal, the fields were soon covered with buildings,
and the King and Queen were overlooked in their most
private walks by the upper windows of a hundred houses.
Nor was this the worst. Grenville was as liberal of words

as he was sparing of guineas.   Instead of explaining himself
in that clear, concise, and lively manner, which alone could
win the attention of a young mind new to business, he
spoke in the closet just as he spoke in the House of
Commons.   When he had harangued two hours, he looked 5
at his watch, as he had been in the habit of looking at the
clock opposite the Speaker's chair, apologised for the length
of his discourse, and then went on for an hour more.   The
members of the House of Commons can cough an orator
down, or can walk away to dinner ; and they were by no 10
means sparing in the use of these privileges when Grenville
was on his legs.   But the poor young King had to endure
all this eloquence with mournful civility.   To the end of
his life he continued to talk with horror of Grenville's
orations.   15

About this time took place one of the most singular
events in Pitt's life.   There was a certain Sir William
Pynsent, a Somersetshire baronet of Whig politics, who
had been a Member of the House of Commons in the
days of Queen Anne, and had retired to rural privacy 20
when the Tory party, towards the end of her reign,
obtained the ascendency in her councils.   His manners
were eccentric.   His morals lay under very odious im-
putations.   But his fidelity to his political opinions was
unalterable.   During fifty years of seclusion he continued 25
to brood over the circumstances which had driven him
from public life, the dismissal of the Whigs, the peace of
Utrecht, the desertion of our allies.   He now thought that
he perceived a close analogy between the well-remembered
events of his youth and the events which he had witnessed 30
in extreme old age ; between the disgrace of Marlborough
and the disgrace of Pitt ; between the elevation of Harley
and the elevation of Bute ; between the treaty negotiated

by St John and the treaty negotiated by Bedford; between the wrongs of the House of Austria in 1712 and the wrongs of the House of Brandenburg in 1762. This fancy took such possession of the old man's mind that he determined 5 to leave his whole property to Pitt. In this way Pitt unexpectedly came into possession of near three thousand pounds a year. Nor could all the malice of his enemies find any ground for reproach in the transaction. Nobody could call him a legacy hunter. Nobody could accuse 10 him of seizing that to which others had a better claim. For he had never in his life seen Sir William; and Sir William had left no relation so near as to be entitled to form any expectations respecting the estate.

The fortunes of Pitt seemed to flourish; but his health 15 was worse than ever. We cannot find that, during the session which began in January 1765, he once appeared in Parliament. He remained some months in profound retirement at Hayes, his favourite villa, scarcely moving except from his armchair to his bed, and from his bed to 20 his armchair, and often employing his wife as his amanuensis in his most confidential correspondence. Some of his detractors whispered that his invisibility was to be ascribed quite as much to affectation as to gout. In truth his character, high and splendid as it was, wanted simplicity. 25 With genius which did not need the aid of stage tricks, and with a spirit which should have been far above them, he had yet been, through life, in the habit of practising them. It was, therefore, now surmised that, having acquired all the consideration which could be derived from eloquence 30 and from great services to the state, he had determined not to make himself cheap by often appearing in public, but, under the pretext of ill health, to surround himself with mystery, to emerge only at long intervals and on momentous occasions, and at other times to deliver his oracles only to a few favoured votaries, who were suffered to make pilgrimages to his shrine. If such were his object, it was for a time fully attained. Never was the magic of his name so powerful, never was he regarded by his country 5 with such superstitious veneration, as during this year of silence and seclusion.

While Pitt was thus absent from Parliament, Grenville proposed a measure destined to produce a great revolution, the effects of which will long be felt by the whole human 10 race. We speak of the Act for imposing stamp duties on the North American colonies. The plan was eminently characteristic of its author. Every feature of the parent was found in the child. A timid statesman would have shrunk from a step, of which Walpole, at a time when 15 the colonies were far less powerful, had said—" He who shall propose it will be a much bolder man than I." But the nature of Grenville was insensible to fear. A statesman of large views would have felt that to lay taxes at West-minster on New England and New York, was a course 20 opposed, not indeed to the letter of the Statute Book, or to any decision contained in the Term Reports, but to the principles of good government, and to the spirit of the constitution. A statesman of large views would also have felt that ten times the estimated produce of the American 25 stamps would have been dearly purchased by even a trans-ient quarrel between the mother country and the colonies. But Grenville knew of no spirit of the constitution distinct from the letter of the law, and of no national interests except those which are expressed by pounds, shillings, and 30 pence. That his policy might give birth to deep discontents in all the provinces, from the shore of the Great Lakes to the Mexican sea; that France and Spain might seize the

opportunity of revenge; that the empire might be dismembered; that the debt, that debt with the amount of which he perpetually reproached Pitt, might, in consequence of his own policy, be doubled; these were possibilities which
5 never occurred to that small, sharp mind.

The Stamp Act will be remembered as long as the globe lasts. But, at the time, it attracted much less notice in this country than another Act which is now almost utterly forgotten. The King fell ill, and was thought to be in a
10 dangerous state. His complaint, we believe, was the same which, at a later period, repeatedly incapacitated him for the performance of his regal functions. The heir apparent was only two years old. It was clearly proper to make provision for the administration of the government, in case
15 of a minority. The discussions on this point brought the quarrel between the court and the ministry to a crisis. The King wished to be entrusted with the power of naming a regent by will. The ministers feared, or affected to fear, that, if this power were conceded to him, he would name
20 the Princess Mother, nay, possibly the Earl of Bute. They, therefore, insisted on introducing into the bill words confining the King's choice to the royal family. Having thus excluded Bute, they urged the King to let them, in the most marked manner, exclude the Princess Dowager also.
25 They assured him that the House of Commons would undoubtedly strike her name out, and by this threat they wrung from him a reluctant assent. In a few days, it appeared that the representations by which they had induced the King to put this gross and public affront on his
30 mother were unfounded. The friends of the Princess in the House of Commons moved that her name should be inserted. The ministers could not decently attack the parent of their master. They hoped that the Opposition

would come to their help, and put on them a force to which they would gladly have yielded. But the majority of the Opposition, though hating the Princess, hated Grenville more, beheld his embarrassment with delight, and would do nothing to extricate him from it. The Princess's name 5 was accordingly placed in the list of persons qualified to hold the regency.

The King's resentment was now at the height. The present evil seemed to him more intolerable than any other. Even the junta of Whig grandees could not treat 10 him worse than he had been treated by his present ministers. In his distress he poured out his whole heart to his uncle, the Duke of Cumberland. The Duke was not a man to be loved ; but he was eminently a man to be trusted. He had an intrepid temper, a strong understanding, and a 15 high sense of honour and duty. As a general, he belonged to a remarkable class of captains, captains, we mean, whose fate it has been to lose almost all the battles which they have fought, and yet to be reputed stout and skilful soldiers. Such captains were Coligni and William the Third. We 20 might, perhaps, add Marshal Soult to the list. The bravery of the Duke of Cumberland was such as distinguished him even among the princes of his brave house. The indifference with which he rode about amidst musket balls and cannon balls was not the highest proof of his fortitude. 25 Hopeless maladies, horrible surgical operations, far from unmanning him, did not even discompose him. With courage, he had the virtues which are akin to courage. He spoke the truth, was open in enmity and friendship, and upright in all his dealings. But his nature was hard ; and what seemed 30 to him justice was rarely tempered with mercy. He was, therefore, during many years one of the most unpopular men in England. The severity with which he had treated

the rebels after the battle of Culloden, had gained for him
the name of the Butcher.   His attempts to introduce into
the army of England, then in a most disorderly state, the
rigorous discipline of Potsdam, had excited still stronger
5 disgust. Nothing was too bad to be believed of him. Many
honest people were so absurd as to fancy that, if he were
left Regent during the minority of his nephews, there would
be another smothering in the Tower.   These feelings, however, had passed away.   The Duke had been living, during
10 some years, in retirement.   The English, full of animosity
against the Scots, now blamed his Royal Highness only for
having left so many Camerons and Macphersons to be
made gaugers and customhouse officers.   He was, therefore,
at present, a favourite with his countrymen, and especially
15 with the inhabitants of London.

He had little reason to love the King, and had shown
clearly, though not obtrusively, his dislike of the system
which had lately been pursued.   But he had high and
almost romantic notions of the duty which, as a prince
20 of the blood, he owed to the head of his house.   He determined to extricate his nephew from bondage, and to
effect a reconciliation between the Whig party and the
throne, on terms honourable to both.

In this mind he set off for Hayes, and was admitted
25 to Pitt's sick room ; for Pitt would not leave his chamber,
and would not communicate with any messenger of inferior
dignity.   And now began a long series of errors on the
part of the illustrious statesman, errors which involved his
country in difficulties and distresses more serious even
30 than those from which his genius had formerly rescued
her.   His language was haughty, unreasonable, almost unintelligible.   The only thing which could be discerned
through a cloud of vague and not very gracious phrases,

was that he would not at that moment take office. The
truth, we believe, was this. Lord Temple, who was Pitt's
evil genius, had just formed a new scheme of politics.
Hatred of Bute and of the Princess had, it should seem,
taken entire possession of Temple's soul. He had quarrelled 5
with his brother George, because George had been connected with Bute and the Princess. Now that George
appeared to be the enemy of Bute and of the Princess,
Temple was eager to bring about a general family reconciliation. The three brothers, as Temple, Grenville, and 10
Pitt, were popularly called, might make a ministry, without
leaning for aid either on Bute or on the Whig connection.
With such views, Temple used all his influence to dissuade
Pitt from acceding to the propositions of the Duke of Cumberland. Pitt was not convinced. But Temple had an 15
influence over him such as no other person had ever
possessed. They were very old friends, very near relations. If Pitt's talents and fame had been useful to
Temple, Temple's purse had formerly, in times of great
need, been useful to Pitt. They had never been parted 20
in politics. Twice they had come into the cabinet together;
twice they had left it together. Pitt could not bear to think
of taking office without his chief ally. Yet he felt that he
was doing wrong, that he was throwing away a great opportunity of serving his country. The obscure and unconcilia- 25
tory style of the answers which he returned to the overtures
of the Duke of Cumberland, may be ascribed to the embarrassment and vexation of a mind not at peace with itself.
It is said that he mournfully exclaimed to Temple,

"Extinxi te meque, soror, populumque, patresque 30
    Sidonios, urbemque tuam."

The prediction was but too just.

Finding Pitt impracticable, the Duke of Cumberland

advised the King to submit to necessity, and to keep
Grenville and the Bedfords. It was, indeed, not a time
at which offices could safely be left vacant. The unsettled
state of the government had produced a general relaxa-
5 tion through all the departments of the public service.
Meetings, which at another time would have been harmless,
now turned to riots, and rapidly rose almost to the dignity
of rebellions. The Houses of Parliament were blockaded
by the Spitalfields weavers. Bedford House was assailed
10 on all sides by a furious rabble, and was strongly garrisoned
with horse and foot. Some people attributed these dis-
turbances to the friends of Bute, and some to the friends
of Wilkes. But, whatever might be the cause, the effect
was general insecurity. Under such circumstances the
15 King had no choice. With bitter feelings of mortification,
he informed the ministers that he meant to retain them.

They answered by demanding from him a promise on
his royal word never more to consult Lord Bute. The
promise was given. They then demanded something more.
20 Lord Bute's brother, Mr Mackenzie, held a lucrative office
in Scotland. Mr Mackenzie must be dismissed. The
King replied that the office had been given under very
peculiar circumstances, and that he had promised never
to take it away while he lived. Grenville was obstinate;
25 and the King, with a very bad grace, yielded.

The session of Parliament was over. The triumph of
the ministers was complete. The King was almost as
much a prisoner as Charles the First had been, when
in the Isle of Wight. Such were the fruits of the policy
30 which, only a few months before, was represented as having
for ever secured the throne against the dictation of insolent
subjects.

His Majesty's natural resentment showed itself in every

look and word. In his extremity he looked wistfully towards that Whig connection, once the object of his dread and hatred. The Duke of Devonshire, who had been treated with such unjustifiable harshness, had lately died, and had been succeeded by his son, who was still 5 a boy. The King condescended to express his regret for what had passed, and to invite the young Duke to court. The noble youth came, attended by his uncles, and was received with marked graciousness.

This and many other symptoms of the same kind 10 irritated the ministers. They had still in store for their sovereign an insult which would have provoked his grandfather to kick them out of the room. Grenville and Bedford demanded an audience of him, and read him a remonstrance of many pages, which they had drawn 15 up with great care. His Majesty was accused of breaking his word, and of treating his advisers with gross unfairness. The Princess was mentioned in language by no means eulogistic. Hints were thrown out that Bute's head was in danger. The King was plainly told that he must not 20 continue to show, as he had done, that he disliked the situation in which he was placed, that he must frown upon the Opposition, that he must carry it fair towards his ministers in public. He several times interrupted the reading, by declaring that he had ceased to hold any 25 communication with Bute. But the ministers, disregarding his denial, went on; and the King listened in silence, almost choked by rage. When they ceased to read, he merely made a gesture expressive of his wish to be left alone. He afterwards owned that he thought he should 30 have gone into a fit.

Driven to despair, he again had recourse to the Duke of Cumberland; and the Duke of Cumberland again had

recourse to Pitt. Pitt was really desirous to undertake
the direction of affairs, and owned, with many dutiful
expressions, that the terms offered by the King were all
that any subject could desire. But Temple was impracti-
5 cable; and Pitt, with great regret, declared that he could
not, without the concurrence of his brother-in-law, undertake the administration.

The Duke now saw only one way of delivering his
nephew. An administration must be formed of the Whigs
10 in opposition, without Pitt's help. The difficulties seemed
almost insuperable. Death and desertion had grievously
thinned the ranks of the party lately supreme in the state.
Those among whom the Duke's choice lay might be divided
into two classes, men too old for important offices, and
15 men who had never been in any important office before.
The cabinet must be composed of broken invalids or
of raw recruits.

This was an evil, yet not an unmixed evil. If the
new Whig statesmen had little experience in business
20 and debate, they were, on the other hand, pure from the
taint of that political immorality which had deeply infected
their predecessors. Long prosperity had corrupted that
great party which had expelled the Stuarts, limited the
prerogatives of the Crown, and curbed the intolerance
25 of the Hierarchy. Adversity had already produced a
salutary effect. On the day of the accession of George
the Third, the ascendency of the Whig party terminated;
and on that day the purification of the Whig party began.
The rising chiefs of that party were men of a very different
30 sort from Sandys and Winnington, from Sir William Yonge
and Henry Fox. They were men worthy to have charged
by the side of Hampden at Chalgrove, or to have exchanged the last embrace with Russell on the scaffold

in Lincoln's Inn Fields. They carried into politics the
same high principles of virtue which regulated their private
dealings, nor would they stoop to promote even the noblest
and most salutary ends by means which honour and probity
condemn.   Such men were Lord John Cavendish, Sir 5
George Savile, and others whom we hold in honour as
the second founders of the Whig party, as the restorers
of its pristine health and energy after half a century
of degeneracy.

The chief of this respectable band was the Marquess 10
of Rockingham, a man of splendid fortune, excellent
sense, and stainless character. He was indeed nervous
to such a degree that, to the very close of his life, he
never rose without great reluctance and embarrassment
to address the House of Lords. But, though not a great 15
orator, he had in a high degree some of the qualities
of a statesman. He chose his friends well; and he
had, in an extraordinary degree, the art of attaching them
to him by ties of the most honourable kind. The cheerful
fidelity with which they adhered to him through many 20
years of almost hopeless opposition was less admirable
than the disinterestedness and delicacy which they showed
when he rose to power.

We are inclined to think that the use and the abuse
of party cannot be better illustrated than by a parallel 25
between two powerful connections of that time, the
Rockinghams and the Bedfords. The Rockingham party
was, in our view, exactly what a party should be. It
consisted of men bound together by common opinions,
by common public objects, by mutual esteem. That 30
they desired to obtain, by honest and constitutional means,
the direction of affairs they openly avowed. But, though
often invited to accept the honours and emoluments of

office, they steadily refused to do so on any conditions inconsistent with their principles. The Bedford party, as a party, had, as far as we can discover, no principle whatever. Rigby and Sandwich wanted public money, and thought that they should fetch a higher price jointly than singly. They therefore acted in concert, and prevailed on a much more important and a much better man than themselves to act with them.

It was to Rockingham that the Duke of Cumberland now had recourse. The Marquess consented to take the treasury. Newcastle, so long the recognized chief of the Whigs, could not well be excluded from the ministry. He was appointed keeper of the privy seal. A very honest clear-headed country gentleman, of the name of Dowdeswell, became Chancellor of the Exchequer. General Conway, who had served under the Duke of Cumberland, and was strongly attached to his royal highness, was made Secretary of State, with the lead in the House of Commons. A great Whig nobleman, in the prime of manhood, from whom much was at that time expected, Augustus Duke of Grafton, was the other Secretary.

The oldest man living could remember no government so weak in oratorical talents and in official experience. The general opinion was, that the ministers might hold office during the recess, but that the first day of debate in Parliament would be the last day of their power. Charles Townshend was asked what he thought of the new administration. "It is," said he, "mere lutestring; pretty summer wear. It will never do for the winter."

At this conjuncture Lord Rockingham had the wisdom to discern the value, and secure the aid, of an ally, who, to eloquence surpassing the eloquence of Pitt, and to industry which shamed the industry of Grenville, united an amplitude

of comprehension to which neither Pitt nor Grenville could
lay claim.   A young Irishman had, some time before, come
over to push his fortune in London.   He had written much
for the booksellers; but he was best known by a little
treatise, in which the style and reasoning of Bolingbroke 5
were mimicked with exquisite skill, and by a theory, of
more ingenuity than soundness, touching the pleasures
which we receive from the objects of taste.   He had also
attained a high reputation as a talker, and was regarded by
the men of letters who supped together at the Turk's Head 10
as the only match in conversation for Dr Johnson.   He
now became private secretary to Lord Rockingham, and
was brought into Parliament by his patron's influence.
These arrangements, indeed, were not made without some
difficulty.   The Duke of Newcastle, who was always 15
meddling and chattering, adjured the First Lord of the
Treasury to be on his guard against this adventurer, whose
real name was O'Bourke, and whom his grace knew to be
a wild Irishman, a Jacobite, a Papist, a concealed Jesuit.
Lord Rockingham treated the calumny as it deserved; 20
and the Whig party was strengthened and adorned by the
accession of Edmund Burke.

     The party, indeed, stood in need of accessions; for it
sustained about this time an almost irreparable loss.   The
Duke of Cumberland had formed the government, and was 25
its main support.   His exalted rank and great name in
some degree balanced the fame of Pitt.   As mediator
between the Whigs and the Court, he held a place which
no other person could fill.   The strength of his character
supplied that which was the chief defect of the new ministry. 30
Conway, in particular, who, with excellent intentions and
respectable talents, was the most dependent and irresolute
of human beings, drew from the counsels of that masculine

mind a determination not his own. Before the meeting
of Parliament the Duke suddenly died. His death was
generally regarded as the signal of great troubles, and on
this account, as well as from respect for his personal
5 qualities, was greatly lamented. It was remarked that
the mourning in London was the most general ever known,
and was both deeper and longer than the Gazette had
prescribed.

In the mean time, every mail from America brought
10 alarming tidings. The crop which Grenville had sown his
successors had now to reap. The colonies were in a state
bordering on rebellion. The stamps were burned. The
revenue officers were tarred and feathered. All traffic
between the discontented provinces and the mother country
15 was interrupted. The Exchange of London was in dismay.
Half the firms of Bristol and Liverpool were threatened
with bankruptcy. In Leeds, Manchester, Nottingham, it
was said that three artisans out of every ten had been
turned adrift. Civil war seemed to be at hand; and it
20 could not be doubted that, if once the British nation were
divided against itself, France and Spain would soon take
part in the quarrel.

Three courses were open to the ministers. The first
was to enforce the Stamp Act by the sword. This was
25 the course on which the King, and Grenville, whom the
King hated beyond all living men, were alike bent. The
natures of both were arbitrary and stubborn. They resembled each other so much that they could never be
friends; but they resembled each other also so much that
30 they saw almost all important practical questions in the
same point of view. Neither of them would bear to be
governed by the other; but they were perfectly agreed as
to the best way of governing the people.

Another course was that which Pitt recommended. He held that the British Parliament was not constitutionally competent to pass a law for taxing the colonies. He therefore considered the Stamp Act as a nullity, as a document of no more validity than Charles's writ of ship- 5 money, or James's proclamation dispensing with the penal laws. This doctrine seems to us, we must own, to be altogether untenable.

Between these extreme courses lay a third way. The opinion of the most judicious and temperate statesmen of 10 those times was that the British constitution had set no limit whatever to the legislative power of the British King, Lords, and Commons, over the whole British Empire. Parliament, they held, was legally competent to tax America, as Parliament was legally competent to commit 15 any other act of folly or wickedness, to confiscate the property of all the merchants in Lombard Street, or to attaint any man in the kingdom of high treason, without examining witnesses against him, or hearing him in his own defence. The most atrocious act of confiscation or of 20 attainder is just as valid an act as the Toleration Act or the Habeas Corpus Act. But from acts of confiscation and acts of attainder lawgivers are bound, by every obligation of morality, systematically to refrain. In the same manner ought the British legislature to refrain from taxing the 25 American colonies. The Stamp Act was indefensible, not because it was beyond the constitutional competence of Parliament, but because it was unjust and impolitic, sterile of revenue, and fertile of discontents. These sound doctrines were adopted by Lord Rockingham and his col- 30 leagues, and were, during a long course of years, inculcated by Burke, in orations, some of which will last as long as the English language.

The winter came; the Parliament met; and the state of
the colonies instantly became the subject of fierce contention. Pitt, whose health had been somewhat restored by the
waters of Bath, reappeared in the House of Commons, and,
5 with ardent and pathetic eloquence, not only condemned
the Stamp Act, but applauded the resistance of Massachusetts and Virginia, and vehemently maintained, in
defiance, we must say, of all reason and of all authority,
that, according to the British constitution, the supreme
10 legislative power does not include the power to tax. The
language of Grenville, on the other hand, was such as
Strafford might have used at the council table of Charles
the First, when news came of the resistance to the liturgy
at Edinburgh. The colonists were traitors; those who
15 excused them were little better. Frigates, mortars, bayonets,
sabres, were the proper remedies for such distempers.

The ministers occupied an intermediate position; they
proposed to declare that the legislative authority of the
British Parliament over the whole Empire was in all cases
20 supreme; and they proposed, at the same time, to repeal
the Stamp Act. To the former measure Pitt objected;
but it was carried with scarcely a dissentient voice. The
repeal of the Stamp Act Pitt strongly supported; but
against the Government was arrayed a formidable assem-
25 blage of opponents. Grenville and the Bedfords were
furious. Temple, who had now allied himself closely
with his brother, and separated himself from Pitt, was no
despicable enemy. This, however, was not the worst.
The ministry was without its natural strength. It had to
30 struggle, not only against its avowed enemies, but against
the insidious hostility of the King, and of a set of persons
who, about this time, began to be designated as the King's
friends.

The character of this faction has been drawn by Burke with even more than his usual force and vivacity. Those who know how strongly, through his whole life, his judgment was biassed by his passions, may not unnaturally suspect that he has left us rather a caricature than a likeness; and yet there is scarcely, in the whole portrait, a single touch of which the fidelity is not proved by facts of unquestionable authenticity.

The public generally regarded the King's friends as a body of which Bute was the directing soul. It was to no purpose that the Earl professed to have done with politics, that he absented himself year after year from the levee and the drawing-room, that he went to the north, that he went to Rome. The notion that, in some inexplicable manner, he dictated all the measures of the court, was fixed in the minds, not only of the multitude, but of some who had good opportunities of obtaining information, and who ought to have been superior to vulgar prejudices. Our own belief is that these suspicions were unfounded, and that he ceased to have any communication with the King on political matters some time before the dismissal of George Grenville. The supposition of Bute's influence is, indeed, by no means necessary to explain the phænomena. The King, in 1765, was no longer the ignorant and inexperienced boy who had, in 1760, been managed by his mother and his Groom of the Stole. He had, during several years, observed the struggles of parties, and conferred daily on high questions of state with able and experienced politicians. His way of life had developed his understanding and character. He was now no longer a puppet, but had very decided opinions both of men and things. Nothing could be more natural than that he should have high notions of his own prerogatives,

should be impatient of opposition, and should wish all
public men to be detached from each other and dependent
on himself alone ; nor could anything be more natural than
that, in the state in which the political world then was, he
5 should find instruments fit for his purposes.

Thus sprang into existence and into note a reptile
species of politicians never before and never since known
in our country. These men disclaimed all political ties,
except those which bound them to the throne. They
10 were willing to coalesce with any party, to abandon any
party, to undermine any party, to assault any party, at a
moment's notice. To them, all administrations, and all
oppositions were the same. They regarded Bute, Grenville,
Rockingham, Pitt, without one sentiment either of pre-
15 dilection or of aversion. They were the King's friends.
It is to be observed that this friendship implied no personal
intimacy. These people had never lived with their master
as Dodington at one time lived with his father, or as
Sheridan afterwards lived with his son. They never hunted
20 with him in the morning, or played cards with him in the
evening, never shared his mutton or walked with him
among his turnips. Only one or two of them ever saw
his face, except on public days. The whole band,
however, always had early and accurate information as to
25 his personal inclinations. These people were never high
in the administration. They were generally to be found
in places of much emolument, little labour, and no
responsibility ; and these places they continued to occupy
securely while the cabinet was six or seven times re-
30 constructed. Their peculiar business was not to support
the ministry against the opposition, but to support the
King against the ministry. Whenever his Majesty was
induced to give a reluctant assent to the introduction of

some bill which his constitutional advisers regarded as necessary, his friends in the House of Commons were sure to speak against it, to vote against it, to throw in its way every obstruction compatible with the forms of Parliament. If his Majesty found it necessary to admit 5 into his closet a Secretary of State or a First Lord of the Treasury whom he disliked, his friends were sure to miss no opportunity of thwarting and humbling the obnoxious minister. In return for these services, the King covered them with his protection. It was to no purpose that his 10 responsible servants complained to him that they were daily betrayed and impeded by men who were eating the bread of the government. He sometimes justified the offenders, sometimes excused them, sometimes owned that they were to blame, but said that he must take time to 15 consider whether he could part with them. He never would turn them out; and, while every thing else in the state was constantly changing, these sycophants seemed to have a life estate in their offices.

It was well known to the King's friends that, though 20 his Majesty had consented to the repeal of the Stamp Act, he had consented with a very bad grace, and that though he had eagerly welcomed the Whigs, when, in his extreme need and at his earnest entreaty, they had undertaken to free him from an insupportable yoke, he had by no means 25 got over his early prejudices against his deliverers. The ministers soon found that, while they were encountered in front by the whole force of a strong opposition, their rear was assailed by a large body of those whom they had regarded as auxiliaries. 30

Nevertheless, Lord Rockingham and his adherents went on resolutely with the bill for repealing the Stamp Act. They had on their side all the manufacturing and

commercial interests of the realm. In the debates the
government was powerfully supported. Two great orators
and statesmen, belonging to two different generations,
repeatedly put forth all their powers in defence of the bill.
5 The House of Commons heard Pitt for the last time, and
Burke for the first time, and was in doubt to which of them
the palm of eloquence should be assigned. It was indeed
a splendid sunset and a splendid dawn.

For a time the event seemed doubtful. In several
10 divisions the ministers were hard pressed. On one occasion, not less than twelve of the King's friends, all men in
office, voted against the government. It was to no purpose
that Lord Rockingham remonstrated with the King. His
Majesty confessed that there was ground for complaint, but
15 hoped that gentle means would bring the mutineers to a
better mind. If they persisted in their misconduct, he
would dismiss them.

At length the decisive day arrived. The gallery, the
lobby, the Court of Requests, the staircases, were crowded
20 with merchants from all the great ports of the island. The
debate lasted till long after midnight. On the division the
ministers had a great majority. The dread of civil war,
and the outcry of all the trading towns of the kingdom,
had been too strong for the combined strength of the court
25 and the opposition.

It was in the first dim twilight of a February morning
that the doors were thrown open, and that the chiefs of
the hostile parties showed themselves to the multitude.
Conway was received with loud applause. But, when Pitt
30 appeared, all eyes were fixed on him alone. All hats were
in the air. Loud and long huzzas accompanied him to his
chair, and a train of admirers escorted him all the way to
his home. Then came forth Grenville. As soon as he was

recognised, a storm of hisses and curses broke forth.   He
turned fiercely on the crowd, and caught one man by the
throat.   The bystanders were in great alarm.   If a scuffle
began, none could say how it might end.   Fortunately
the person who had been collared only said, " If I may 5
not hiss, sir, I hope I may laugh," and laughed in Grenville's
face.

The majority had been so decisive, that all the opponents of the ministry, save one, were disposed to let the
bill pass without any further contention.   But solicitation 10
and expostulation were thrown away on Grenville.   His
indomitable spirit rose up stronger and stronger under the
load of public hatred.   He fought out the battle obstinately
to the end.   On the last reading he had a sharp altercation
with his brother-in-law, the last of their many sharp alter- 15
cations.   Pitt thundered in his loftiest tones against the
man who had wished to dip the ermine of a British King
in the blood of the British people.   Grenville replied with
his wonted intrepidity and asperity.   " If the tax," he said,
" were still to be laid on, I would lay it on.   For the evils 20
which it may produce my accuser is answerable.   His
profusion made it necessary.   His declarations against the
constitutional powers of King, Lords, and Commons, have
made it doubly necessary.   I do not envy him the huzza.
I glory in the hiss.   If it were to be done again, I would 25
do it."

The repeal of the Stamp Act was the chief measure of
Lord Rockingham's government.   But that government is
entitled to the praise of having put a stop to two oppressive
practices, which, in Wilkes's case, had attracted the notice 30
and excited the just indignation of the public.   The House
of Commons was induced by the ministers to pass a
resolution condemning the use of general warrants, and

another resolution, condemning the seizure of papers in cases of libel.

It must be added, to the lasting honour of Lord Rockingham, that his administration was the first which, during a long course of years, had the courage and the virtue to refrain from bribing members of Parliament. His enemies accused him and his friends of weakness, of haughtiness, of party spirit; but calumny itself never dared to couple his name with corruption.

Unhappily his government, though one of the best that has ever existed in our country, was also one of the weakest. The King's friends assailed and obstructed the ministers at every turn. To appeal to the King was only to draw forth new promises and new evasions. His Majesty was sure that there must be some misunderstanding. Lord Rockingham had better speak to the gentlemen. They should be dismissed on the next fault. The next fault was soon committed, and His Majesty still continued to shuffle. It was too bad. It was quite abominable; but it mattered less as the prorogation was at hand. He would give the delinquents one more chance. If they did not alter their conduct next session, he should not have one word to say for them. He had already resolved that, long before the commencement of the next session, Lord Rockingham should cease to be minister.

We have now come to a part of our story which, admiring as we do the genius and the many noble qualities of Pitt, we cannot relate without much pain. We believe that, at this conjuncture, he had it in his power to give the victory either to the Whigs or to the King's friends. If he had allied himself closely with Lord Rockingham, what could the court have done? There would have been only one alternative, the Whigs or Grenville; and there could be no doubt what the King's choice would be. He still remembered, as well he might, with the uttermost bitterness, the thraldom from which his uncle had freed him, and said about this time, with great vehemence, that he would sooner see the Devil come into his closet than 5 Grenville.

And what was there to prevent Pitt from allying himself with Lord Rockingham? On all the most important questions their views were the same. They had agreed in condemning the peace, the Stamp Act, the general warrant, 10 the seizure of papers. The points on which they differed were few and unimportant. In integrity, in disinterestedness, in hatred of corruption, they resembled each other. Their personal interests could not clash. They sat in different Houses, and Pitt had always declared that nothing 15 should induce him to be first lord of the treasury.

If the opportunity of forming a coalition beneficial to the state, and honourable to all concerned, was suffered to escape, the fault was not with the Whig ministers. They behaved towards Pitt with an obsequiousness which, had it 20 not been the effect of sincere admiration and of anxiety for the public interests, might have been justly called servile. They repeatedly gave him to understand that, if he chose to join their ranks, they were ready to receive him, not as an associate, but as a leader. They had proved their 25 respect for him by bestowing a peerage on the person who, at that time, enjoyed the largest share of his confidence, Chief Justice Pratt. What then was there to divide Pitt from the Whigs? What, on the other hand, were there in common between him and the King's friends, that he should lend 30 himself to their purposes, he who had never owed any thing to flattery or intrigue, he whose eloquence and independent spirit had overawed two generations of slaves and jobbers,

he who had twice been forced by the enthusiasm of an
admiring nation on a reluctant Prince?

Unhappily the court had gained Pitt, not, it is true, by
those ignoble means which were employed when such men
as Rigby and Wedderburn were to be won, but by allure-
ments suited to a nature noble even in its aberrations. The
King set himself to seduce the one man who could turn the
Whigs out without letting Grenville in. Praise, caresses,
promises, were lavished on the idol of the nation. He, and
he alone, could put an end to faction, could bid defiance to
all the powerful connections in the land united, Whigs and
Tories, Rockinghams, Bedfords, and Grenvilles. These
blandishments produced a great effect. For though Pitt's
spirit was high and manly, though his eloquence was often
exerted with formidable effect against the court, and though
his theory of government had been learned in the school of
Locke and Sidney, he had always regarded the person of
the sovereign with profound veneration. As soon as he was
brought face to face with royalty, his imagination and
sensibility were too strong for his principles. His Whiggism thawed and disappeared; and he became, for the
time, a Tory of the old Ormond pattern. Nor was he by
any means unwilling to assist in the work of dissolving all
political connections. His own weight in the state was
wholly independent of such connections. He was therefore
inclined to look on them with dislike, and make far too
little distinction between gangs of knaves associated for
the mere purpose of robbing the public, and confederacies
of honourable men for the promotion of great public
objects. Nor had he the sagacity to perceive that the
strenuous efforts which he made to annihilate all parties
tended only to establish the ascendency of one party, and
that the basest and most hateful of all.

It may be doubted whether he would have been thus
misled, if his mind had been in full health and vigour. But
the truth is that he had for some time been in an unnatural
state of excitement. No suspicion of this sort had yet got
abroad. His eloquence had never shone with more splen- 5
dour than during the recent debates. But people afterwards
called to mind many things which ought to have roused
their apprehensions. His habits were gradually becoming
more and more eccentric. A horror of all loud sounds,
such as is said to have been one of the many oddities of 10
Wallenstein, grew upon him. Though the most affectionate
of fathers, he could not at this time bear to hear the voices
of his own children, and laid out great sums at Hayes in
buying up houses contiguous to his own, merely that he
might have no neighbours to disturb him with their noise. 15
He then sold Hayes, and took possession of a villa at
Hampstead, where he again began to purchase houses to
right and left. In expense, indeed, he vied, during this
part of his life, with the wealthiest of the conquerors of
Bengal and Tanjore. At Burton Pynsent, he ordered a 20
great extent of ground to be planted with cedars. Cedars
enough for the purpose were not to be found in Somersetshire.
They were therefore collected in London, and sent down by
land carriage. Relays of labourers were hired ; and the
work went on all night by torchlight. No man could be 25
more abstemious than Pitt ; yet the profusion of his kitchen
was a wonder even to epicures. Several dinners were
always dressing ; for his appetite was capricious and
fanciful ; and at whatever moment he felt inclined to eat, he
expected a meal to be instantly on the table. Other cir- 30
cumstances might be mentioned, such as separately are of
little moment, but such as, when taken together, and when
viewed in connection with the strange events which followed,

justify us in believing that his mind was already in a morbid state.

Soon after the close of the session of Parliament, Lord Rockingham received his dismissal. He retired, accompanied by a firm body of friends, whose consistency and uprightness enmity itself was forced to admit. None of them had asked or obtained any pension or any sinecure, either in possession or in reversion. Such disinterestedness was then rare among politicians. Their chief, though not a man of brilliant talents, had won for himself an honourable fame, which he kept pure to the last. He had, in spite of difficulties which seemed almost insurmountable, removed great abuses and averted a civil war. Sixteen years later, in a dark and terrible day, he was again called upon to save the state, brought to the very brink of ruin by the same perfidy and obstinacy which had embarrassed, and at length overthrown, his first administration.

Pitt was planting in Somersetshire when he was summoned to court by a letter written by the royal hand. He instantly hastened to London. The irritability of his mind and body was increased by the rapidity with which he travelled; and when he reached his journey's end he was suffering from fever. Ill as he was, he saw the King at Richmond, and undertook to form an administration.

Pitt was scarcely in the state in which a man should be who has to conduct delicate and arduous negotiations. In his letters to his wife, he complained that the conferences in which it was necessary for him to bear a part heated his blood and accelerated his pulse. From other sources of information we learn, that his language, even to those whose cooperation he wished to engage, was strangely peremptory and despotic. Some of his notes written at this time have been preserved, and are in a style which

Lewis the Fourteenth would have been too well bred to employ in addressing any French gentleman.

In the attempt to dissolve all parties, Pitt met with some difficulties. Some Whigs, whom the court would gladly have detached from Lord Rockingham, rejected all 5 offers. The Bedfords were perfectly willing to break with Grenville; but Pitt would not come up to their terms. Temple, whom Pitt at first meant to place at the head of the treasury, proved intractable. A coldness indeed had, during some months, been fast growing between the 10 brothers-in-law, so long and so closely allied in politics. Pitt was angry with Temple for opposing the repeal of the Stamp Act. Temple was angry with Pitt for refusing to accede to that family league which was now the favourite plan at Stowe. At length the Earl proposed an equal 15 partition of power and patronage, and offered, on this condition, to give up his brother George. Pitt thought the demand exorbitant, and positively refused compliance. A bitter quarrel followed. Each of the kinsmen was true to his character. Temple's soul festered with spite, and 20 Pitt's swelled into contempt. Temple represented Pitt as the most odious of hypocrites and traitors. Pitt held a different and perhaps a more provoking tone. Temple was a good sort of man enough, whose single title to distinction was, that he had a large garden, with a large 25 piece of water, and a great many pavilions and summer-houses. To his fortunate connection with a great orator and statesman he was indebted for an importance in the state which his own talents could never have gained for him. That importance had turned his head. He had 30 begun to fancy that he could form administrations, and govern empires. It was piteous to see a well meaning man under such a delusion.

In spite of all these difficulties, a ministry was made
such as the King wished to see, a ministry in which all
his Majesty's friends were comfortably accommodated, and
which, with the exception of his Majesty's friends, con-
5 tained no four persons who had ever in their lives been
in the habit of acting together.   Men who had never
concurred in a single vote found themselves seated at the
same board.   The office of paymaster was divided between
two persons who had never exchanged a word.   Most of
10 the chief posts were filled either by personal adherents of
Pitt, or by members of the late ministry, who had been
induced to remain in place after the dismissal of Lord
Rockingham.   To the former class belonged Pratt, now
Lord Camden, who accepted the great seal, and Lord Shel-
15 burne, who was made one of the Secretaries of State.   To
the latter class belonged the Duke of Grafton, who became
First Lord of the Treasury, and Conway, who kept his
old position both in the government and in the House
of Commons.   Charles Townshend, who had belonged to
20 every party, and cared for none, was Chancellor of the
Exchequer.   Pitt himself was declared prime minister, but
refused to take any laborious office.   He was created Earl
of Chatham, and the privy seal was delivered to him.

It is scarcely necessary to say, that the failure, the
25 complete and disgraceful failure, of this arrangement, is not
to be ascribed to any want of capacity in the persons whom
we have named.   None of them was deficient in abilities ;
and four of them, Pitt himself, Shelburne, Camden, and
Townshend, were men of high intellectual eminence.   The
30 fault was not in the materials, but in the principle on which
the materials were put together.   Pitt had mixed up these
conflicting elements, in the full confidence that he should
be able to keep them all in perfect subordination to himself,

and in perfect harmony with each other. We shall soon
see how the experiment succeeded.

On the very day on which the new prime minister kissed
hands, three-fourths of that popularity which he had long
enjoyed without a rival, and to which he owed the greater 5
part of his authority, departed from him. A violent outcry
was raised, not against that part of his conduct which really
deserved severe condemnation, but against a step in which
we can see nothing to censure. His acceptance of a peerage
produced a general burst of indignation. Yet surely no 10
peerage had ever been better earned; nor was there ever
a statesman who more needed the repose of the Upper
House. Pitt was now growing old. He was much older
in constitution than in years. It was with imminent risk
to his life that he had, on some important occasions, at- 15
tended his duty in Parliament. During the session of 1764,
he had not been able to take part in a single debate. It
was impossible that he should go through the nightly labour
of conducting the business of the government in the House
of Commons. His wish to be transferred, under such 20
circumstances, to a less busy and a less turbulent assembly,
was natural and reasonable. The nation, however, overlooked all these considerations. Those who had most
loved and honoured the Great Commoner were loudest in
invective against the new made Lord. London had hitherto 25
been true to him through every vicissitude. When the
citizens learned that he had been sent for from Somersetshire, that he had been closeted with the King at Richmond, and that he was to be first minister, they had been
in transports of joy. Preparations were made for a grand 30
entertainment and for a general illumination. The lamps
had actually been placed round the Monument, when the
Gazette announced that the object of all this enthusiasm

was an Earl. Instantly the feast was countermanded. The
lamps were taken down. The newspapers raised the roar
of obloquy. Pamphlets, made up of calumny and scurrility,
filled the shops of all the booksellers; and of those pam-
5 phlets, the most galling were written under the direction
of the malignant Temple. It was now the fashion to
compare the two Williams, William Pulteney and William
Pitt. Both, it was said, had, by eloquence and simulated
patriotism, acquired a great ascendency in the House of
10 Commons and in the country. Both had been entrusted
with the office of reforming the government. Both had,
when at the height of power and popularity, been seduced
by the splendour of the coronet. Both had been made earls,
and both had at once become objects of aversion and scorn
15 to the nation which a few hours before had regarded them
with affection and veneration.

The clamour against Pitt appears to have had a serious
effect on the foreign relations of the country. His name
had till now acted like a spell at Versailles and Saint
20 Ildefonso. English travellers on the Continent had remarked that nothing more was necessary to silence a
whole room full of boasting Frenchmen than to drop
a hint of the probability that Mr Pitt would return to
power. In an instant there was deep silence: all shoulders
25 rose, and all faces were lengthened. Now, unhappily,
every foreign court, in learning that he was recalled to
office, learned also that he no longer possessed the hearts
of his countrymen. Ceasing to be loved at home, he
ceased to be feared abroad. The name of Pitt had been
30 a charmed name. Our envoys tried in vain to conjure
with the name of Chatham.

The difficulties which beset Chatham were daily increased by the despotic manner in which he treated all

around him. Lord Rockingham had, at the time of the
change of ministry, acted with great moderation, had
expressed a hope that the new government would act
on the principles of the late government, and had even
interfered to prevent many of his friends from quitting 5
office. Thus Saunders and Keppel, two naval commanders
of great eminence, had been induced to remain at the
Admiralty, where their services were much needed. The
Duke of Portland was still Lord Chamberlain, and Lord
Besborough Postmaster. But within a quarter of a year, 10
Lord Chatham had so deeply affronted these men, that
they all retired in disgust. In truth, his tone, submissive
in the closet, was at this time insupportably tyrannical
in the cabinet. His colleagues were merely his clerks
for naval, financial, and diplomatic business. Conway, 15
meek as he was, was on one occasion provoked into
declaring that such language as Lord Chatham's had
never been heard west of Constantinople, and was with
difficulty prevented by Horace Walpole from resigning,
and rejoining the standard of Lord Rockingham. 20

The breach which had been made in the government
by the defection of so many of the Rockinghams, Chatham
hoped to supply by the help of the Bedfords. But with
the Bedfords he could not deal as he had dealt with other
parties. It was to no purpose that he bade high for one 25
or two members of the faction, in the hope of detaching
them from the rest. They were to be had; but they were
to be had only in the lot. There was indeed for a moment
some wavering and some disputing among them. But at
length the counsels of the shrewd and resolute Rigby 30
prevailed. They determined to stand firmly together, and
plainly intimated to Chatham that he must take them all,
or that he should get none of them. The event proved

that they were wiser in their generation than any other connection in the state. In a few months they were able to dictate their own terms.

The most important public measure of Lord Chatham's 5 administration was his celebrated interference with the corn trade. The harvest had been bad ; the price of food was high ; and he thought it necessary to take on himself the responsibility of laying an embargo on the exportation of grain. When Parliament met, this proceeding was 10 attacked by the opposition as unconstitutional, and defended by the ministers as indispensably necessary. At last an Act was passed to indemnify all who had been concerned in the embargo.

The first words uttered by Chatham, in the House 15 of Lords, were in defence of his conduct on this occasion. He spoke with a calmness, sobriety, and dignity, well suited to the audience which he was addressing. A subsequent speech which he made on the same subject was less successful. He bade defiance to aristocratical con- 20 nections, with a superciliousness to which the Peers were not accustomed, and with tones and gestures better suited to a large and stormy assembly than to the body of which he was now a member. A short altercation followed, and he was told very plainly that he should not be suffered to 25 browbeat the old nobility of England.

It gradually became clearer and clearer that he was in a distempered state of mind. His attention had been drawn to the territorial acquisitions of the East India Company, and he determined to bring the whole of that 30 great subject before Parliament. He would not, however, confer on the subject with any of his colleagues. It was in vain that Conway, who was charged with the conduct of business in the House of Commons, and Charles

Townshend, who was responsible for the direction of
the finances, begged for some glimpse of light as to what
was in contemplation.   Chatham's answers were sullen and
mysterious.   He must decline any discussion with them;
he did not want their assistance; he had fixed on a person 5
to take charge of his measure in the House of Commons.
This person was a member who was not connected with
the government, and who neither had, nor deserved to
have, the ear of the House, a noisy, purseproud, illiterate
demagogue, whose Cockney English and scraps of mispro- 10
nounced Latin were the jest of the newspapers, Alderman
Beckford.   It may well be supposed that these strange
proceedings produced a ferment through the whole political
world.   The city was in commotion.   The East India
Company invoked the faith of charters.   Burke thundered 15
against the ministers.   The ministers looked at each other,
and knew not what to say.   In the midst of the confusion,
Lord Chatham proclaimed himself gouty, and retired to
Bath.   It was announced, after some time, that he was
better, that he would shortly return, that he would soon 20
put everything in order.   A day was fixed for his arrival
in London.   But when he reached the Castle inn at
Marlborough, he stopped, shut himself up in his room,
and remained there some weeks.   Every body who travelled
that road was amazed by the number of his attendants. 25
Footmen and grooms, dressed in his family livery, filled
the whole inn, though one of the largest in England,
and swarmed in the streets of the little town.   The truth
was, that the invalid had insisted that, during his stay,
all the waiters and stable-boys of the Castle should wear 30
his livery.

His colleagues were in despair.   The Duke of Grafton
proposed to go down to Marlborough in order to consult

the oracle.   But he was informed that Lord Chatham must
decline all conversation on business.   In the mean time,
all the parties which were out of office, Bedfords, Grenvilles,
and Rockinghams, joined to oppose the distracted govern-
5 ment on the vote for the land tax.   They were reinforced
by almost all the county members, and had a considerable
majority.   This was the first time that a ministry had
been beaten on an important division in the House of
Commons since the fall of Sir Robert Walpole.   The
10 administration, thus furiously assailed from without, was
torn by internal dissensions.   It had been formed on
no principle whatever.   From the very first, nothing but
Chatham's authority had prevented the hostile contingents
which made up his ranks from going to blows with each
15 other.   That authority was now withdrawn, and every
thing was in commotion.   Conway, a brave soldier, but
in civil affairs the most timid and irresolute of men, afraid
of disobliging the King, afraid of being abused in the newspapers, afraid of being thought factious if he went out, afraid
20 of being thought interested if he stayed in, afraid of every
thing, and afraid of being known to be afraid of any thing,
was beaten backwards and forwards like a shuttlecock
between Horace Walpole who wished to make him prime
minister, and Lord John Cavendish who wished to draw
25 him into opposition.   Charles Townshend, a man of splendid eloquence, of lax principles, and of boundless vanity and
presumption, would submit to no control.   The full extent
of his parts, of his ambition, and of his arrogance, had not
yet been made manifest ; for he had always quailed before
30 the genius and the lofty character of Pitt.   But now that
Pitt had quitted the House of Commons, and seemed
to have abdicated the part of chief minister, Townshend
broke loose from all restraint.

While things were in this state, Chatham at length
returned to London.   He might as well have remained
at Marlborough.   He would see nobody.   He would give
no opinion on any public matter.   The Duke of Grafton
begged piteously for an interview, for an hour, for half an 5
hour, for five minutes.   The answer was, that it was
impossible.   The King himself repeatedly condescended
to expostulate and implore.   " Your duty," he wrote,
" your own honour, require you to make an effort."   The
answers to these appeals were commonly written in Lady 10
Chatham's hand, from her lord's dictation ; for he had not
energy even to use a pen.   He flings himself at the King's
feet.   He is penetrated by the royal goodness, so signally
shown to the most unhappy of men.   He implores a little
more indulgence.   He cannot as yet transact business. 15
He cannot see his colleagues.   Least of all can he bear
the excitement of an interview with majesty.

Some were half inclined to suspect that he was, to use a
military phrase, malingering.   He had made, they said, a
great blunder, and had found it out.   His immense popu- 20
larity, his high reputation for statesmanship, were gone for
ever.   Intoxicated by pride, he had undertaken a task
beyond his abilities.   He now saw nothing before him
but distresses and humiliations ; and he had therefore
simulated illness, in order to escape from vexations which 25
he had not fortitude to meet.   This suspicion, though it
derived some colour from that weakness which was the
most striking blemish of his character, was certainly
unfounded.   His mind, before he became first minister,
had been, as we have said, in an unsound state ; and 30
physical and moral causes now concurred to make the
derangement of his faculties complete.   The gout, which
had been the torment of his whole life, had been suppressed

by strong remedies. For the first time since he was a boy
at Oxford, he had passed several months without a twinge.
But his hand and foot had been relieved at the expense
of his nerves. He became melancholy, fanciful, irritable.
5 The embarrassing state of public affairs, the grave responsibility which lay on him, the consciousness of his errors, the
disputes of his colleagues, the savage clamours raised by
his detractors, bewildered his enfeebled mind. One thing
alone, he said, could save him. He must repurchase
10 Hayes. The unwilling consent of the new occupant was
extorted by Lady Chatham's entreaties and tears; and her
lord was somewhat easier. But if business were mentioned
to him, he, once the proudest and boldest of mankind,
behaved like a hysterical girl, trembled from head to
15 foot, and burst into a flood of tears.

His colleagues for a time continued to entertain the
expectation that his health would soon be restored, and
that he would emerge from his retirement. But month
followed month, and still he remained hidden in mysterious
20 seclusion, and sunk, as far as they could learn, in the
deepest dejection of spirits. They at length ceased to
hope or to fear any thing from him; and though he was
still nominally Prime Minister, took without scruple steps
which they knew to be diametrically opposed to all his
25 opinions and feelings, allied themselves with those whom
he had proscribed, disgraced those whom he most esteemed,
and laid taxes on the colonies, in the face of the strong
declarations which he had recently made.

When he had passed about a year and three quarters in
30 gloomy privacy, the King received a few lines in Lady
Chatham's hand. They contained a request, dictated by
her lord, that he might be permitted to resign the Privy
Seal. After some civil show of reluctance, the resignation

was accepted. Indeed Chatham was, by this time, almost as much forgotten as if he had already been lying in Westminster Abbey.

At length the clouds which had gathered over his mind broke and passed away. His gout returned, and freed him 5 from a more cruel malady. His nerves were newly braced. His spirits became buoyant. He woke as from a sickly dream. It was a strange recovery. Men had been in the habit of talking of him as of one dead, and, when he first showed himself at the King's levee, started as if they 10 had seen a ghost. It was more than two years and a half since he had appeared in public.

He, too, had cause for wonder. The world which he now entered was not the world which he had quitted. The administration which he had formed had never been, at any 15 one moment, entirely changed. But there had been so many losses and so many accessions, that he could scarcely recognize his own work. Charles Townshend was dead. Lord Shelburne had been dismissed. Conway had sunk into utter insignificance. The Duke of Grafton had fallen 20 into the hands of the Bedfords. The Bedfords had deserted Grenville, had made their peace with the King and the King's friends, and had been admitted to office. Lord North was Chancellor of the Exchequer, and was rising fast in importance. Corsica had been given up to France 25 without a struggle. The disputes with the American colonies had been revived. A general election had taken place. Wilkes had returned from exile, and, outlaw as he was, had been chosen knight of the shire for Middlesex. The multitude was on his side. The Court was obstinately 30 bent on ruining him, and was prepared to shake the very foundations of the constitution for the sake of a paltry revenge. The House of Commons, assuming to itself an

authority which of right belongs only to the whole legislature, had declared Wilkes incapable of sitting in Parliament. Nor had it been thought sufficient to keep him out. Another must be brought in. Since the freeholders of
5 Middlesex had obstinately refused to choose a member acceptable to the Court, the House had chosen a member for them. This was not the only instance, perhaps not the most disgraceful instance, of the inveterate malignity of the Court. Exasperated by the steady opposition of the
10 Rockingham party, the King's friends had tried to rob a distinguished Whig nobleman of his private estate, and had persisted in their mean wickedness till their own servile majority had revolted from mere disgust and shame. Discontent had spread throughout the nation, and was
15 kept up by stimulants such as had rarely been applied to the public mind. Junius had taken the field, had trampled Sir William Draper in the dust, had well nigh broken the heart of Blackstone, and had so mangled the reputation of the Duke of Grafton, that his grace had become sick of
20 office, and was beginning to look wistfully towards the shades of Euston. Every principle of foreign, domestic, and colonial policy which was dear to the heart of Chatham had, during the eclipse of his genius, been violated by the government which he had formed.

25   The remaining years of his life were spent in vainly struggling against that fatal policy which, at the moment when he might have given it a death blow, he had been induced to take under his protection. His exertions redeemed his own fame, but they effected little for his
30 country.

He found two parties arrayed against the government, the party of his own brothers-in-law, the Grenvilles, and the party of Lord Rockingham. On the question of the

Middlesex election these parties were agreed.   But on
many other important questions they differed widely; and
they were, in truth, not less hostile to each other than to
the Court.   The Grenvilles had, during several years,
annoyed the Rockinghams with a succession of acrimonious 5
pamphlets.   It was long before the Rockinghams could be
induced to retaliate.   But an ill natured tract, written
under Grenville's direction, and entitled a State of the
Nation, was too much for their patience.   Burke undertook
to defend and avenge his friends, and executed the task 10
with admirable skill and vigour.   On every point he was
victorious, and nowhere more completely victorious than
when he joined issue on those dry and minute questions
of statistical and financial detail in which the main strength
of Grenville lay.   The official drudge, even on his own 15
chosen ground, was utterly unable to maintain the fight
against the great orator and philosopher.   When Chatham
reappeared, Grenville was still writhing with the recent
shame and smart of this well merited chastisement.   Cordial
co-operation between the two sections of the Opposition 20
was impossible.   Nor could Chatham easily connect himself
with either.   His feelings, in spite of many affronts given
and received, drew him towards the Grenvilles.   For he had
strong domestic affections ; and his nature, which, though
haughty, was by no means obdurate, had been softened by 25
affliction.   But from his kinsmen he was separated by a wide
difference of opinion on the question of colonial taxation.
A reconciliation, however, took place.   He visited Stowe :
he shook hands with George Grenville ; and the Whig freeholders of Buckinghamshire, at their public dinners, drank 30
many bumpers to the union of the three brothers.

In opinions, Chatham was much nearer to the Rockinghams than to his own relatives.   But between him and

the Rockinghams there was a gulf not easily to be passed.
He had deeply injured them, and in injuring them, had
deeply injured his country. When the balance was
trembling between them and the Court, he had thrown
5 the whole weight of his genius, of his renown, of his
popularity, into the scale of misgovernment. It must be
added, that many eminent members of the party still
retained a bitter recollection of the asperity and disdain
with which they had been treated by him at the time
10 when he assumed the direction of affairs. It is clear from
Burke's pamphlets and speeches, and still more clear from
his private letters, and from the language which he held in
conversation, that he regarded Chatham with a feeling not
far removed from dislike. Chatham was undoubtedly
15 conscious of his error, and desirous to atone for it. But
his overtures of friendship, though made with earnestness,
and even with unwonted humility, were at first received
by Lord Rockingham with cold and austere reserve.
Gradually the intercourse of the two statesmen became
20 courteous and even amicable. But the past was never
wholly forgotten.

Chatham did not, however, stand alone. Round him
gathered a party, small in number, but strong in great and
various talents. Lord Camden, Lord Shelburne, Colonel
25 Barré, and Dunning, afterwards Lord Ashburton, were the
principal members of this connection.

There is no reason to believe that, from this time till
within a few weeks of Chatham's death, his intellect suffered
any decay. His eloquence was almost to the last heard
30 with delight. But it was not exactly the eloquence of the
House of Lords. That lofty and passionate, but somewhat
desultory declamation, in which he excelled all men, and
which was set off by looks, tones, and gestures, worthy of

Garrick or Talma, was out of place in a small apartment
where the audience often consisted of three or four drowsy
prelates, three or four old judges, accustomed during many
years to disregard rhetorick, and to look only at facts and
arguments, and three or four listless and supercilious men 5
of fashion, whom any thing like enthusiasm moved to a
sneer. In the House of Commons, a flash of his eye, a
wave of his arm, had sometimes cowed Murray. But, in
the House of Peers, his utmost vehemence and pathos
produced less effect than the moderation, the reasonable- 10
ness, the luminous order, and the serene dignity, which
characterized the speeches of Lord Mansfield.

On the question of the Middlesex election, all the three
divisions of the Opposition acted in concert. No orator in
either House defended what is now universally admitted to 15
have been the constitutional cause with more ardour or
eloquence than Chatham. Before this subject had ceased
to occupy the public mind, George Grenville died. His
party rapidly melted away; and in a short time most of his
adherents appeared on the ministerial benches.   20

Had George Grenville lived many months longer, the
friendly ties which, after years of estrangement and hostility,
had been renewed between him and his brother-in-law,
would, in all probability, have been a second time violently
dissolved. For now the quarrel between England and the 25
North American colonies took a gloomy and terrible aspect.
Oppression provoked resistance; resistance was made the
pretext for fresh oppression. The warnings of all the
greatest statesmen of the age were lost on an imperious
court and a deluded nation. Soon a colonial senate con- 30
fronted the British Parliament. Then the colonial militia
crossed bayonets with the British regiments. At length
the commonwealth was torn asunder. Two millions of

Englishmen, who, fifteen years before, had been as loyal to their prince and as proud of their country as the people of Kent or Yorkshire, separated themselves by a solemn act from the Empire. For a time it seemed that the insurgents
5 would struggle to small purpose against the vast financial and military means of the mother country. But disasters, following one another in rapid succession, rapidly dispelled the illusions of national vanity. At length a great British force, exhausted, famished, harassed on every side by a
10 hostile peasantry, was compelled to deliver up its arms. Those governments which England had, in the late war, so signally humbled, and which had during many years been sullenly brooding over the recollections of Quebec, of Minden, and of the Moro, now saw with exultation that
15 the day of revenge was at hand. France recognized the independence of the United States; and there could be little doubt that the example would soon be followed by Spain.

Chatham and Rockingham had cordially concurred in
20 opposing every part of the fatal policy which had brought the state into this dangerous situation. But their paths now diverged. Lord Rockingham thought, and, as the event proved, thought most justly, that the revolted colonies were separated from the Empire for ever, and that the only
25 effect of prolonging the war on the American continent would be to divide resources which it was desirable to concentrate. If the hopeless attempt to subjugate Pennsylvania and Virginia were abandoned, war against the House of Bourbon might possibly be avoided, or, if inevit-
30 able, might be carried on with success and glory. We might even indemnify ourselves for part of what we had lost, at the expense of those foreign enemies who had hoped to profit by our domestic dissensions. Lord Rockingham,

therefore, and those who acted with him, conceived that the wisest course now open to England was to acknowledge the independence of the United States, and to turn her whole force against her European enemies.

Chatham, it should seem, ought to have taken the same side. Before France had taken any part in our quarrel with the colonies, he had repeatedly, and with great energy of language, declared that it was impossible to conquer America, and he could not without absurdity maintain that it was easier to conquer France and America together than America alone. But his passions overpowered his judgment, and made him blind to his own inconsistency. The very circumstances which made the separation of the colonies inevitable made it to him altogether insupportable. The dismemberment of the Empire seemed to him less ruinous and humiliating, when produced by domestic dissensions, than when produced by foreign interference. His blood boiled at the degradation of his country. Whatever lowered her among the nations of the earth, he felt as a personal outrage to himself. And the feeling was natural. He had made her so great. He had been so proud of her; and she had been so proud of him. He remembered how, more than twenty years before, in a day of gloom and dismay, when her possessions were torn from her, when her flag was dishonoured, she had called on him to save her. He remembered the sudden and glorious change which his energy had wrought, the long series of triumphs, the days of thanksgiving, the nights of illumination. Fired by such recollections, he determined to separate himself from those who advised that the independence of the colonies should be acknowledged. That he was in error will scarcely, we think, be disputed by his warmest admirers. Indeed, the treaty, by which, a few years later, the republic of the

United States was recognized, was the work of his most attached adherents and of his favourite son.

The Duke of Richmond had given notice of an address to the throne, against the further prosecution of hostilities 5 with America. Chatham had, during some time, absented himself from Parliament, in consequence of his growing infirmities. He determined to appear in his place on this occasion, and to declare that his opinions were decidedly at variance with those of the Rockingham party. He was 10 in a state of great excitement. His medical attendants were uneasy, and strongly advised him to calm himself, and to remain at home. But he was not to be controlled. His son William, and his son-in-law Lord Mahon, accompanied him to Westminster. He rested himself in the 15 Chancellor's room till the debate commenced, and then, leaning on his two young relations, limped to his seat. The slightest particulars of that day were remembered, and have been carefully recorded. He bowed, it was remarked, with great courtliness to those peers who rose 20 to make way for him and his supporters. His crutch was in his hand. He wore, as was his fashion, a rich velvet coat. His legs were swathed in flannel. His wig was so large, and his face so emaciated, that none of his features could be discerned, except the high curve of his nose, and 25 his eyes, which still retained a gleam of the old fire.

When the Duke of Richmond had spoken, Chatham rose. For some time his voice was inaudible. At length his tones became distinct and his action animated. Here and there his hearers caught a thought or an expression 30 which reminded them of William Pitt. But it was clear that he was not himself. He lost the thread of his discourse, hesitated, repeated the same words several times, and was so confused that in speaking of the Act

of Settlement, he could not recall the name of the Electress
Sophia.   The House listened in solemn silence, and with
the aspect of profound respect and compassion.   The
stillness was so deep that the dropping of a handkerchief
would have been heard.   The Duke of Richmond replied 5
with great tenderness and courtesy ; but while he spoke,
the old man was observed to be restless and irritable.   The
Duke sat down.   Chatham stood up again, pressed his
hand on his breast, and sank down in an apoplectic fit.
Three or four lords who sat near him caught him in his 10
fall.   The House broke up in confusion.   The dying man
was carried to the residence of one of the officers of
Parliament, and was so far restored as to be able to bear
a journey to Hayes.   At Hayes, after lingering a few weeks,
he expired in his seventieth year.   His bed was watched to 15
the last, with anxious tenderness, by his wife and children ;
and he well deserved their care.   Too often haughty and
wayward to others, to them he had been almost effeminately
kind.   He had through life been dreaded by his political
opponents, and regarded with more awe than love even by 20
his political associates.   But no fear seems to have mingled
with the affection which his fondness, constantly overflowing
in a thousand endearing forms, had inspired in the little
circle at Hayes.

Chatham, at the time of his decease, had not, in both 25
Houses of Parliament, ten personal adherents.   Half the
public men of the age had been estranged from him by his
errors, and the other half by the exertions which he had
made to repair his errors.   His last speech had been an
attack at once on the policy pursued by the government, 30
and on the policy recommended by the opposition.   But
death restored him to his old place in the affection of his
country.   Who could hear unmoved of the fall of that

which had been so great, and which had stood so long?
The circumstances, too, seemed rather to belong to the
tragic stage than to real life. A great statesman, full of
years and honours, led forth to the Senate House by a son
5 of rare hopes, and stricken down in full council while
straining his feeble voice to rouse the drooping spirit of
his country, could not but be remembered with peculiar
veneration and tenderness. The few detractors who ventured to murmur were silenced by the indignant clamours
10 of a nation which remembered only the lofty genius, the
unsullied probity, the undisputed services, of him who was
no more. For once, the chiefs of all parties were agreed.
A public funeral, a public monument, were eagerly voted.
The debts of the deceased were paid. A provision was
15 made for his family. The City of London requested that
the remains of the great man whom she had so long loved
and honoured might rest under the dome of her magnificent
cathedral. But the petition came too late. Every thing
was already prepared for the interment in Westminster
20 Abbey.

Though men of all parties had concurred in decreeing
posthumous honours to Chatham, his corpse was attended
to the grave almost exclusively by opponents of the government. The banner of the lordship of Chatham was borne
25 by Colonel Barré, attended by the Duke of Richmond and
Lord Rockingham. Burke, Savile, and Dunning upheld
the pall. Lord Camden was conspicuous in the procession.
The chief mourner was young William Pitt. After the
lapse of more than twenty-seven years, in a season as dark
30 and perilous, his own shattered frame and broken heart
were laid, with the same pomp, in the same consecrated
mould.

Chatham sleeps near the northern door of the Church,

in a spot which has ever since been appropriated to statesmen, as the other end of the same transept has long been
to poets.   Mansfield rests there, and the second William
Pitt, and Fox, and Grattan, and Canning, and Wilberforce.
In no other cemetery do so many great citizens lie within 5
so narrow a space.   High over those venerable graves towers
the stately monument of Chatham, and from above, his
effigy, graven by a cunning hand seems still, with eagle face
and outstretched arm, to bid England be of good cheer, and
to hurl defiance at her foes.   The generation which reared 10
that memorial of him has disappeared.   The time has come
when the rash and indiscriminate judgments which his
contemporaries passed on his character may be calmly
revised by history.   And history, while, for the warning of
vehement, high, and daring natures, she notes his many 15
errors, will yet deliberately pronounce, that, among the
eminent men whose bones lie near his, scarcely one has
left a more stainless, and none a more splendid name.

NOTES.

PAGE 1.

5. **Mr Thackeray:** the Rev. Francis Thackeray, cousin of the novelist, and author of the Life of Pitt criticised in this essay.

State Paper Office: a department of the "Record Office" in which state papers not of use for current reference are preserved.

7. **Gifford,** whose real name was Richards Green, was a voluminous writer and supporter of the more objectionable aspects of the Tory reaction against Revolutionary principles at the beginning of this century. His life of Pitt was more voluminous than valuable. Of **Tomline's** it may suffice to quote Lord Rosebery's comment that "there are worse books."

10. **The Annual Register** was designed and for many years edited by Edmund Burke. It was an annual record of the year's events, partly in the form of a narrative, partly of a chronological register; with supplementary essays.

PAGE 2.

5. **Lues Boswelliana:** the "Boswellian Madness" which Macaulay speaks of in the "Warren Hastings," in similar fashion, as the "*furor biographicus*"; the enthusiasm of the biographer for the person of whom he writes, leading to "undiscerning panegyric." The phrase is of course taken from Johnson's biographer.

22. **cornet:** the junior commissioned officer in a regiment of horse, corresponding to the ensign of a foot regiment, whose special office was to carry the colours. The title has now been abolished.

27. **to establish an inquisition** etc.: this refers to the appointment of a secret Committee to examine charges against Walpole, and the proposal to pass an Act of Indemnity for all who should give evidence against him. The matter is further discussed in the Essay at p. 24.

31. **peace...with Spain.** The war known as that of "Jenkins's ear" broke out with Spain in 1739 when Walpole was in office and Pitt in Opposition. It closed in 1748 with the Peace of Aix-la-Chapelle, when Pitt was in office under the Pelhams. The **"right of search"** had been the exciting cause of the war. British ships were not allowed to trade on the Spanish Main except by privilege, and the Spanish coast-guard were entitled to search all vessels within Spanish waters for contraband goods. As a matter of fact, British ships did carry on a very extensive smuggling traffic; but it was asserted on the other hand that the Spaniards transgressed their own legitimate claims by enforcing the right of search not only in Spanish waters but on the high seas. As to the right itself, the Spaniards had all law on their side, and the ultimate acquiescence therein was necessary; it was however naturally and quite honestly challenged in the excitement which accompanied the outbreak of the war. See also note on "Maritime right," p. 22.

PAGE 3.

4. **When he left** etc.: it is noteworthy that as a matter of fact, inconsistent as these various positions appear when placed thus antithetically, real inconsistency was not necessarily involved. Pitt **left Newcastle** because the latter insisted on a policy which Pitt could not accept: he coalesced with him when the Duke consented to give up the direction of policy and content himself with a free hand for jobbery. He attacked **subsidies** and the **Hanoverian connection,** when Hanoverian interests appeared to be controlling British policy to England's detriment; he supported both, when Hanover was plunged into a war in which not she but England was directly interested, and a continental army could only be maintained by subsidies because sound policy demanded concentration of the fighting energies of Britain on the fleet. Pitt however was undoubtedly prepared when in opposition to believe the worst, and when in office to believe the best, of the motives of ministers. Had it not been so his judicial impartiality would have been unique in the history of Parliament.

14. **not complete and well-proportioned.** This paragraph conveys Macaulay's ideals of political character with precision. Extravagance of every kind was his bug-bear. His admiration is given to the men who check the elements of disorder rather than to those who arouse enthusiasm. The calm resolution of Hampden, the cool consistency of Somers, were great qualities, but cannot be properly compared with the genius of Cromwell or of Chatham. It may be that if Hampden had not fallen at Chalgrove Field he would have achieved a place in the first rank of statesmen, but he fell too soon to be judged; while the place of

Somers, high as it is, is definitely not in the first rank. Neither Hampden nor Somers made blunders, but it does not appear that, if neither of them had lived, the course of English history would have been materially different. To be steadily consistent, a man must be dispassionate; and the dispassionate character rarely, very rarely, attains the highest eminence, at least in the political field.

15. **John Hampden** entered Parliament in 1621; in the second Parliament of Charles I. he became prominent, by his resistance to the crown obtaining money by forced loans, and was imprisoned in 1627. From 1629 to 1640, the king attempted to govern without a Parliament, obtaining funds by the exaction of "ship-money," an impost which Hampden refused to pay. Parliament being again called in 1640 Hampden was recognised as a chief remarkable for calm and energetic resolution. He was one of the "five members" whom Charles attempted to arrest in 1642. He then took an active part in the Committee of Public Safety; but was killed at the skirmish of Chalgrove Field before the Civil War had lasted a year, in June 1643.

16. **Somers** first attracted notice by his defence of the Seven Bishops, in the reign of James II. His sound and unvarying sense gave him rapidly increasing weight in the counsels of the Whigs, and in 1695 he was one of the four leaders known as the "Junto" who displaced the Tory ministry. He was at different times Lord Keeper, Lord President, and Lord Chancellor; and took a leading part on the Whig side throughout the reign of William and the greater part of that of Anne. With him lies the chief credit of the skill with which the Act of Union with Scotland was carried in 1707. After George I.'s accession ill health precluded him from any further share in active politics.

25. **pride and resentment**: the reference here would seem to be chiefly to the period of his career treated in the second essay. If Pitt's conduct towards Walpole was due in part to resentment at his exclusion from office, it was far more due to the belief for which there was much justification, that the great minister's foreign policy was pusillanimous. The same comment applies to his relations with Newcastle before the coalition. Later in life, he demanded a dictatorship or nothing, but his whole character shows that it was not practicable for him to rule except as a dictator; the one case in which it seems impossible to defend his action was in his refusal to join the Rockinghams.

30. **without simplicity.** This term seems to be used in a somewhat forced sense, as if in contrast to theatricality; whereas "simplicity" as a characteristic of great men would naturally be taken to mean singleness of aim. It is however true that Pitt sought after stage effects with a remarkable persistency. Many great men, since the great Scipio

tore up the accounts in the face of the Roman Senate, have known how
to strike a theatrical note on occasion.   At least one contemporary of
Pitt's can be named who is fairly entitled to rank as a man of genius,
and was at the same time perpetually employing histrionics—the
Frenchman Dupleix.   Great Englishmen however have inclined to an
affectation of the blunt rather than the grand manner.

PAGE 4.

8. Belisarius : the great captain who, in the time of Justinian,
thrice beat back the hordes of the barbarian invader.   The jealousy of
the court repeatedly robbed him of the honour which his splendid
services merited; and popular tradition went so far as to invent that the
saviour of the empire was to be seen in his old age begging for the
charity of passers by.   From this fiction his name has become a type
for the heroic victim of ingratitude; pointing the moral of tragedians
in prose and verse.

20. Dodington : George Bubb Dodington acquired a certain
political influence in the reign of George II. chiefly by being able to
control half-a-dozen rotten boroughs.   With an entire disregard of
principle, he alternated between supporting Walpole, Prince Frederick,
the Pelhams, the Princess Dowager, and in short anyone and everyone
from whom something was to be had.   His ambitions were satisfied
when he succeeded in getting made a peer, as Baron Melcombe.   He
is one of the odd collection of "people of importance" addressed by
Robert Browning in the volume entitled "Parleyings"—a poem which
may be unravelled by the curious.

Sandys was conspicuous for ceaseless parliamentary attacks upon
Walpole throughout that statesman's career.   On Walpole's fall he
obtained office, and forthwith turned his back upon every one of his
earlier political professions.

21. might have been tempted : the innuendo is hardly justifiable.
The worst that could be said of Pitt was that he would not accept the
task of saving his country—would not undertake its government—except
on his own terms, and that he allowed personal feelings to enter into
those terms.

PAGE 5.

11. from a wish : again it seems distinctly ungenerous to imply
that personal ambition was the motive, service to the state only the
means.   What he desired for himself was not profit but glory; but the
patriotic intent, if it did not dominate the personal, was at any rate an
equally strong motive with him.

15. Governor of Madras : at that time—about the accession of

Queen Anne—the British colony in India consisted of mercantile establishments at Calcutta, Madras, and Bombay : each establishment having its own governor.   No territory, and no sort of sovereignty over the natives of India had been acquired.   The governors were merely officers appointed by a trading company.

16. **the diamond**, known as the Pitt or sometimes the Orleans diamond.   There is only one larger one in Europe, the " Orloff " : it is larger than the celebrated "Koh-i-noor."

17. **Orleans :** became regent on the death of Louis XIV.   During his government, the relations between the French court and Britain were very friendly.   Philip of Spain, though barred by treaty from the French succession, was next heir by blood, while under the treaty Orleans was Heir Presumptive.   A disputed succession was exceedingly probable in the event of the young king dying without issue ; and Orleans relied on British support for his claim.   His death in 1723 paved the way for the alliance between the French and Spanish Families of Bourbon.

18. **two millions of livres:** the sum is also stated to have been two and a half million "livres," or francs, valued at the time as equivalent to £130,000.   Pitt is said to have given £20,000 for it, in 1702.

Saint Simon ; one of the old French noblesse, who was closely associated with Orleans.   He left behind him a great mass of MS. records of the people and events with whom he had been connected ; forming an invaluable repository of information about the earlier part of the 18th century.

20. **bought rotten boroughs :** this was a favourite practice with the men who returned with large fortunes from India, who in later days were known as the "Nabobs."   "Rotten" boroughs were those in which the number of electors was exceedingly small, and practically under the control of the owner.

30. **the second year :** i.e. in 1727.

PAGE 6.

6 **làbenti :** *làbi* and *làbare* may both be used for "to totter," "to fall."

9. **Themis :** Justice.   **Cocytus** one of the rivers of the under-world, but having an actual existence in Epirus ; like Acheron.

24. **the Blues.**   The Household Cavalry consists of three regiments— the 1st and 2nd Life Guards, and the Royal Horse Guards (Blue) commonly called the Blues.   The corresponding foot-regiments, composing the Brigade of Guards, are the Coldstream, the Grenadier Guards, and the Scots Guards.

31. **Fourteen years** since 1721.

PAGE 7.

7. **out of office**: in 1716, George I. had gone to Hanover, with Stanhope. Rumours were sedulously circulated that Townshend, the secretary of state, was intriguing with the Prince of Wales. Sunderland fomented the king's feeling against Townshend, who was forced to resign and was accompanied by Walpole. Sunderland remained at the head of affairs till the South-Sea crash.

the South-Sea Act was passed in 1720, converting a large portion of the National Debt into stock in the South-Sea Company (which had been founded by Harley), and giving a violent impetus to the craze for its shares. The shares went up to enormous prices, and when it was suddenly discovered that the vast profits looked for were quite illusory, thousands of people found themselves ruined.

PAGE 8.

2. **Aislabie** was Chancellor of the Exchequer, and had made great profits out of the South-Sea scheme; most of which were forfeited on his fall. **Craggs**, the secretary of state, was a comparatively young man, of considerable ability, and high character, a friend of both Addison and Pope. He himself was probably quite free from guilt in the South-Sea affair, but his father, who subordinated politics to finance, was deeply involved in it.

7. **Sunderland** was fully acquitted on the evidence, but the popular verdict held him guilty—as it appears, quite unjustly. The removal of himself and his most prominent followers from public life made the renewed association of the rest with Townshend and Walpole a comparatively simple matter.

31. **Pulteney**, after heading the Whig opposition to Walpole, and being mainly instrumental in his fall, would probably have succeeded him as first Minister but that he wrecked his own prestige by taking a peerage as Lord Bath; a blunder which closed his active political career.

PAGE 9.

16. **Carteret**, afterwards Lord Granville, is brilliantly described by Macaulay towards the close of his Essay on the Letters of Horace Walpole. After Sir Robert's fall, he was the statesman in whom George II. reposed most confidence; but he was never popular in the country or successful as a leader. With all his brilliancy, he appeared to regard foreign politics as an exciting game; and did not adopt a sufficiently insular tone to satisfy Englishmen. He came into power shortly after Walpole's fall, but soon had to make way for the Pelhams.

27. Townshend had held higher office than Walpole in the earlier stages of their career, and it was against him rather than Walpole that Sunderland's attack had been directed.

28. by marriage; Townshend married Walpole's sister as his second wife.

31. Godolphin was recognised as a man of great tact and business ability under James II. He remained a member of the Tory party, but being chiefly concerned with finance retained office when the Whig Junto came in in 1695. In 1702 he became Lord High Treasurer; and though nominally at the head of the Tory party found himself gradually growing more and more in sympathy with the Whig element which shared in the administration. It was during this period that Townshend and Walpole took office under him. He was driven from power by Harley and St John (Bolingbroke) in 1710, and died two years later.

32. Harley, one of the Tory leaders under Queen Anne, who became Earl of Oxford at the close of her reign. For some time he was associated with St John, with whom he shared the responsibility for the treaty of Utrecht (1713). He would not, however, finally commit himself on the question of the succession, and Bolingbroke managed to drive him from office, but too late to carry out his own plans.

Page 10.

2. Sunderland, *v. supra*, p. 8, note.

30. Chesterfield is best known now as the author of the celebrated "Letters," and as the "patron" who so excited the wrath of Samuel Johnson. His truest title to fame however rests on his Irish administration of 1745, which was distinguished by a unique combination of firmness, justice, and regard for the welfare of the country.

Page 11.

3. the Excise Bill. This was a measure introduced by Walpole; with the primary intention that tobacco and spirits—instead of paying a customs duty on being landed (which was an obvious incitement to smuggling)—might be landed and warehoused; not paying duty till withdrawn for consumption, or being reembarked without paying duty at all. The advantage to trade seems obvious now, but at that time the proposal excited frantic opposition, and Walpole withdrew it.

17. Argyle. Queen Anne was seized with a mortal illness the day after Oxford's dismissal (*v.* p. 9, note on Harley). Bolingbroke's attempt to effect a Jacobite restoration by a *coup de main* was frustrated by the Council being broken in upon by Argyle and Somerset, who with

the Duke of Shrewsbury there and then secured the reins of government; and the Queen's death two days later found the Hanoverian
succession secured. He took the command in Scotland when the
"Fifteen" took place.

19. **Act of Settlement**; the Act by which the succession to the
throne was attached to the house of Hanover.

PAGE 12.

11. **Horace.** The more famous Horace was Sir Robert's son.
The brother Horace was employed in various diplomatic and other
offices.

15. **Fox**: Henry Fox, subsequently Lord Holland, father of the
greater Charles James Fox. His name recurs frequently in these two
essays.

30. **Squire Western**: the reference is to Fielding's novel, *Tom
Jones*; where Squire Western is presented as the type of the hopelessly illiterate and boorish Tory squire of the day. The Osbaldistones
in *Rob Roy* are an example of the same type. But a very different
aspect of the country squire is given in Addison's "Sir Roger de
Coverley."

33. **the October Club**; a Tory Club of Queen Anne's time, in
Westminster. It consisted of country Tories of the type which considered that every Whig ought to be impeached—thereby causing
considerable embarrassment to the party leaders. The name was taken
from the "October" ale which was drunk.

PAGE 13.

5. **Wyndham** was a recognised chief among the Tories in Parliament, with a reputation for both brains and honour. He was always
under suspicion as a Jacobite.

21. Lord William **Russell's** name was coupled with that of Algernon
Sidney in the regard of the Whigs of the Revolution. He was one
of the boldest advocates of the exclusion of James (James II) from the
succession. On the occasion of the "Rye House Plot," he and Sidney
were both accused of complicity, condemned in defiance of all real
evidence, and beheaded.

26. **Lyttelton, George**: afterwards Lord Lyttelton, a man of talent,
but not of first-rate ability. He remained in Pitt's circle till 1754, when
he held to Newcastle: becoming his Chancellor of the Exchequer. He
was however too much of a dreamer and too unpractical to remain in
the front rank. Later he became reconciled to Pitt, but his influence
was unimportant.

31. **Prince of Wales** : Frederick, father of George III. He was a man of little ability; but his perpetual quarrels with his father encouraged the Opposition Whigs to group themselves round him. He died in 1751. The habitual opposition between the Hanoverian kings and their Heirs Apparent is sufficiently explained in the text.

PAGE **14.**

21. **Granville** ; the same as Carteret.

30. **four Princes:** George II., whose opposition to his father led to the Sunderland administration, as related; Frederick, son of George II.; George III., who became Prince of Wales on his father's death, but could hardly be called a leader of opposition to his grandfather; and George IV., whose most intimate associates included Fox (C. J.) and Sheridan.

PAGE **15.**

5. **dividing with** : i.e. on the same side with.

PAGE **16.**

17. **Henry the Fourth:** Henri IV., the great French king; not the English monarch.

31. **unmeaning phrase** ; this is hardly as unmeaning as Macaulay would imply. Tindal would clearly have us to understand that Pitt while possessing the merits of both Demosthenes and Cicero avoided the notorious defect of each.

PAGE **17.**

3. **Coxe** : William, Archdeacon of Wiltshire; a very industrious writer, who among other works edited a life of Sir R. Walpole.

23. **the audience,** etc. : Macaulay in this comparison leaves out of count the fact that unless a man has certain qualities of delivery, he remains to this day unheard by the nation, because the reporters omit to report him. He must get the ear of his actual audience before his words are allowed to travel beyond the House.

31. **A hundred years ago.** Up to 1771, the publication of reports of parliamentary debates was forbidden. Before that time, however, reports—usually very inaccurate, and with fictitious names attached—had occasionally appeared. In 1771 the House of Commons endeavoured to punish the printers of some reports which had been published; the cause of the printers was taken up by the Lord Mayor and Aldermen of London, John Wilkes taking a vigorous share in the proceedings; and the struggle ended in the "Standing Order" forbidding reports being tacitly dropped. After that time the reporting of debates became generally recognised, and ultimately demanded as a matter of course.

PAGE **18.**

10. **Brutus or Coriolanus:** i.e. the qualities which would have enabled him to play those characters also made his oratory successful. The illustration however seems a little unfortunate in this place, because in Shakspeare both Brutus and Coriolanus as orators proved conspicuous failures. Later in this paragraph it is implied—as we should expect—that it was Pitt's skill as an actor and in the arts of the actor that made him so effective as a speaker; while for him, the parts of either Coriolanus or Brutus would hardly have demanded acting at all. The scornfulness of the one, and the air of moral rectitude of the other, were his by nature.

PAGE **19.**

26. **Shelburne** was one of Chatham's supporters during the reign of George III. He was not thirty when he joined the Chatham administration of 1766; he resigned during the period of his chief's incapacitation, and remained out of office till the fall of Lord North's administration in '82. He became a leading member of the Rockingham administration, but was driven out of office by the Fox and North coalition; after which he to a great extent withdrew from public affairs.

33. **the late Mr Fox,** i.e. Charles James Fox.

PAGE **20.**

7. **Mr Stanley,** the "Rupert of Debate," afterwards Earl of Derby and leader of the Conservative party. Though one of the most brilliant debaters of his day, he is said to have declared that he never rose in the House without feeling his knees shake under him.

PAGE **21.**

9. **Walpole,** i.e. Horace Walpole.

30. **Appeal to the Old Whigs.** This was a pamphlet written after Burke's quarrel with Fox. It was in essence an appeal against the support given by the "New" i.e. the Fox Whigs to the French Revolution.

PAGE **22.**

11. **maritime right.** Spain had the right to control commerce with her American territories; she had conceded to an English company the right to send one trading vessel per annum to the Spanish main. The traffic of other British ships was contraband, but lucrative. The Spanish coastguard had the right to board and search suspected vessels

in Spanish waters; to this they were charged with adding the practice of boarding vessels on the High Seas. This the British were fully entitled to resent, though the resentment came with a bad grace from sailors who hardly disguised the fact that they were in those seas with illegal objects. But in fact at that time—indeed from the days of Elizabeth—the British had always felt about Spanish colonies very much what European nations are now wont to feel about British colonies; that if we *could* only pick a quarrel and turn the other side out, we should be justified in doing so. The allegations about "boarding on the High Seas" accompanied by details of insolence and violence were a handy means to the quarrel. There was no moral justification, but it was not difficult to arrive at a point of indignation which made it quite easy to believe that there was; cf. p. 2, l. 31, note.

PAGE 23.

13. **Hardwicke**, a famous Lord Chancellor, best known in history in connection with his "Marriage Act," passed during the Pelham administration, abolishing the old scandal of marriages in the "Fleet," i.e. the precincts of the Fleet prison.

16. **Pitt and those persons**, etc. A few lines later Macaulay describes this story as "supported by strong testimony," but he treats it throughout as if it was unquestionable, which is quite another thing. For Pitt himself it seems thoroughly out of character: while the worst aspect of his subsequent attack on Walpole disappears, if this be untrue.

33. **He was not......and he therefore**: the imputation conveyed is not proved. Judging by all Pitt's career, the chances are that if he had become a placeman he would have given the new government nearly if not quite as much trouble as he did in opposition. He never showed any inclination to be subservient to any chief for the sake of office; though his freedom of action would no doubt have been in some degree impaired.

PAGE 24.

5. **Sandys**, *v.* p. 4, note.

18. **Orford**: this was the title taken by Walpole on his retirement.

29. **to force his way**: it is to be noted that Macaulay deliberately assumes the desire of office as the only real motive by which Pitt was actuated: and translates all his actions in that light.

PAGE 25.

9. **paying Hanoverian troops.** By this time, the War of the

Austrian Succession had broken out. Maria Theresa was being attacked on all sides; George, as Elector of Hanover, was very anxious to give her hearty support; but England was not directly interested in the war, except so far as Austria could be used on the Continent to counterbalance France and Spain. Carteret therefore was supposed to be allowing the interests of Hanover to outweigh those of Britain, and hence the opposition to Hanoverian subsidies.

12. **Wyndham**, the Tory leader mentioned *supra*, p. 13.

15. **The Duchess of Marlborough**. Sarah, Duchess of Marlborough, one of the most masterful and disagreeable women in history, was for some time the bosom friend of Queen Anne. Owing to the violence of her temper, a rival, Mrs Masham, succeeded in supplanting her, and in transferring the royal favour to the leaders of the Tory party: thereby leading to the reversal of Marlborough's war policy, and to the Treaty of Utrecht in 1713.

PAGE **26**.

15. **omitted nothing** : Carteret being driven from office and the Pelhams in power there was now no reason why Pitt should not support the Government.

PAGE **28**.

8. **vails**: a term properly used of gifts to servants or retainers—for which the modern equivalent is "tip." The original form was "avails," i.e. "helps."

25. **eight years** till the death of Henry Pelham in 1754.

PAGE **29**.

21. **intellectually** : this statement may be taken as true or not, according to the precise sense in which the word is used. But there was one quality which may properly be called intellectual, in which Pitt surpassed every contemporary except Burke : that is, Imagination: the quality which differentiates Genius from Talent or Ability.

PAGE **30**.

3. **Fox**: Henry Fox, afterwards Lord Holland. If this comparison between Pitt and Fox is read with care, it will at once be remarked that Macaulay seems always to be finding an excuse for Fox's weak points, whereas even to Pitt's virtues he attaches some uncomplimentary suggestion—e.g. his "ostentatious purity."

PAGE **32**.

7. **Cutler**, in spite of his avarice, was capable of occasional munificence : the Grocers' Company, the Royal College of Physicians,

the Royal Society, and others, benefiting by his donations. Arbuthnot said of him that "his worsted stockings had been darned with silk so often that they became silk stockings."

23. **Craggs,** *v.* p. 8, note.

Page 34.

23. **In India.** While the war between France and England had lasted, the English and French companies had been at open war in India. After the peace, they could only fight each other by taking sides with other belligerents. The thrones of Hyderabad and of the Carnatic becoming vacant, one pair of claimants joined hands and got French support, and the other pair got English support. Success attended the French, inspired by Dupleix, until Clive came to the front, and re-established British prestige by the defence of Arcot; and the French were finally forced to surrender before Trichinopoli. Dupleix himself was recalled in 1754, so that the moving spirit of French rivalry was withdrawn.

26. **in America.** The English colonists, holding the coast, claimed all the territory westward. The French, holding Canada on the north and Louisiana on the south, claimed the river basins which would unite the two, cooping the British colonists up in the eastern strip of continent. Therefore, British and French colonists fought each other on the Ohio.

Page 35.

17. **The negotiations** in connection with the disputed rights in America. Throughout 1755 it was becoming evident that matters would end in an appeal to arms. But ministers were completely blind to the fact that, whilst France was likely to go to war with Britain, Austria was preparing in association with Russia to try to crush Prussia. The ministry were in fact in so hopeless a state of confusion that they attempted simultaneously to form alliances with Russia and Prussia. Meantime France was making up her mind between a Prussian or an Austrian alliance, finally deciding in favour of the latter.

24. **disastrous events:** referring to the establishment by the French of Fort Duquesne on the Ohio; their defeat of George Washington at Great Meadows; and the subsequent destruction of General Braddock's force—an event commemorated by Thackeray in *The Virginians.*

Page 36.

11. **the young Prince of Wales:** afterwards George III. His father, Frederick, had died in 1751—mourned in the rhyme

"But since 'tis only Fred
Who was alive and is dead,
There is no more to be said."

25. **the Russian subsidy**: Pitt was probably alive to the fact
that Prussia, not Russia, was the ally we wanted. He was also
aware that if Hanover was attacked, it would only be as a means of
harassing England, and therefore he recognised that subsidies in defence
of Hanover were reasonable.

PAGE 37.

9. **Gerard Hamilton,** after this time known as "single-speech
Hamilton," because he never afterwards achieved any striking feat
of oratory. His success on this occasion was so remarkable that
various other persons were credited with having composed the speech
for him.

PAGE 38.

4. **events disastrous to England.** The French fleet sailed for
Minorca from Toulon, without any declaration of war. Byng, in
command of the British Mediterranean fleet, came to the conclusion
that if he attacked and was defeated, not Minorca only but Gibraltar
also would fall : therefore he held back. This was in April '56.

11. **Port-Mahon,** the fort of Minorca.

PAGE 41.

7. **The Reform Bill** of 1832, a measure by which Macaulay seems
to have gauged all parliamentary history ; regarding it as the apex of
Whig achievement.

13. **a remedy**: the remedy practically has always been found—
when a "necessary" person has been unseated—in the voluntary
resignation of a safe party seat by someone sufficiently disinterested—
or interested—to be willing to retire, in favour of the excluded chief.

29. **an error such as** etc.: on the contrary, it was an error
such as the great commanders do not commit, but second-class men
do. Frederick's blunders for instance were invariably the blunders of
over-confidence. Byng's blunder implied not cowardice but complete
lack of confidence in himself and his fleet—a point fully realised in
the French critic's sarcasm, that Byng was shot "pour encourager les
autres."

PAGE 42.

15. **Marie Louise,** second wife of Napoleon I., who divorced
Josephine in order to marry her for the sake of political advantages.
She was the daughter of the Emperor Francis of Austria.

PAGE **43.**

8. **Vattel**, a great jurist. His most valuable work, the *Droit des Gens*, a treatise on International Law and the " Law of Nature," was not published till 1758 ; so that George's complaint is a little remarkable.

13. **at Oudenarde**; one of Marlborough's victories, fought in 1708: where George was present as a lad. His courage however was a quality never questioned, and was notably if somewhat ludicrously displayed at Dettingen, the last occasion when a British reigning monarch appeared in the field. The incident is related as none but Thackeray could relate it, in *The Four Georges*.

16. **in April**—1757.

PAGE **48.**

12. **Leicester House** : the residence of the Prince of Wales.

17. **of Godolphin** : the ministry under whose *régime* Marlborough's triumphs had been won.

PAGE **49.**

14. **Louisburg** is on the island of Cape Breton, commanding the mouth of the St Lawrence, which is the maritime gate of Canada. The whole island at this time was French. Louisburg had been captured during the previous war, but restored in exchange for Madras, which had fallen into the hands of the French.

25. **the Grand Alliance** : the European combination against Louis XIV., formed by William III. on ascending the throne of Britain. The name was also given to the later alliance whose armies were directed by Marlborough.

26. **Goree** is on the west coast of Africa : **Guadaloupe** is one of the West Indian Islands : **Ticonderoga** and **Niagara** were the Canadian forts the capture of which opened the way for invasion by land.

28. **the Toulon Squadron.** The French fleets were harboured at Toulon in the Mediterranean, and at Brest in Brittany. Boscawen from Gibraltar kept guard over the former: Hawke from Torbay over the latter. Apparently the French Admiral at Toulon—De la Clue—wished to evade Boscawen, join Conflans at Brest, and with the combined fleet crush Hawke. He succeeded in passing Boscawen, but was pursued, his rear overtaken and destroyed, and himself with only half his fleet blocked up in Cadiz.

30. **the heights of Abraham.** Wolfe had been lying before Quebec, but found it impossible to make any impression on the

enemy's lines. At last he conceived the daring plan of scaling the heights of Abraham—which was only possible by effecting a complete surprise. It was done however; and on the open plateau at the top a decisive victory was won, Quebec was captured, the brilliant commander Montcalm slain, and the French army compelled to surrender.

PAGE 50.

8. **The Brest Fleet** was larger than that of Toulon which Boscawen had shattered. After the great triumph of Quiberon, instead of twenty-three sail of the line at Brest and twelve at Toulon, the French were left with only twenty-one sail of the line scattered in detachments at Rochefort, Cadiz, Toulon, and the mouth of the Vilaine river; so that they were entirely unable to put to sea.

28. **Cortes** and **Pizarro**; the Spanish conquerors of Mexico and Peru.

31. **India.** Here the French resistance had practically been confined to the Carnatic or Madras district: where Lally was vanquished by Coote at Wandewash. Before this however, Clive, at the head of an expedition sent to the Hooghly to obtain satisfaction for the outrage known as the "Black Hole of Calcutta," had conquered Bengal at the battle of Plassey, virtually adding it to the possessions of the East India Company.

Chandernagore: the French settlement on the Hooghly.

PAGE 51.

2. **Acbar**, the third of the Great Moguls, grandson of Baber. He re-established and organised the Mogul Empire: his reign coinciding with that of Elizabeth in England.

Aurungzebe, the sixth great Mogul, extended the empire over Southern India; but at the same time sowed the seeds of disintegration, by enlarging his borders beyond manageable limits. After his death, the empire broke up into great provinces, each virtually independent though acknowledging the Suzerainty of the Mogul.

20. **conquer America in Germany,** by forcing France to divide her attention between the Continental and Naval wars. Thus the British naval superiority, on which Pitt concentrated all British activity, was promptly asserted; while Frederick of Prussia was enabled by subsidies to make head against the common enemy in Europe.

PAGE 52.

12. **three months.** Pitt and Newcastle came in together in July 1757. Before the new ministry had the war in hand, the Duke of Cumberland, commanding the allies on the Weser, blundered so badly

that he was forced to dismiss part of his troops, and retire beyond the Elbe with the rest, at the convention of Closterseven following the battle of Hastenbeck (Sept.). The appointment of Ferdinand of Brunswick in place of Cumberland placed a thoroughly efficient general in command, and the French were first checked and then hurled back from Minden in 1759.

20. **Minden** was a victory won by Ferdinand in great part through the magnificent conduct of the British troops serving under him. Here however it was that Lord George Sackville, in command of the British cavalry, refused to charge at a critical time, thereby rendering the disaster to the French somewhat less crushing than it should have been.

PAGE 53.

20. **not planned by him**: they were however secured by his policy, of which the fundamental feature was the development of overwhelming predominance on the sea—a policy which made it impossible for France, alike in America and India, to send any succour when her arms met with a reverse.

PAGE 54.

11. **Sackville**: see note on Minden, p. 52.

PAGE 55.

11. **A few years**: it is of course to be observed that the change which Macaulay describes was mainly due to the fact that Pitt was driven from power; and that—except for the brief period of the Rockingham administration—the ministerial policy in every crisis was the reverse of what Pitt would have carried out. Even when Pitt himself was Prime Minister in name, he was hopelessly invalided and his cabinet acted in consistent defiance of his principles.

PAGE 58.

3. **Malebolge**: the name given to the eighth circle of Hell. This scene is described in the *Inferno*, Canto 25.

28. **Locke**: John Locke, who may be regarded as the father of the peculiarly English school of philosophy, political and mental; his essay on *The Human Understanding* occupying in the latter field the position taken in the other by his *Civil Government*. The central idea of the latter is that there is no sanctity in any special form of government, the sovereign power being maintained for the benefit of the community at large.

Milton: as representing the Republicans of the Great Rebellion. His principal contributions to Political Theory are to be found in his *Areopagitica, Eikonoklastes*, and *Tenure of Kings and Magistrates*; as well as, by implication, in his numerous pamphlets on Church Government. Freedom of opinion and discussion was his fundamental demand.

29. **Pym**: John Pym was one of the leaders of Parliamentary resistance to Charles I. Like Hampden, he was one of the Five Members whose attempted arrest hastened the Rebellion. (v. "Hampden," p. 3, note.)

30. **thirtieth of January**: the day on which Charles I. was executed. The "**man in the mask**" was his executioner, whose identity was never ascertained.

Page 59.

1. **Strafford**: Thomas Wentworth, Earl of Strafford, was the minister who—after acting as a leader of the popular side—threw in his lot with King Charles I. and devoted his abilities to the establishment of an absolute monarchy. Impeached, it was impossible to obtain a conviction against him; and he was condemned to death by an Act of Attainder to which the king gave his assent.

9. **fifteen years ago**, in 1829: when the king of France was ejected from the throne, and Louis Philippe placed there.

10. **Guizot**, a French historian and statesman whose chief period of activity was during the second quarter of this century. His political principles were much akin to those of the Whigs; but his attitude had never been (as might be supposed from this passage) of an incendiary type. The rule of the Orleans family and their supporters was resented by the Bourbon legitimists, a little as that of the house of Hanover was resented by the Jacobites. Thus **M. de la Roche Jaquelin** belonged to one of the Vendéan families which had fought against the Revolution, but had no mind for Louis Philippe.

19. **Sidney**: Algernon Sidney, a Whig leader of avowedly Republican principles, in the reign of Charles II. He and Russell (p. 13, note) were both judicially murdered in connexion with the Rye House Plot, and were enshrined as martyrs of the cause of Freedom.

Page 60.

18. **Walpole's resignation** took place in Feb. 1742.

20. **the Russells**: the family of which the Duke of Bedford was head.

the Cavendishes: the family of the Duke of Devonshire.

24. **the Mendips** in Somerset: **the Wrekin** in Shropshire.

26. **Oxford:** Harley, who was associated with St John at the head of the Tory party in Queen Anne's time. He held the **white staff** as Treasurer and head of the Government, in the ministry which concluded the Peace of Utrecht.

PAGE 61.

7. **Timoleon:** a Corinthian, who is said to have slain his brother Timophanes for attempting to make himself "tyrant"—i.e. autocratic ruler—of Corinth. Most of his career however was spent in Sicily, where he expelled the ruling tyrants of Greek "Colonies," substituting democratic governments.

Brutus in this context is the Marcus Brutus who stabbed Caesar, not the other Republican hero, Lucius Junius Brutus, the traditional expeller of the Tarquins.

15. **the Rump:** in 1648, the majority of the "Long Parliament," then still sitting, being in favour of making terms with the king, eighty members were forcibly excluded by the army. After the beheading of Charles, the remnant of members, known as "The Rump," continued to act as a properly constituted House of Commons, until Cromwell suppressed it in 1653.

PAGE 62.

28. **schedules A and B:** a reference to the Reform Bill of 1832, when the "rotten boroughs," i.e. those which were in the gift of a landowner or local magnate, were abolished.

PAGE 63.

19. **lawn sleeves,** i.e. bishops, whose official robes have lawn sleeves.

25. **prebend:** an office, or the stipend of an office, paid out of the revenues of a cathedral.

28. **potwallopers:** lit. pot-boilers: lodgers who had a vote on the ground that they cooked their own meals.

PAGE 64.

23. **tide-waiter:** see note, p. 101.

PAGE 65.

25. **Cavendish:** while this family is here named as of the Newcastle connexion, it is to be noted that its head, the Duke of Devonshire,

had been the nominal head of the brief ministry in which Pitt attempted to govern without Newcastle, 1756—7.

Lennox: the family name of the Dukes of Richmond. The Duke, of Walpole's day, supported Sir Robert. Lady Sarah Lennox, mentioned later in this essay, was the daughter of the Duke of Richmond.

Fitzroy: the Dukes of Grafton descended from Charles II. Hence the name of Fitzroy.

26. **Bentinck**: a family which came over with William III. The first Bentinck was made Duke of Portland.

Manners: the family of the Dukes of Rutland, whose eldest sons bore the courtesy title of Marquess of Granby. The Lord Granby at this date was a good soldier, but a wavering statesman.

Conway: the family of the Earl of Hertford. Its most distinguished member was General Conway, of whom frequent mention is made in this essay.

Wentworth: the family of the Marquess of Rockingham.

PAGE **66**.

19. **Sandwich** held office in subsequent ministries; but is most notorious for his intimacy with John Wilkes, and his shameless desertion of that companion in profligacy when the scandalous *Essay on Woman* was condemned by the Lords.

Rigby began his career by courting Frederick, Prince of Wales: but after joining Bedford, he held steadily by the Duke, very much to his own profit. He has been taken as the type of the entirely unprincipled "wire-puller."

PAGE **67**.

22. **Oswald**: a Scotchman, who was described by H. Walpole as a match for Fox in debate.

23. **Nugent**: a clever and witty Irishman of whom Lord G. Sackville said that he was the "most uninformed man in his position" in the country. To him, under his title of Lord Clare, Goldsmith addressed the lines *The Haunch of Venison*.

Charles Townshend subsequently became responsible for the tax upon tea which led to the emptying, by an organised mob, of the tea-ships in Boston harbour—the first organised defiance of Westminster by the American colonists.

24. **Elliot**: Sir Gilbert Elliot, Lord Minto, who became George's confidant and to a great extent his personal adviser. He was a very able debater.

Barrington: principally known as one of the "King's Friends," who after George III.'s accession retained office in his interests through one administration after another.

North: Lord North, afterwards head of the North administration which ruled from 1770 to 1782.

Pratt became Chief Justice of the Common Pleas and subsequently Lord Camden.

31. **Sackville**: see note on Minden, p. 52.

Dodington: v. *supra*, p. 4, note.

PAGE 68.

6. **the Cocoa Tree**: a Tory club, which the superior members of the party attended. Gibbon was a member.

PAGE 69.

11. **Francis**: Austrian Emperor; whose daughter Marie Louise was married by Napoleon.

PAGE 71.

11. **Derwentwater**: one of the most important of the English leaders of the rising of 1715. He was taken, and was executed for high treason.

Kilmarnock was executed after the '45, in which he took an active part, though not at the outset.

12. **Balmerino**. Lord Balmerino was implicated in the '15, and out in the '45. When condemned, he flatly refused to acknowledge to treason, maintaining that James was the rightful sovereign.

Cameron: Lochiel was attainted, but escaped to France. This was his younger brother Archibald, a doctor, who rendered assistance to Charles Edward in his wanderings. Cameron escaped to France, but returning privately to Scotland in 1753, he was betrayed, arrested, and executed, in spite of the strongest remonstrances.

28. **Apis**: an Egyptian deity. When a calf was discovered having certain peculiar marks, the animal was regarded as a manifestation of the god; the discovery was attended by public rejoicings, and the calf was called Apis, and treated with all possible respect and attention by the priests of Apis. (Herodotus, Book III. cc. 27—29.)

33. **Doge**: the title of the first magistrate in Venice; **Stadtholder**, that of the head of the Dutch Republic. The point is that these offices had in them none of the sanctity of *hereditary* rule, being elective, at any rate in theory. The office of Stadtholder subsequently became hereditary to the house of Orange.

PAGE **72.**

9. **Doddridge**: a Presbyterian divine, who was active in promoting the cause of unity among Nonconformists.

10. **Whiston**; a mathematician and theologian, who left the Church because of his Arian views; i.e. he denied the equality of the Persons of the Trinity.

11. **South**: a witty and quarrelsome divine, born in 1633. He began as a Calvinist, but after the Restoration developed strong views in favour of Non-resistance.

Atterbury: the high-church bishop of Rochester, who was prepared, on Queen Anne's death, to head a procession and proclaim King James: and who was subsequently suspected of having a hand in every Jacobite plot or intrigue.

PAGE **73.**

17. **Scotch Peers**: the Peers of Scotland who are not also Peers of the United Kingdom elect sixteen representatives who have seats in the House of Lords, whenever a general election takes place. If a vacancy is caused by death a fresh representative is chosen.

PAGE **74.**

5. **Sir Charles Grandison**, by Samuel Richardson, author of *Pamela* and *Clarissa Harlowe*, was published in 1753.

24. **the Princess Dowager**: Augusta of Saxe-Gotha.

PAGE **75.**

7. **Filmer**: Sir Robert Filmer, about 1680, published a work called *Patriarcha*, maintaining the Divine origin of the rights of primogeniture, and consequently of the Divine Right of kings. John Locke's (p. 58, note) treatises *On Civil Government* were written in part as a direct refutation of Filmer.

Sacheverell: Dr Sacheverell, whose sermon advocating the doctrine of non-resistance led to his impeachment and to the "Sacheverell riots," in 1710.

8. **Perceval**: prime minister from 1809 to 1812, when he was assassinated. He is usually named as the type of narrow-minded and inadequate respectability. His Toryism, like that of John Scott Lord **Eldon** (Lord Chancellor), rested not so much on the Divine Right of the ruler as on the fear of popular control engendered by the French Revolution: while it took expression chiefly in a blind antagonism to anything which could be called "Reform."

9. **Bolingbroke**, more particularly after being driven from any open share in politics by the failure of his Jacobite schemes on the one hand and his quarrel with the Stuarts on the other, posed as the philosophical statesman, with a curious blend of the high monarchical and the Roman Republican.

24. **the instrument:** known as the Declaration of Right, Jan. 1689.

PAGE 76.

4. **responsible to the nation :** Macaulay desires again to remind his readers that the Reform Bill of 1832 was the crown and apex of the Revolution of 1688.

5. **constituent bodies** or "constituencies"—the bodies which returned members to Parliament.

7. **the debates** etc. : cf. note on p. 17, line 31.

PAGE 77.

28. **Sudbury** and **Old Sarum** were two of the rotten boroughs which had the smallest pretensions to representation.

PAGE 78.

3. **Dodington :** see p. 4, note.

PAGE 79.

19. **Montague** (Lord Halifax) and **Godolphin** were the great finance ministers of the reigns of William III. and Anne. See p. 9, note on Godolphin, and p. 92, note on Halifax.

22. **now** that the French were beaten out of both America and India. The fact that France was by no means prepared as yet to believe that she was thoroughly beaten—was in fact seeking to draw Spain into the contest—was left out of count.

25. **Hapsburg**, or more correctly Habsburg ; the Austrian Royal Family, represented at this time by Maria Theresa.

Brandenburg : i.e. the Prussian Royal Family. The King of Prussia was also Elector of Brandenburg ; the "Mark" of Brandenburg, within which Berlin lies, being the original territory. After the acquisition of Prussia the Prussian title was extended to the whole dominion ; but it was from Brandenburg that the king still derived his title as an Elector of the Holy Roman Empire.

26. **Silesia** was the great bone of contention between Frederick of Prussia and Maria Theresa. Frederick had acquired it in the war of the Austrian Succession, terminated by the Treaty of Aix-la-Chapelle in

1748: the desire to recover it was at the root of Maria Theresa's determination to crush Frederick, and consequently of her alliance with France and Frederick's alliance with Britain in the "seven years' war," which began in 1756.

27. **on the Main**: i.e. defending the western frontier of Prussia. They were fighting there for two reasons: one, that Hanover, drawn into the war on account of her connexion with England, was entitled to our protection: the other, that every obligation of honour demanded that we should support Frederick to the end—his magnificent resistance having been of the utmost service to this country in distracting the attention and exhausting the resources of France.

PAGE **80.**

33. **Vattel**: see p. 43, note.

PAGE **81.**

16. **Onslow**: one of the ablest occupants of the Speaker's chair in the House of Commons. He was appointed Speaker in 1728, and was reappointed without a break till his retirement in 1761.

PAGE **82.**

16. **army extraordinaries**: i.e. extraordinary credits for the army.

18. **eight millions**: Pitt's war expenditure was unprecedented; but was greatly exceeded subsequently. "The National Debt, which was fifty-two millions in 1727, had risen to nearly one hundred and thirty-nine millions in 1763." The wars of William and Anne had involved an annual expenditure averaging from below four millions under William to a little over five millions under Anne. But sixteen millions were voted in 1760 alone. On the other hand, the large expenditure meant that the war was one of the most decisive ever waged between Powers which began on an equality.

28. **Charles III. of Spain.** The course of the Spanish Succession is confusing. Philip V., uncle of Louis XV. of France, was established on the Spanish throne by the Peace of Utrecht. On his death in 1746 he was succeeded by Ferdinand, his son by his first wife, a princess of the house of Savoy. In 1759, Ferdinand was succeeded by his half-brother Charles, son of Philip's second wife Elizabeth Farnese. While it had appeared that there was very little prospect of her own sons succeeding to the Spanish throne, Elizabeth had been careful to secure for them the Italian duchies or kingdoms wrested from Austria: and thus in 1737 Charles had become king of Naples, or "the two Sicilies." The sceptre of the Sicilies passed from his hands on his accession to the

throne of **Spain**. The accession of Ferdinand had changed Spanish policy: because up till that time Elizabeth had guided it, and she was vehemently anti-British. Ferdinand, her *step*-son, was not under her influence; but Charles her *son*, who succeeded him, was as hostile to England as his mother had been.

29. **Twenty years before**: i.e. on the outbreak of the war of the Austrian Succession. At that time Spain was divided between hostility to Britain and to Austria. The war with England had already broken out. The king of Naples would undoubtedly have joined Spain in an attack on the Italian possessions of Austria but for the sudden appearance of Captain Martin with five ships of the line and a demand that a treaty of neutrality should be signed in an hour.

PAGE 83.

14. **Minorca** at this particular time was not in the hands of the British, having been captured by the French in 1756, when Byng failed to rescue it. When the war did terminate, however, Minorca reverted to Britain, being exchanged by the French for the island of Belle Isle.

17. **the Family Compact**: this was in fact a ratification of the first Family Compact of 1733—both being treaties for the aggrandisement of the united Bourbon sovereigns.

27. **Havanna**, the port of Cuba in the West Indies; the **Philippines** being in the East Indies.

PAGE 84.

13. **Canada**: this proposal is a very remarkable commentary on the prevailing theory of Governorships. It was about two years since Quebec had fallen; Canada was an absolutely new acquisition—yet it was proposed that its Governor should reside in England.

PAGE 87.

18. **the Fleet**: i.e. the precincts of the Fleet prison.

PAGE 89.

27. **Egremont**: son of Sir William Wyndham.

PAGE 90.

7. **Ciceronian treason**: i.e. talking treason in Ciceronian Latin.

8. **the theatre**: the Sheldonian "theatre" in which the public ceremonies of the University were performed.

PAGE 91.

12. **a deep stain**: France and England mutually agreed to withdraw from the continental war. Happily for Frederick, Russia was now neutral, and Austria came to terms; but the British withdrawal

was a flagrant breach of faith. Bute indeed had even attempted to come
to a separate understanding with Austria.

14. **a peace.** The peace of Paris, signed in 1763. The prelimi-
naries were signed in Nov. of the preceding year. By 1762 Britain was
sweeping the seas without check and practically conquering where she
chose. By the terms of the peace, however, it was agreed that all
conquests of which the news had not arrived before the signature
should be restored : the fruits of the latest expeditions to distant seas
being thus entirely thrown away. The peace secured England in
possession of Canada. Havanna was returned to Spain in exchange
for Florida, France transferring Louisiana to her as compensation and
thus withdrawing entirely from the American Continent. In India,
France was left without a military foothold, while Britain was practically
mistress of Bengal, and predominant on the Coromandel coast. But
the conquests in the Philippines were resigned, and it was only extreme
pressure from his fellow ministers which made Bute retain as much as
he did.

PAGE 92.

4. **Felton.** George Villiers, Duke of Buckingham, the favourite of
Charles I., urged the king forward in his attempts to defy Parliament.
The Parliamentary leaders, headed by Eliot, in their demands for the
remedy of grievances, placed the removal of Buckingham in the front of
their requirements. To this, however, Charles refused to accede : and
in 1628 Buckingham was assassinated by John Felton.

9. **Strafford**, see note, p. 59.

Falkland, one of the moderate Parliamentarians under Charles I.,
took the king's side when it appeared that the struggle was likely to
mean war. He was killed in the first battle of Newbury, in 1643.

Clarendon (Hyde), the historian of the Great Rebellion, was a
Parliamentarian who joined the king in 1641 : like Falkland. In the
time of the Commonwealth, he remained abroad, holding a high
position among the counsellors of Charles ; and on the Restoration, he
was made Lord High Chancellor. He failed however to satisfy either
the Puritans or the Court, and never held a very assured position, though
his judgment was respected on all hands.

Clifford, Sir Thomas, one of the members of the "Cabal" (Clifford,
Arlington, Buckingham, Ashley, Lauderdale) who ruled in England
after the fall of Clarendon in 1667. Clifford and Arlington were privy
to the disgraceful secret "treaty of Dover" by which Charles virtually
sold England to Louis XIV.

Shaftesbury : Anthony Ashley Cooper, Lord Shaftesbury, was one of the ablest and most unscrupulous of Charles II.'s ministers. As a young man, in the days of the Commonwealth, he assumed extreme Puritanism: on the Restoration, he plunged in the debaucheries of the court, still for political ends. For a long time, religious toleration was the cause to which he mainly devoted himself; but, recognising to the full the danger of Romanism becoming predominant, he changed his attitude, and turned vehemently against the Catholics. He was thus driven into opposition to the king. He was succeeded in office in 1674 by Danby.

Lauderdale: the Scottish member of the Cabal, to whom Scottish administration was entrusted. This he organised with a view to strengthening the hands of the monarchy at the expense of liberty. Lauderdale began his career as a Covenanter; perhaps the one principle to which he held consistently was that of retaining Scottish affairs in the hands of Scottish ministers. He retained the confidence of Charles II. and James till his death in 1782.

10. **Danby:** a monarchist, but in the first place a Churchman, who was equally anxious to check Catholic and Protestant-Nonconformist predominance. This suited neither the king nor the opposition, and Danby fell in 1678.

Temple (Sir William), the subject of one of Macaulay's essays, was never at the head of government. He attained high rank as a diplomatist in the reign of Charles II., serving mainly as ambassador at the Hague.

Halifax: presumably the reference is to the Lord Halifax who was a minister of Charles II. after the fall of Danby. He was known as "the Trimmer," having a natural aptitude for avoiding extreme courses and discovering compromises. Another Lord Halifax—known through the greater part of his career by his surname of Montague—stood in the front rank of the finance ministers of the time (the reign of William III.); his most memorable achievements being the creation of a "National Debt," and of the Bank of England.

Rochester is better known as a wit, a typical member of the Restoration Court, than as a statesman. He was high in favour with Charles II., and was associated with Sunderland and Halifax in supporting the succession of James, under whom he became Lord Treasurer. He was dismissed from office on his refusal to adopt the Roman Catholic religion.

Sunderland: a statesman whose ability was only surpassed by his duplicity. He attained a leading position in the latter years of Charles II., as an opponent of the exclusion policy—i. e. of the exclusion of James from the succession. When James came to the throne, Sunderland became his most trusted minister, yet he intrigued with the party of William. The change of kings made it necessary for him to leave the country, but he succeeded in gaining favour with William, became one of his ministers, and originated the system of governing through a Cabinet the members of which should all belong to one Parliamentary party.—The Sunderland whom Macaulay reproaches for having intrigued for the ejection of Walpole in George II.'s time— who also designed the "Peerage Bill," the rejection of which was in great part due to Walpole's vigorous opposition—and who was finally driven from public life by the South Sea disaster—was his son. (See p. 8.)

17. **in opposition.** This is a somewhat broad statement. It is true of five out of the first six named, the exception being Clifford; Temple was hardly a party politician: and the rest did not gain distinction, as Macaulay's words imply, by opposition to the king, even if they were in opposition to his ministers for the time being.

19. **Carr,** or Ker, a favourite of James I., who was made Earl of Somerset. He had no pretence to statesmanship, and is most notorious for his marriage with Lady Essex who murdered Sir Thomas Overbury, with or without Somerset's connivance.

Villiers: referring to the first Duke of Buckingham. The second Duke of Buckingham—one of the "Cabal"—owed his power more to court favour than ability; but he was always a subordinate member even of the Cabal.

PAGE 93.

1. **Englishman against Scot.** The Union between the two countries had only been accomplished in 1707, till which time a Scots parliament sat in Edinburgh. The ancient antagonism between the two nations was like Charles II., "an unconscionable time a-dying." Readers of *Rob Roy* will remember Andrew Fairservice's diatribes on "the sad and sorrowfu' Union." Scotland had exercised pressure on her wealthier neighbour by threatening to repudiate for herself the Hanoverian succession. In the rising of 1745, the abolition of the Union had been held out as a bait to some of those Scots who had otherwise no desire to see a "Papist" on the throne. Both in the '15 and the '45, it was Scottish chiefs who had been most active, and on whom the penalties of non-success fell most severely. The Prince's march to Derby had been looked upon as a Scottish invasion : and the Prince himself had probably intensified the feeling by emphasising the Scottish origin of his family, and wearing the kilt.

7. **Grampians:** the Highland hills bordering on the Lowlands.

12. **the severity** etc. : the cruelties of the Government troops in

punishing the rebellion caused the Duke of Cumberland to be nicknamed the "Butcher."

27. **the princess** Parizade. The reference is to an episode in the
concluding tale (called that of *The Two Sisters*) related by Scheherazade.
The princess, desiring to obtain "the talking bird, the singing tree, and
water from the golden fountain" had to climb a hill without once
looking back. The air was full of mocking and threatening voices;
but the princess stuffed her ears with wool, so that the voices did not
alarm her. Whereby she succeeded in her quest.

33. **Maecenas**, the friend of Augustus the first Roman Emperor, is
the standing type of the judicious and munificent patron of Art and
Letters. He deserved his credit; but he was fortunate in patronising
and winning in return the praises of the most popular of Roman writers,
Horace, who made his name a household word.

Page 94.

12. **Vanity of Human Wishes:** a didactic poem of Dr Johnson's,
more quoted than read at the present day.

13. **Adam**: Robert Adam, one of a group of brothers who built
several of the great houses of this period. The "Adelphi" is so named
because the brothers designed it.

14. **Ramsay**: Allan Ramsay, son of the poet, and generally
esteemed very highly as a portrait painter, though of a lower rank
than Reynolds and Gainsborough.

17. **Home's** tragedy of Douglas was for a short time regarded as a
masterpiece. It is however an exceedingly stilted production, and his
subsequent attempts were received with derision.

20. **the author of the Bard**: Gray; whose poetical output was
singularly small, but was of the finest quality. He resided most of
his life at Cambridge. He was buried at Stoke Pogis, but his *Elegy* has
placed him among the Immortals. The professorship was that of History:
a post to which he was appointed on its again becoming vacant in 1758.

25. **the pedagogue**: one Laurence Brockett. He was killed some
six years later by a fall from his horse when riding home drunk, after
dining with Lord Sandwich.

26. **Sir James Lowther**: described by Mr Lecky as a man "whose
violence, arrogance, despotism, and caprice rose almost to the point of
madness." See also note, p. 152, line 11.

Page 95.

14. **Wilkes**: John Wilkes, of whom a good deal is to be read in
this essay.

15. **the mother of Edward III.**: Isabella, wife of Edward II., was unfaithful to her husband; and first secretly, and at last openly, sided with the barons against him. Edward was deposed and murdered; the young king was still a boy; and power fell into the hands of the queen and her favourite Roger Mortimer. The barons however rose against Mortimer's supremacy, and he was put to death.

17. **Churchill**: a satirist of great repute; known chiefly by his poem the *Rosciad*, published in 1761. He was intimately associated with Wilkes. The work referred to in the text was a satire entitled *A Prophecy of Famine*.

PAGE **97.**

4. **Fox** : Mr Lecky's summary of Fox's character leaves little room for the compensating merits which Macaulay is so anxious to impress upon his readers. "A bold, bad man, educated in the school of Walpole, but almost destitute of principle, patriotism, and consistency" (vol. II. p. 441).

PAGE **99.**

3. **Virgil's foot-race**: *Aen.* V. 314 ff. The victorious Nisus slipped on mire, and fell. The parallel is by no means complete however, for Nisus having fallen himself, secured the victory for his friend Euryalus, who was running third, by tripping up the leading runner. But Nisus, like Fox, received a "consolation" prize.

PAGE **101.**

12. **tidewaiter**: an official in the Customs; the title coming from his awaiting the tide which brought up the vessels from which dues were to be levied.

gauger: an excise official, whose duty is to gauge or measure casks with excisable contents such as spirits.

15. **Grafton**: the Duke had been Groom of the Stole to George III. when Prince of Wales: but, being a great admirer of Pitt, he opposed the peace, and was one of those who were deprived of the Lord Lieutenancies of their counties in consequence. Later he was in Chatham's ministry, becoming its nominal head when Chatham withdrew.

32. **Tellers of the Exchequer**: four officials of the Exchequer appointed to receive and pay moneys due to or from the Crown. The office was abolished in 1834.

Justices in Eyre. This term means Itinerant Justices, who passed from place to place in a given district, dealing with the local cases. The title was abolished with the establishment of the modern system of

Circuits. The word Eyre is from the Old French "erre," a contraction from "*itinere*" "on journey."

PAGE 103.

11. **excise**: see p. 11, note.

15. **definition**: the terms of this definition were: "a hateful tax levied upon commodities, and adjudged not by the common judges of property, but wretches hired by those to whom excise is paid."

19. **John Philips** flourished in the first decade of the eighteenth century. *The Splendid Shilling* is probably his best known work, but Macaulay refers to his poem on Cider—a poem "in imitation of the Georgics."

20. **the Cider-land** roughly covers Devon, Somerset, Herefordshire and Worcestershire.

29. **Dashwood**: already described in the Essay, p. 89.

PAGE 104.

4. **the profusion**: Grenville had been treasurer to the Navy while it was going on. It would hardly be possible now for a man who had held such a position to act as if he had not, by holding it, accepted responsibility for the financial policy he himself carried out.

16. **Gentle Shepherd**: the opening lines of this song are

"Tell me, Shepherd, have you seen
My Flora pass this way."

The song has been used for political purposes since Pitt's day. The author was Samuel Howard.

PAGE 106.

25. **his father-in-law**: the husband of Lady Mary Wortley Montagu.

27. **for his son**: the House of Lords had ruled in 1711 that a peer of Scotland could not act as a peer of Great Britain; but his son, being a Commoner, was eligible for the peerage. This decision was not set aside till 1782.

32. **he retired** in April 1763.

33. **in the House of Lords** as Lord Holland.

PAGE 107.

1. **George Grenville**: with whom, till the month of August, were associated Lord Halifax and Lord Egremont (son of Sir William Wyndham); their government was known as the Triumvirate.

PAGE **108.**

6. **Mayor of the Palace**: a favourite historical illustration of
Macaulay's. The later Merovingian kings of the Franks lost all reality
of power, which was absorbed by the family of Pepin le Vieux, whose
descendant Pepin le Bref became king in name as well as in fact. The
glory of his house culminated in Charlemagne. **Childeric** was the last
of the Merovingians. "Mayor of the Palace" was the title given to these
powerful ministers who held the kings in awe.

16. **the worst administration:** this is applied to the whole period
when Grenville was at the head of affairs—to the "Bedford" administration as well as the "Triumvirate." George Grenville was
responsible for initiating (1) the attempt to override colonial opinion in
dealing with the colonies, (2) the attempt to set the wishes of a
temporary majority of the House of Commons above the law. The
result of the first was the American war : the result of the second was
ignominious defeat, in the long run. Grenville represented the reaction
to guidance by petty technicalities from the audacious idealism of Pitt.
His administration was worse than that of Lord North, only because it
was he who set the example of an evil policy ; it was worse than that of
Newcastle from 1754 to 1756 because it was actively ruinous instead of
being merely incompetent—as the pilot who steers on to the rocks is
worse than the pilot who lets his ship drift on them.

19. **on the liberty of the people:** in the case of Wilkes and of the
American colonies.

20. **on the dignity of the crown:** by the personally offensive
demeanour displayed to George by Grenville and Bedford.

PAGE **109.**

6. **the North Briton:** Churchill (p. 95, note) was associated with
him in the conduct of this paper, which was more particularly devoted
to attacking Bute and the Scots.

12. **the forty-fifth number** was an attack on the king's speech on
the closing of Parliament after Bute's resignation. Although constitutional usage fully recognised that the "king's speech" was subject to
comment as the work of ministers, the attack on it was treated and
regarded as a personal attack on George himself.

20. **a general warrant :** i.e. a warrant was issued directing the
apprehension of the "authors printers and publishers" of Number
Forty-Five ; without specifying names. Under this warrant forty-nine
persons were apprehended, as it appears to have been held to cover all
persons suspected of a share in the writing, printing or publishing.

General warrants were declared illegal shortly afterwards, in the Rockingham administration.

25. **pronounced unlawful** on the ground of privilege, Wilkes being a member of the House of Commons. Chief Justice Pratt at the same time declared general warrants to be illegal: and that warrants for the seizure of papers on a charge of libel were illegal.

<h3 style="text-align:center">PAGE 110.</h3>

18. **Buckingham House**, i.q. Buckingham Palace.

<h3 style="text-align:center">PAGE 111.</h3>

27. **Cornet Joyce.** In June 1647 Charles I was at Holmby House, under the surveillance of the Parliamentary Commissioners. "Five hundred troopers suddenly appeared before Holmby House...and displaced its guards. 'Where is your commission for this act?' Charles asked the cornet who commanded them. 'It is behind me,' said Joyce, pointing to his soldiers. 'It is written in very fine and legible characters,' laughed the king." This is the account given by Mr Green (*Short History*, p. 548). The cornet in fact appears to have been peremptory, but not flagrantly rude.

President Bradshaw. A court of 150 commissioners was named to try Charles I., John Bradshaw being appointed President. In the course of the trial Bradshaw treated the king with an insolence which would have been unseemly in any case.

<h3 style="text-align:center">PAGE 112.</h3>

1. **Warburton's Commentary.** William Warburton was appointed to the Bishopric of Gloucester in 1760. He was distinguished for his theological works, and is also remembered for his annotations and emendations to Shakespeare, usually more ingenious than judicious. The *Commentary* was a series of seven letters published under the title of *A Vindication of Mr Pope's Essay on Man* (1740).

18. **Lord March** may be remembered as appearing in Thackeray's *Virginians* where the novelist makes him challenge Harry Esmond to a jumping match, and subsequently turn the cold shoulder on the Virginian, when the latter is in difficulties.

<h3 style="text-align:center">PAGE 113.</h3>

9. **one of the most dissolute clubs;** a society of which Wilkes was himself the moving spirit, entitled the "Medmenham Brotherhood," which took for its motto the Rabelaisian "Fay ce que vouldras"—"Do what you want." The members habitually acted up to the motto.

11. **the Beggar's Opera**: a play by John Gay, written at Swift's suggestion; an extremely popular work, in which the characters were chiefly thieves, and containing political and topical hits. Captain Macheath is the hero.

PAGE 115.

28. **the desertion of our allies**, notably the Catalonians; who had resisted the Bourbon monarchy on the faith of British support, and were left absolutely without protection by the Treaty of Utrecht. But that peace was in fact also a desertion of the House of Austria.

32. **the elevation of Harley** through the influence over Queen Anne of Harley's cousin, Mrs Masham, who supplanted the Duchess of Marlborough in the Queen's affections.

PAGE 117.

11. **stamp duties**: i.e. taxes on legal and other documents; on the execution of which fees were to be paid to the revenue, and the Government stamp affixed. Stamp duties form a material part of the revenue of the United Kingdom; the novelty was in the attempt to increase the revenue of *Great Britain* by a tax on the *Colonies*. The point which requires to be grasped is this. It had always been held that the mother country had a right to interfere with the freedom of trade in the interest of the British merchant. It was considered legitimate for instance to establish Customs duties in order to enable *British* articles of commerce to enter the colonies and be sold at a lower price than *foreign* goods. But it was understood that such taxation was imposed not in order to swell the receipts of the Exchequer—i.e. not in order to provide Government with funds—but for the benefit of British trade. Taxation in this sense had never been seriously complained of. But the Stamp Act imposed a tax avowedly and exclusively to provide Government with additional funds: the root principle on which the Parliament had fought Charles I. was that the Government should not be supplied with money except by consent of the governed; and this principle of the Constitution was set at nought the moment that taxes, for filling the Government coffers, were laid upon the Colonists who were not represented in the body (the British Parliament) which imposed those taxes.

19. **to lay taxes**: that is, in the sense conveyed in the preceding note. Taxes *for commercial purposes* were already laid on the colonies. It was the introduction of taxation *for revenue* which was a novel burden. Being not only novel, but contrary to the recognised principles of the British Constitution as established by the Stuart struggle, it was

at once felt as a grievance; and by an easy transition, the right hitherto admitted of taxation for commercial purposes came to be called in question.

PAGE 118.

2. **the debt:** the national debt. The argument might be expressed by saying that Grenville's finance was penny wise and pound foolish. He wanted some thousands of pounds of revenue: which his tax would bring in. But the policy produced a war which cost millions. In contrast, Pitt's policy had required an enormous expenditure; but while it increased the national debt, it increased the national assets to a much greater degree.

10. **His complaint** is described by Macaulay in somewhat ambiguous terms. It was in fact the threatening of insanity.

PAGE 119.

20. **Coligni.** Admiral Coligni, a leader of the French Huguenots who was murdered in the massacre of St Bartholomew. To associate Cumberland's name with that of Coligni and William is a somewhat rhetorical device. These two great leaders were usually compelled to fight under the most unfavourable conditions; and both evinced extreme ability in neutralising the effects of the defeats they suffered in the field. Their reputation would find a much closer parallel in that of Washington. But it is difficult to see what Cumberland's reputation was based upon. He commanded British and Hanoverian forces during the war of the Austrian succession, but never showed signs of being fit to cope with such a leader as Marshal Saxe. His one successful achievement was the Culloden campaign; and he allowed himself to be out-manœuvred at Hastenbeck in 1757 by a totally inefficient commander.

21. **Soult:** one of Napoleon's great generals who had the misfortune to be frequently pitted against Wellington.

PAGE 120.

4. **of Potsdam:** i.e. of the Prussian army; which had been built up by the father of Frederick the Great into extraordinary efficiency.

9. **during some years:** since the affairs of Hastenbeck and Closterseven.

27. **a long series of errors** which may however be resolved into the one obstinate resolution not to take office unless Temple would join him. To say that Pitt's mind was unhinged by his sufferings from disease would be an overstatement; yet it may fairly be doubted

whether his obstinacy in this particular matter was not a kind of monomania. For he did not make it a condition merely that Temple should be offered office, but that he should get it on terms for which Pitt himself had no liking. Pitt's position in fact remains to all appearance strictly irrational; nor is it possible to attribute this either to the lust for power or the personal pique in which Macaulay usually finds an explanation of his errors and a detraction from his merits.

PAGE 121.

30. **Extinxi** etc.: the words are taken from Virgil, *Aen.* IV. 682: the speaker being Anna the sister of Dido. "I have brought ruin upon thee and me, my sister, and upon the Sidonian fathers and people, and upon thy city." The reading "extinxti," "*thou* hast brought ruin" is preferred by the commentators, and would have been still more appropriate in Pitt's mouth, addressing Temple. In some editions of this essay "extinxti" is the reading given.

PAGE 122.

9. **the Spitalfields weavers** were suffering seriously from the competition of French silks, and petitioned the Government for their exclusion from the English market. The terms in which Bedford refused exasperated them; and a number of them marched to the House of Lords carrying black flags, the mob subsequently attacking the Duke of Bedford, and nearly wrecking Bedford house. There is no sort of reason to suppose that Wilkes—much less Bute—had anything to do with the matter: but it is easy to perceive that any mob would have been disposed to invoke the name of Wilkes. (May 1765.)

20. **a lucrative office**: Privy Seal, which was a sinecure office, i.e. one to which virtually no duties were attached.

29. **in the Isle of Wight**: Charles was confined at Carisbrooke Castle in November 1647, remaining there till his removal to Hurst Castle shortly before the decision was formed to try him for his life.

PAGE 123.

3. **the Duke of Devonshire** had been nominal head of Pitt's first administration before the coalition with Newcastle; and had been bitterly insulted by the king, as related at p. 100, for his opposition to Bute.

31. **a fit**: he is reported to have said—" If I had not broken into a profuse sweat, I should have suffocated with indignation."

Page **124.**

32. **Chalgrove Field,** the skirmish at which Hampden received his mortal wound.

33. **Russell :** see p. 13, note.

Page **125.**

5. **Lord John Cavendish** joined the Rockingham ministry, supporting the opposition throughout North's ministry, and associating himself with Charles Fox when the younger Pitt came to the front.

6. **Sir George Savile** supported the Rockingham principles without joining their Ministry, considering his services more useful outside. He died before the coalition of Fox and North.

Page **126.**

7. **a much better man :** the Duke of Bedford, v. p. 66.

15. **Conway,** see p. 65, note.

20. **Grafton,** see p. 101, note.

27. **Charles Townshend,** see p. 67, note.

28. **lutestring :** a kind of glossy silk. The word is a corruption of *lustring* (from *lustre*), and has no connexion with the lute.

Page **127.**

4. **a little treatise** entitled *A Vindication of Natural Society,* a parody or rather an intentionally extravagant exposition of Bolingbroke's philosophy : published in 1756.

6. **a theory** embodied in the treatise *On the Sublime and Beautiful,* published in 1757.

10. **the Turk's Head.** There was a Turk's Head in the Strand, and another in Soho, both frequented by the Johnson group. The latter was the meeting place of "The Literary Club" started by Reynolds, Johnson, Burke, Goldsmith, Nugent, and other select spirits, which later on developed into the Johnson club.

13. **into Parliament** as member for Wendover.

19. **a Papist :** as a matter of fact, Burke was a Protestant and his father was a Protestant ; but his mother came of a Roman Catholic family.

Page **128.**

13. **revenue officers.** Grenville's measures for raising revenue from the colonies had taken two forms—one being the Stamp Act, the other the strict enforcement of the existing revenue laws. Now it was

pointed out (p. 117, notes) that the taxation of imports in the way of protecting British products against foreign competition had never been objected to; moreover, in the days before Grenville, smuggling had to a great extent been winked at. The burden therefore had not been heavy enough to develope a grievance. The suddenly roused activity of the customs officers would in itself have roused ill-feeling; coupled with the new impost, it was not only irritating, but led to the whole right of taxation, whether for revenue or for commercial purposes, being called in question; and the whole population took the part of the smugglers as against the officials.

13. **All traffic**: throughout the American colonies, the attempt to tax was met by the formation of associations pledged, as we should now put it, to boycott British commerce: so that practically the American markets were closed to British goods.

16. **Bristol and Liverpool** were the largest ports devoted to the American trade.

PAGE 129.

2. **not constitutionally competent**: Pitt's view was based on the principles of the constitution as declared in sundry Acts of Parliament —that the people may not be taxed except by consent of their representatives. The colonies being unrepresented in the Parliament at Westminster, that Parliament was not competent to impose taxes. Legally, Pitt's view broke down, because the right of taxation was reserved under the Colonial Charters. Moreover, admitting the abstract truth that representation is recognised as a condition of taxation, it was at least possible to argue that this again was conditional on representation being practicable; since it was not possible for the colonies to be represented at Westminster, it would have been necessary on Pitt's principles to admit that the colonies might force a huge expenditure on Britain, and then repudiate any obligation to bear a part of the burden. Now there is no doubt that on the technical point Grenville was right. The sense of taxation through representatives must obviously be reduced to taxation by consent of Parliament, since even in Great Britain there were and still are whole classes who are without the franchise. But the application of the principle was a piece of legal pedantry, under circumstances which the existing machinery had not been organised to meet. The colonies had a moral right to a voice in settling what they were to pay: and the only method of giving them such a voice was to leave it to their own sense of justice to fix the contribution.

5. **Shipmoney**: Charles I. endeavoured to raise money by issuing

a writ by Royal Authority. James similarly issued a proclamation suspending the Penal Laws against Nonconformists, by Royal Authority. In both cases, it was argued that no authority was sufficient but that of the Sovereign, i.e. the Crown and Parliament together. Pitt would seem to have held that the sovereignty of Crown and Parliament together—i.e. the *legal* right to enforce any enactment whatsoever—did not extend to the colonies because they were unrepresented.

21. **the Toleration and Habeas Corpus Acts** are selected as typical measures for the public good; the one securing freedom of conscience, the other freedom of the person. They were passed in 1689 and 1679 respectively.

PAGE **130**.

6. **Massachusetts and Virginia**, the two colonies which took the lead in opposing the demands of Parliament. Boston, the port of Massachusetts, was at all times most defiant; riots took place there; and the Bostonians were urgent in their endeavours to gather a General Congress for combined action. The Virginian Assembly was the first to formally and categorically deny the right of taxation.

12. **Strafford**, see p. 59, note.

PAGE **135**.

21. **his profusion**: i.e. the enormous expenditure on the great war. Grenville had argued, not without justice, that the war had been fought in great part to deliver the colonies from the rivalry of France in Canada and on the Ohio: the expenditure had been incurred for their benefit; it had been greater than the unaided resources of Great Britain could support; therefore the colonies were bound to pay their quota. He had no choice but to demand it, and it was Pitt's fault that he had no choice. Of course the answer was that if the colonies benefited, British trade also benefited: and that, granting the right to call for a Colonial contribution, still the demand was made in the wrong way—for which the responsibility lay entirely on Grenville.

33. **general warrants**, etc.: thereby confirming the opinion already expressed from the bench by Chief Justice Pratt.

PAGE **137**.

28. **Pratt**: see note on p. 67.

30. **lend himself**: Macaulay is probably unjust to Pitt in the following paragraph. It is true that the great minister had always been peculiarly susceptible to the personal influence of royalty: he

had used expressions about the crushing force of royal disfavour which would hardly have been out of place in an Oriental court. But the true motive of his action at this time appears to have lain in a conviction that the rule of the Whig houses was an evil which must be got rid of. If they formed a solid party, the revival of that Oligarchy which he had fought against before would be brought about. It was only under stress of a terrific national crisis that he had consented to form the coalition with Newcastle; and he would not be a party to the formation of a fresh group which would hold government in the hollow of its hand. Both Pitt and the king wished to make a permanent Whig Oligarchy impossible; and Pitt still believed himself capable of forming a powerful administration which should not depend upon the resuscitated power of the Whig nobles. Whether it would have been possible for him to carry on government on those lines if he had retained all his mental powers may be questioned; but that he would not have played into the hands of the king's friends is no less certain than that there was no other man alive who could conceivably have carried out his scheme—a scheme which in the end required neither more nor less than a Pitt dictatorship.

Page 138.

5. Wedderburn subsequently became Lord Loughborough. He commenced his career by posing as a defender of popular liberties in the case of Wilkes, and attacking Lord North's American policy. This paved the way for him to join Lord North's ministry; and later on he became Lord Chancellor under the younger Pitt. •

22. Ormond, a leading Jacobite Tory who was associated with Bolingbroke in the attempt to overthrow the Act of Settlement and replace the Stuarts on the death of Queen Anne. He was obliged to fly the country, and was not only implicated in the '15 but in later attempts, of a futile character, to bring in the Stuarts.

Page 139.

11. Wallenstein, Duke of Friedland, commander of the armies of the Emperor during the Thirty Years' War, was one of the ablest generals of his time, proving himself little less than a match for Gustavus Adolphus. Among his peculiarities was a strong superstition, taking the form of belief in Astrology. As with Clive also, it is said that the unsuccessful snapping of a pistol led him to believe that his life had been saved by a Destiny which had specially reserved him for great deeds.

29. at whatever moment: it may be observed that Napoleon was also given to this very trying habit.

13. **sixteen years later**: on the resignation of Lord North in 1782.
At that date, the American war had been virtually terminated by the
British surrender of Yorktown: in the West Indies there was a
powerful French fleet, and the Spanish fleet was on the way to join it:
Gibraltar had been besieged year after year: the allies had recently
appeared in immense force in the Channel: in India Hyder Ali was
threatening the existence of the British power. Great Britain was in
the most perilous situation she had faced since the days of the Armada.
During the year, the Fleet emerged triumphantly: Rodney won the
great victory of "The Saints," Gibraltar was relieved, Hyder Ali was
checked. This recovery was hardly due to the second Rockingham
administration: but they synchronized. The country had North's
government to thank for the position to which it had sunk : and it was
well known that the king dictated North's policy.

Page **143**.

13. **growing old**: he was in fact only 58, which is by no means a
great age for discharging the highest functions of the state according to
present day usage. Of the six leading members of the 1897 cabinet,
five are as old as Pitt was at this time.

Page **144**.

7. **William Pulteney,** the most active leader of the opposition to
Walpole, had more than once refused a peerage; but was politically
annihilated by his acceptance of the Earldom of Bath, on the fall of
Sir Robert.

18. **on the foreign relations**: this statement is open to question.
The fact that Pitt's retirement prevented him from controlling his
cabinet, and that foreign countries soon discovered that government was
in a state of chaos, is true. But that they immediately discovered that
his peerage involved a serious loss of popular prestige is another matter.
It was some little time before they began to assume that they could act
without fear of Chatham.

19. **Saint Ildefonso,** i.e. the Court of Spain.

Page **145**.

6. **Saunders** had been the admiral in command of the fleet in the
St Lawrence, and rendered signal service to Wolfe during the siege of
Quebec.

Keppel commanded the vessel which led Hawke's fleet into Quiberon

Bay: and was second in command on the fleet which captured Havanna. In the French war of '78—'83, a scandalous attempt on the part of Sandwich (who was at the head of the admiralty) to ruin Keppel by a series of charges of misconduct in command of the Channel fleet, was completely foiled, and only added to the admiral's reputation.

7. **take on himself.** The embargo was declared by an Order in Council, on the ground that Parliament not being in session and the matter being urgent, such a step was the Constitutional method of dealing with an emergency, Parliament having the power to refuse indemnity.

28. **the territorial acquisitions.** The East India Company had practically acquired the dominion over Bengal and Behar, and over a great part of the Madras district. Their rule had been exceedingly bad. The conquest had been completed in 1760: when Clive had been obliged to leave India. The removal of his strong governing hand had resulted in grave misrule by the Company's servants—a mixture of tyranny and anarchy. In 1765 Clive reappeared, reconstructed the system, and came home again: but any system was as yet entirely experimental—there was no precedent to serve as guide; the Company's officers were responsible to a body of London merchants, without assured supervision; and Clive himself had remarked on the probability that the Crown would be obliged to take over the control of the Company's territories. There is very little doubt that in some form or another, such a scheme was in Chatham's contemplation; and hence arose the indignation of the East India Company, and the outcry against the violation of their charter, involved in a transfer of control from the Company to the Crown.

11. **Alderman Beckford** had been a Westminster boy, and was pronounced by the head-master Dr Freind to be one of the best scholars he ever taught. He was twice Lord Mayor, and was the sturdiest of Wilkes's supporters in the resistance to the infringement of the rights of citizenship. Beckford was a man to make enemies, but he had many friends, and was a genuine if aggressive devotee of liberty.

22. **the Castle Inn**, some 70 miles from London, was one of the great inns of the old coaching days, between London and Bath. Before becoming an inn, it was the country seat of the Earl of Hertford. During the present century, the building was appropriated to form the "Old House" of Marlborough College.

Page **148.**

24. **Lord John Cavendish** already referred to as one of those who renewed the life of the true Whig party : a member of the family of the Duke of Devonshire, and of the party at this time known as the Rockinghams.

Page **150.**

25. **allied themselves,** etc: more specifically, the Bedfords (not the Grenvilles) were introduced into the ministry, while first Conway and then Shelburne were driven to resign. Charles Townshend, before death removed him from the power of further mischief, dragged his colleagues into laying on the American colonies a group of small, useless, but still vexatious import duties which cancelled the beneficial results of the repeal of the Stamp Act ; among other things, leading directly to the emptying of the tea ships in Boston Harbour which is frequently regarded as the crossing of the Rubicon by the colonists.

Page **151.**

23. **Lord North** was shortly to become head of the ministry under which Britain lost the thirteen colonies and found herself shorn of half an empire, with even her maritime supremacy at stake : the king dominating Parliament, and the European Nations acting with a complete and perfect disregard for the wishes and interests of the Power which in 1762 had been in a position to dictate her own terms to each and all of them.

25. **Corsica** was a province of the Genoese. Revolting against their rule, the Corsican leaders were prepared to offer the island to England, but in the existing condition of affairs they found that she was not prepared to use the opportunity. France was permitted to buy Corsica from the Genoese, with the significant accidental result that Napoleon might have been born a British subject, but was born a French one.

29. **Middlesex.** On the return of John Wilkes for Middlesex the validity of his election was challenged. The old charges against him were revived, and he was expelled from the House once more. A new writ was issued : Wilkes was re-elected. The House declared the election invalid, on the ground that he was incapacitated by his expulsion. At a fresh election, a candidate was put up against him, Colonel Luttrell. Wilkes was at the head of the poll : the House declared that the votes cast for him were invalid, and that, by consequence, Luttrell was duly elected. It was evident that if this method

of settling elections were pressed, the majority of the House would soon be in a position to adopt the practice of expelling members obnoxious to it, and declaring the defeated candidates elected : i.e. the majority of the House was claiming the right to override the choice of the electors.

PAGE 152.

11. **a Whig nobleman**: the Duke of Portland. Sir James Lowther (see p. 94, note) discovered that certain lands, held as a Crown grant by the Dukes of Portland without question for two generations, were not fully specified in the grant. The Crown resumed the lands and leased them to Lowther, notoriously with the object of transferring voters from the Rockingham interest to the Lowther—i.e. the Court— interest. The scandal was so great that in 1769 the "Nullum Tempus" Act of Sir G. Savile was passed securing landowners from all dormant claims on the part of the Crown after an undisputed possession of 60 years. (cf. Lecky, vol. iii. p. 125.)

16. **Junius**, the author of the celebrated "letters," commonly identified with Sir Philip Francis. This question is discussed by Macaulay in his essay on Warren Hastings. "Junius" published a series of attacks on the public men of the day, in the form of letters addressed to them, which are commonly accepted as models of virulent invective.

17. **Sir William Draper** rashly entered the lists against Junius in defence of Lord Granby. His controversial powers were not equal to the task, and Junius used his unequalled powers of misrepresentation to hold Sir William up to wholly undeserved contempt.

18. **Blackstone**, Sir William, author of the *Commentaries*, a learned lawyer, but capable of serious error. He committed himself in Parliament to the doctrine that expulsion from the House disqualified for election, *à propos* of Wilkes ; whereupon the list of disqualifications was cited from his own work, and was found not to include expulsion.

PAGE 153.

7. **An ill natured tract**: the answer was given in Burke's *Observations on a late state of the Nation.* The tract on *The Present Discontents* was written a year later.

31. **the three brothers**: it will be remembered that Lady Chatham was the sister of Temple and Grenville.

PAGE 154.

25. **Barré**: an officer who had served in Canada, and was a vigorous advocate in Parliament of the Colonial cause : he had also

taken an active part in the opposition to "general warrants." He suffered heavily in loss of appointments on account of his political attitude, but was rewarded later on in the second Rockingham ministry, and by the younger Pitt.

Dunning in April 1780 brought in and carried by a majority of eighteen the celebrated resolution that "the power of the crown has increased, is increasing, and ought to be diminished." Both Barré and Dunning owed their subsequent rewards to Shelburne.

PAGE 155.

1. **Talma ;** a great French actor, famous at the beginning of the present century.

12. **Mansfield :** the title which Murray had taken.

30. **a colonial senate :** a general Congress was summoned to meet at Philadelphia in Sept. 1774 ; which affirmed the unconstitutional character of the taxes imposed since 1763 ; declared that these ought to be resisted ; but accepted the practice recognised before 1763, and repudiated all desire for independence.

32. **crossed bayonets** at the skirmish of Lexington, April 18, 1775. The British general in command, Gage, sent a body of troops to destroy some military stores being collected at Concord : and hence arose the first engagement.

PAGE 156.

3. **a solemn act :** the Declaration of Independence was not adopted till July 4, 1776, by which time it was felt that no alternative remained.

4. **for a time :** up till the end of 1776, the Colonial armies met with no success. When the British did move, they almost invariably accomplished their immediate object ; but they hardly ever considered a movement necessary, perhaps expecting that the opposing forces would break up of themselves. In that winter, Washington took the offensive with some success : and in the following autumn, an army descending from the North under Burgoyne in order to form a junction with the main body was cut off at Saratoga, and compelled to surrender by General Gates. This was the turning point of the war. (Oct. 1777.)

PAGE 158.

13. **William :** his second son, afterwards prime minister.

Lord Mahon, the courtesy title of the eldest son of Lord Stanhope. The title had its origin in the capture of Port Mahon in Minorca by General Stanhope, afterwards the Lord Stanhope who was at the head of the ministry under George I. before the South Sea Bubble brought Walpole into power.

17. **that day**: April 7th, 1778. The French treaty with the now recognised United States had been made known three weeks earlier: having undoubtedly been the direct outcome of the surrender of Saratoga.

PAGE 159.

1. **Electress Sophia**, mother of George I. and granddaughter of James I.

PAGE 161.

4. **Fox**: Charles James Fox, the rival of the younger Pitt.

Grattan: the great Irishman, one of the leaders in the struggle for legislative independence. His efforts resulted in the Constitution of 1782, and what is known as Grattan's Parliament. He was opposed to the Act of Union of 1801, but after it was passed he sat for many years as a member in the Imperial Parliament at Westminster. He died in 1820.

Canning became prominent in Parliament at the close of the century; after the death of the younger Pitt became the leading representative of that political school.

Wilberforce is remembered chiefly for his long and ultimately successful struggle for the abolition of the slave trade.

APPENDIX.

CHRONOLOGICAL TABLE OF EVENTS
FROM 1708—1783.

In column 1, italics are used to denote incidents personal to Pitt.

In columns 2 and 3, italics are used to denote beginning and termination of wars.

DOMESTIC	CONTINENTAL AND NAVAL
1708 *Birth of William Pitt*	
1714 Accession of George I.	
1717 Walpole in opposition	
1721 South Sea Bubble	
1722 Walpole in power	
1727 Accession of George II.	
1730 Walpole supreme	
1733 Walpole's Excise Scheme	First Family Compact
1735 *Pitt enters Parliament, and joins the Whig opposition*	
1737 Leicester House the centre of opposition	
1739	*War declared with Spain*
1740	Frederick attacks Maria Theresa
1742 Fall of Walpole. Carteret	
1743 Henry Pelham Prime Minister	Battle of Dettingen
Pitt supports Government	
1744	*War declared with France*
1745 Landing of Charles Edward	
1746 *Pitt brought into the Ministry*	
Culloden	
1748	*Peace of Aix-la-Chapelle*
1749	... ...
1751	... ...
1752 ⎫	
1753 ⎭	... ...
1754 Death of Pelham	... ...
Newcastle Prime Minister	

AMERICAN				INDIAN

...	...	...	...	Dupleix attacks the English. He is **1744** generally successful, but at the Peace Madras is restored
...	...	...	...	The struggle renewed, French and **1749** British supporting rival claimants to native thrones. The French successful, until
...	...	...	...	Clive's capture and defence of Arcot **1751**
...	...	...	...	British capture Trichinopoli, and { **1752** establish their candidates { **1753**
...	...	...	...	Dupleix recalled **1754**

14—2

	DOMESTIC	CONTINENTAL AND NAVAL
1755	*Pitt in opposition*	... ...
	Fox and Newcastle coalition	
1756	... ...	Alliance with Prussia
		Byng at Minorca
		Beginning of Seven Years' War
	Pitt's first administration	Frederick attacks Saxony
	(Duke of Devonshire)	
1757	*Pitt dismissed* (April)	Hastenbeck and Closterseven
	Coalition of Pitt and New-	Ferdinand given the command
	castle (June)	on the Weser
		Frederick wins Rosbach and
		Leuthen
1758	... ...	British Navy begins to control
		the sea
1759	... ...	Minden
		Boscawen's victory at Lagos
		Quiberon
1760	... ...	... ...
	Accession of George III.	
1761	Bute Secretary of State	Second Family Compact
	Pitt resigns	
1762	Bute supreme	Declaration of *War with Spain*
	Dismissal of Bute's opponents	Capture of Havanna and Manilla
1763	... ...	*Peace of Paris*
	Bute resigns. The Triumvi-	
	rate	
	Wilkes and " Number 45 "	
	Pitt refuses office without the	
	Whig connexion	
	Bedford Ministry	
1764	Wilkes expelled	
1765	Regency Bill	... ...
	Pitt again refuses office, with-	
	out Temple	
	Rockingham Ministry	
1766	Condemnation of General	... ...
	Warrants	
	Fall of Rockingham	

AMERICAN	INDIAN	
Fighting about Fort Duquesne	... ...	**1755**
Braddock's disaster	... ...	**1756**
... ...	Black Hole of Calcutta	
... ...	Acquisition of Bengal at Battle of Plassey	**1757**
Capture of Cape Breton	... ...	**1758**
Capture of Quebec	Lally in the Carnatic	**1759**
Montreal taken	Wandewash ends the French rivalry. Clive leaves India	**1760**
... ...	Misgovernment in Bengal, lasting till the return of Clive in 1765	**1761**
Stamp Act	Clive returns to India. Reorganises administration so as to check its worst evils. The system lasts till 1773	**1765**
Repeal of Stamp Act	... ...	**1766**

	DOMESTIC	CONTINENTAL AND NAVAL
1766	*Pitt forms a ministry* and becomes Earl of Chatham	... ...
1767	*Chatham incapacitated* Grafton	... ...
1768	*Chatham resigns* Wilkes elected for Middlesex	
1769	Series of "Middlesex elections" *Revival of Chatham:* who acts with Opposition	France annexes Corsica
1770	Lord North Prime Minister	... ...
1771	Publication of debates secured	
1772	... ...	Partition of Poland
1773	... ...	... ...
1774	... ...	... ...
1775	... ...	... ...
1776	... ...	... ...
1777	... ...	... ...
1778	... ... *Chatham's last speech* (April) *Chatham's death* (May)	*France declares War* (March)
1779	... ...	*Spain joins the War* Siege of Gibraltar begins
1780	... ...	... ...
1781	... ...	... ...
1782	North resigns. Second Rockingham Ministry Shelburne Ministry	... ... Battle of the Saints Relief of Gibraltar
1783	Coalition of Fox and North William Pitt the younger Prime Minister	*Peace of Versailles*

AMERICAN	INDIAN	
... ...	Plan of transferring territorial acquisitions to Crown	1766
New taxes imposed by Townshend	... ...	1767
... ...	Warren Hastings in Bengal	1770
Emptying of Tea Ships in Boston Harbour	North's Regulating Act Warren Hastings Governor-General	1773
Boston Port Act	... ...	1774
Lexington Bunker Hill	... ...	1775
Declaration of Independence Washington near New York	... ...	1776
Surrender of Saratoga	... ...	1777
... ...	Hyder Ali in the Carnatic	1780
Surrender of York Town	... ...	1781
Independence of United States acknowledged	Death of Hyder Ali	1782

INDEX.

The reference given is to the page in the text of the essay in which, or in a note on which, the subject is mentioned.

220   INDEX.

For EU product safety concerns, contact us at Calle de José Abascal, 56–1°,
28003 Madrid, Spain or eugpsr@cambridge.org.

www.ingramcontent.com/pod-product-compliance
Ingram Content Group UK Ltd.
Pitfield, Milton Keynes, MK11 3LW, UK
UKHW020319140625
459647UK00018B/1934